DRAW CLOSE
TO
JEHOVAH

© 2002
WATCH TOWER BIBLE AND TRACT SOCIETY OF PENNSYLVANIA
All Rights Reserved

Publishers
WATCHTOWER BIBLE AND TRACT SOCIETY OF NEW YORK, INC.
INTERNATIONAL BIBLE STUDENTS ASSOCIATION
Brooklyn, New York, U.S.A.

First Printing in English:
5,000,000 Copies

Unless otherwise indicated, Scripture quotations
are from the modern-language
New World Translation of the Holy Scriptures—With References

Draw Close to Jehovah
English (*cl*-E)

Made in the United States of America

Dear Reader:

Do you feel close to God? To many, that seems just impossible. Some fear that he is too remote; others feel hopelessly unworthy. However, the Bible lovingly urges us: "Draw close to God, and he will draw close to you." (James 4:8) He even assures his worshipers: "I, Jehovah your God, am grasping your right hand, the One saying to you, 'Do not be afraid. I myself will help you.'"—Isaiah 41:13.

How can we reach out for such a close relationship with God? In any friendship we forge, the bond is based on knowing the person, admiring and valuing his distinctive traits. So God's qualities and ways, as revealed in the Bible, are a vital field of study. Pondering the way Jehovah manifests each of his qualities, seeing how Jesus Christ perfectly reflected them, and understanding how we too may cultivate them will draw us closer to God. We will see that Jehovah is the rightful and ideal Sovereign of the universe. What is more, he is the Father we all need. Strong, just, wise, and loving, he never abandons his faithful children.

May this book help you draw ever closer to Jehovah God, to forge a bond with him that will never be broken, so that you may live to praise him forever.

The Publishers

Contents

Chapter

"Look! This Is Our God"

CAN you imagine having a conversation with God? The very thought inspires awe—the Sovereign of the universe speaking to you! You hesitate at first, but then you manage to reply. He listens, he responds, and he even makes you feel free to ask any question you want. Now, what question would you ask?

2 Long ago, there was a man who was in just such a position. His name was Moses. The question he chose to ask God, though, might surprise you. He did not ask about himself, his future, or even the plight of mankind. Rather, he asked God's name. You might find that odd, for Moses already knew God's personal name. His question, then, must have had deeper meaning. In fact, it was the most significant question Moses could have asked. The answer touches us all. It can help you take a vital step in drawing close to God. How so? Let us take a look at that remarkable conversation.

3 Moses was 80 years old. He had spent four decades exiled from his people, the Israelites, who were slaves in Egypt. One day, while tending his father-in-law's flocks, he saw a strange phenomenon. A thornbush was on fire, but it was not being consumed. It just kept burning, shining like a beacon on the mountainside. Moses approached to inspect. How startled he must have been when a voice spoke to him from the midst of the fire!

1, 2. (a) What questions would you like to ask God? (b) What did Moses ask God?

3, 4. What events led up to Moses' conversation with God, and what was the gist of that interchange?

By means of an angelic spokesman, God and Moses then conversed at length. And, as you may know, God there commissioned a hesitant Moses to leave his peaceful life and return to Egypt to deliver the Israelites from slavery. —Exodus 3:1-12.

⁴ Now, Moses could have asked God any question whatsoever. Note, though, the question he chose to ask: "Suppose I am now come to the sons of Israel and I do say to them, 'The God of your forefathers has sent me to you,' and they do say to me, 'What is his name?' What shall I say to them?"—Exodus 3:13.

⁵ That question teaches us first of all that God has a name. We must not take this simple truth for granted. Yet, many do. God's personal name has been removed from countless Bible translations and replaced with titles, such as "Lord" and "God." This is one of the saddest and most reprehensible things that has been done in the name of religion. After all, what is the first thing you do when you meet someone? Do you not ask his name? It is similar with getting to know God. He is not a nameless, distant entity, beyond knowing or understanding. Although invisible, he is a person, and he has a name—Jehovah.

⁶ Furthermore, when God reveals his personal name, something great and thrilling is in the offing. He is inviting us to come to know him. He wants us to make the best choice we can make in life—to draw close to him. But Jehovah has done more than tell us his name. He has also taught us what it means.

5, 6. (a) Moses' question teaches us what simple, vital truth? (b) What reprehensible thing has been done with God's personal name? (c) Why is it so significant that God has revealed his name to mankind?

The Meaning of God's Name

[7] Jehovah chose his own name, one rich in meaning. "Jehovah" literally means "He Causes to Become." True, he brought all things into existence. That in itself is an awe-inspiring thought. But is that the point of God's name? Moses evidently wanted to learn more. You see, the divine name was not new. People had been using it for centuries. Really, in asking God's name, Moses was asking about *the person represented by the name.* In effect, he was saying: 'What can I tell your people Israel about you that will build their faith in you, that will convince them that you really will deliver them?'

[8] In response Jehovah explained the meaning of his name. He said to Moses: "I shall prove to be what I shall prove to be." (Exodus 3:14) Many Bible translations here read: "I am that I am." But the careful rendering in the *New World Translation* shows that God was not merely affirming his own existence. Rather, he was teaching Moses —and by extension all of us—what that name implies. Jehovah would "prove to be," or cause himself to become, whatever was needed in order to fulfill his promises. J. B. Rotherham's translation pointedly renders this verse: "I Will Become whatsoever I please." One authority on Biblical Hebrew explains the phrase this way: "Whatever the situation or need . . . , God will 'become' the solution to that need."

[9] What did that mean to the Israelites? No matter what obstacle loomed before them, no matter how difficult

---

7. (a) What does God's personal name literally mean? (b) What did Moses really want to know when he asked God His name?
8, 9. (a) How did Jehovah answer Moses' question, and what is wrong with the way His response is often translated? (b) What is the meaning of the statement "I shall prove to be what I shall prove to be"?

the predicament in which they might find themselves, Jehovah would become whatever was needed in order to deliver them from slavery and bring them into the Promised Land. Surely that name inspired confidence in God. It can do the same for us today. (Psalm 9:10) Why?

10 To illustrate: Parents know how versatile and adaptable they must be in caring for their children. In the course of a single day, a parent may be called upon to act as a nurse, a cook, a teacher, a disciplinarian, a judge, and much more. Many feel overwhelmed by the wide range of roles they are expected to fill. They remark upon the absolute faith put in them by their little ones, who never doubt that Daddy or Mommy can make the hurt better, settle all disputes, fix any broken toy, and answer whatever question pops into their endlessly inquisitive minds. Some parents are humbled and occasionally frustrated by their own limitations. They feel woefully inadequate to fill many of these roles.

11 Jehovah too is a loving parent. Yet, within the framework of his own perfect standards, there is *nothing* he cannot become in order to care for his earthly children in the best possible way. So his name, Jehovah, invites us to think of him as the best Father imaginable. (James 1:17) Moses and all other faithful Israelites soon learned that Jehovah is true to his name. They watched in awe as he caused himself to become an unbeatable Military Commander, the Master of all natural elements, a peerless Lawgiver, Judge, Architect, Provider of food and water, Preserver of clothing and footgear—and more.

12 So God has made his personal name known, has ex-

_____

10, 11. How does Jehovah's name invite us to think of him as the most versatile and the best Father imaginable? Illustrate.
12. How did Pharaoh's attitude toward Jehovah differ from that of Moses?

plained its meaning, and has even demonstrated that the meaning is true. Unquestionably, God wants us to know him. How do we respond? Moses wanted to know God. That intense desire shaped Moses' life course and led him to draw very close to his heavenly Father. (Numbers 12: 6-8; Hebrews 11:27) Sadly, few of Moses' contemporaries had the same desire. When Moses mentioned Jehovah by name to Pharaoh, that haughty Egyptian monarch retorted: "Who is Jehovah?" (Exodus 5:2) Pharaoh did not want to learn more about Jehovah. Rather, he cynically dismissed the God of Israel as being unimportant or irrelevant. That outlook is all too common today. It blinds people to one of the most important of all truths—Jehovah is the Sovereign Lord.

The Sovereign Lord Jehovah

[13] Jehovah is so versatile, so adaptable, that he rightly bears a wide array of titles in Scripture. These do not compete with his personal name; rather, they teach us more about what his name represents. For example, he is called the "Sovereign Lord Jehovah." (2 Samuel 7:22) That lofty title, which occurs hundreds of times in the Bible, tells us Jehovah's position. He alone has the right to be Ruler of all the universe. Consider why.

[14] Jehovah is unique as the Creator. Revelation 4:11 says: "You are worthy, Jehovah, even our God, to receive the glory and the honor and the power, because you created all things, and because of your will they existed and were created." These majestic words could apply to no other being. Everything in the universe owes its existence

---

13, 14. (a) Why is Jehovah given many titles in the Bible, and what are some of them? (See box on page 14.) (b) Why is Jehovah uniquely qualified to be called the "Sovereign Lord"?

to Jehovah! Without question, Jehovah is worthy of the honor, power, and glory that come with being the Sovereign Lord and Creator of all things.

[15] Another title applied exclusively to Jehovah is "King of eternity." (1 Timothy 1:17; Revelation 15:3) What does this mean? It is difficult for our limited minds to comprehend, but Jehovah is eternal in both directions—past and future. Psalm 90:2 says: "Even from time indefinite to time indefinite you are God." So Jehovah never began; he has always been. He is rightly called "the Ancient of Days"—he existed for an eternity before anyone or anything else in the universe came into being! (Daniel 7:9, 13, 22) Who can validly question his right to be the Sovereign Lord?

[16] Yet, some do question that right, as did Pharaoh. Part of the problem is that imperfect men put too much stock in what they can see with their eyes. We cannot see the Sovereign Lord. He is a spirit being, invisible to human eyes. (John 4:24) Besides, if a flesh-and-blood human were to stand in the immediate presence of Jehovah God, the experience would prove fatal. Jehovah himself told Moses: "You are not able to see my face, because no man may see me and yet live."—Exodus 33:20; John 1:18.

[17] That should not surprise us. Moses got to see just a part of Jehovah's glory, evidently through an angelic representative. With what effect? Moses' face "emitted rays" for some time afterward. The Israelites feared even to look directly at Moses' face. (Exodus 33:21-23; 34:5-7, 29, 30) Surely, then, no mere human could look upon the

---

15. Why is Jehovah called "King of eternity"?
16, 17. (a) Why can we not see Jehovah, and why should that not surprise us? (b) In what sense is Jehovah more real than anything we can see or touch?

Sovereign Lord himself in all his glory! Does this mean that he is any less real than what we can see and touch? No, we readily accept the reality of many things we cannot see—wind, radio waves, and thoughts, for example. Furthermore, Jehovah is permanent, unaffected by the passage of time, even untold billions of years! In that sense, he is far more real than anything we can touch or see, for the physical realm is subject to age and decay. (Matthew 6:19) Should we think of him, though, as merely some abstract, impersonal force or a vague First Cause? Let us see.

A God With Personality

¹⁸ Although we cannot see God, there are thrilling passages in the Bible that afford us glimpses into heaven itself. The first chapter of Ezekiel is one example. Ezekiel was given a vision of Jehovah's heavenly organization, which he saw as a vast celestial chariot. Especially impressive is the description of the mighty spirit creatures around Jehovah. (Ezekiel 1:4-10) These "living creatures" are closely associated with Jehovah, and their appearance tells us something important about the God they serve. Each one has four faces—that of a bull, a lion, an eagle, and a man. These evidently symbolize the four outstanding qualities of Jehovah's personality.—Revelation 4:6-8, 10.

¹⁹ In the Bible, a bull often represents power, and fittingly so, for it is an immensely strong animal. A lion, on the other hand, often pictures justice, for true justice requires courage, a quality for which lions are renowned. Eagles

---

18. What vision was Ezekiel given, and what do the four faces of the "living creatures" near Jehovah symbolize?
19. What quality is represented by (a) the bull's face? (b) the lion's face? (c) the eagle's face? (d) the man's face?

Some of Jehovah's Titles

Almighty. His power is limitless, irresistible.—Revelation 15:3.

Father. The source of all life, including everlasting life, he has fatherly love for his servants.—Proverbs 27:11; John 5:21.

Grand Instructor. He is the all-wise Teacher, to whom we should look for instruction and guidance.—Isaiah 30:20; 48:17.

The Rock. Unchanging, he is a secure refuge.—Deuteronomy 32:4.

Shepherd. He guides and protects his sheeplike servants and arranges for their spiritual sustenance.—Psalm 23:1.

---

are well-known for their keen eyesight, seeing even tiny objects miles away. So the eagle's face would well picture God's farsighted wisdom. And the man's face? Well, man, made in God's image, is unique in his ability to reflect God's dominant quality—love. (Genesis 1:26) These facets of Jehovah's personality—power, justice, wisdom, and love—are so frequently highlighted in Scripture that they may be referred to as God's cardinal attributes.

[20] Should we worry that God might have changed in the thousands of years since he was described in the Bible? No, God's personality does not alter. He tells us: "I am Jehovah; I have not changed." (Malachi 3:6) Rather than arbitrarily changing, Jehovah proves himself an ideal Father in the way he responds to each situation. He brings to the fore those aspects of his personality that are most appropriate. Of the four qualities, the one that predominates is love. It permeates everything God does. He exercises his power, justice, and wisdom in a loving way.

---

20. Do we need to worry that Jehovah's personality might have changed, and why do you so answer?

In fact, the Bible says something extraordinary regarding God and this quality. It says: "God is love." (1 John 4:8) Note that it does not say that God *has* love or that God is *loving*. Rather, it says that God *is* love. Love, his very essence, motivates him in all that he does.

"Look! This Is Our God"

21 Have you ever seen a small child point out his father to his friends and then say with innocent joy and pride, "That's my daddy"? God's worshipers have every reason to feel similarly about Jehovah. The Bible foretells a time when faithful people will exclaim: "Look! This is our God." (Isaiah 25:8, 9) The more insight you gain into Jehovah's qualities, the more you will feel that you have the best Father imaginable.

22 This Father is not cold, aloof, or distant—despite what some austere religionists and philosophers have taught. We would hardly feel drawn to a cold God, and the Bible does not portray our heavenly Father that way. On the contrary, it calls him "the happy God." (1 Timothy 1: 11) He has feelings both strong and tender. He is "hurt at his heart" when his intelligent creatures violate the guidelines that he provides for their well-being. (Genesis 6:6; Psalm 78:41) But when we act wisely according to his Word, we make his "heart rejoice."—Proverbs 27:11.

23 Our Father wants us to be close to him. His Word encourages us to "grope for him and really find him, although, in fact, he is not far off from each one of us." (Acts 17:27) How, though, is it possible for mere humans to draw close to the Sovereign Lord of the universe?

---

21. How will we feel as we get to know Jehovah's qualities better?
22, 23. How does the Bible portray our heavenly Father, and how do we know that he wants us to be close to him?

CHAPTER 2

Can You Really
"Draw Close to God"?

HOW would you feel if the Creator of heaven and earth said of you, "This is my friend"? To many, that might sound farfetched. After all, how could a mere human ever enter into a friendship with Jehovah God? Yet, the Bible assures us that we really can be close to God.

² Abraham of old was one who enjoyed such closeness. Jehovah identified that patriarch as "my friend." (Isaiah 41:8) Yes, Jehovah considered Abraham to be a personal friend. Abraham was granted that close relationship because he "put faith in Jehovah." (James 2:23) Today, too, Jehovah looks for opportunities to "get attached" to those who serve him out of love. (Deuteronomy 10:15) His Word urges: "Draw close to God, and he will draw close to you." (James 4:8) In these words we find both an invitation and a promise.

³ Jehovah invites us to draw near to him. He is ready and willing to receive us into his favor as friends. At the same time, he promises that if we take steps to draw close to him, he will take corresponding action. He will draw close to us. Thus we may enter into something truly precious—"intimacy with Jehovah."* (Psalm 25:14) "Intima-

---

* Interestingly, the Hebrew word rendered "intimacy" is used at Amos 3:7, which says that the Sovereign Lord Jehovah reveals his "confidential matter" to his servants, making known to them in advance what he purposes to do.

1, 2. (a) What might sound farfetched to many, but of what does the Bible assure us? (b) Abraham was granted what close relationship, and why?
3. What invitation does Jehovah extend to us, and what promise is connected with it?

cy" conveys the idea of confidential talk with a special friend.

⁴ Do you have an intimate friend in whom you can confide? Such a friend is one who cares about you. You trust him, for he has proved to be loyal. Your joys are heightened when you share them with him. His sympathetic ear lightens the burden of your sorrows. Even when no one else seems to understand you, he does. Similarly, when you draw close to God, you come to have a special Friend who truly values you, deeply cares about you, and fully understands you. (Psalm 103:14; 1 Peter 5:7) You trust him with your inmost feelings, for you know that he is loyal to those who are loyal to him. (Psalm 18:25) However, this privileged intimacy with God is within our reach only because he has made it possible.

Jehovah Has Opened the Way

⁵ Left on our own, we as sinners could never be close to God. (Psalm 5:4) "But God recommends his own love to us in that, while we were yet sinners, Christ died for us," wrote the apostle Paul. (Romans 5:8) Yes, Jehovah arranged for Jesus "to give his soul a ransom in exchange for many." (Matthew 20:28) Our faith in that ransom sacrifice makes it possible for us to be close to God. Since God "first loved us," he laid the foundation for us to enter into friendship with him.—1 John 4:19.

⁶ Jehovah has taken another step: He has revealed himself to us. In any friendship, closeness is based on truly knowing a person, valuing his qualities and ways. So

4. How would you describe an intimate friend, and in what way does Jehovah prove to be such a friend to those who draw close to him?
5. What did Jehovah do to make it possible for us to be close to him?
6, 7. (a) How do we know that Jehovah is not a hidden, unknowable God? (b) In what ways has Jehovah revealed himself?

if Jehovah were a hidden, unknowable God, we could never be close to him. Yet, far from concealing himself, he wants us to know him. (Isaiah 45:19) Furthermore, what he reveals about himself is available to all, even to those of us who may be considered lowly by the world's standards.—Matthew 11:25.

⁷ How has Jehovah revealed himself to us? His creative works make known certain aspects of his personality —the vastness of his power, the richness of his wisdom, the abundance of his love. (Romans 1:20) But Jehovah's revelation of himself does not stop with the things he created. Ever the Great Communicator, he provided a written revelation of himself in his Word, the Bible.

Beholding "the Pleasantness of Jehovah"

⁸ The Bible itself is evidence of Jehovah's love for us. In his Word, he reveals himself in terms we can comprehend—proof not only that he loves us but that he wants us to know and love him. What we read in this precious book enables us to behold "the pleasantness of Jehovah" and moves us to want to be close to him. (Psalm 90:17) Let us discuss some of the heartwarming ways in which Jehovah reveals himself in his Word.

⁹ The Scriptures contain many direct statements identifying God's qualities. Note some examples. "Jehovah is a lover of justice." (Psalm 37:28) God is "exalted in power." (Job 37:23) "'I am loyal,' is the utterance of Jehovah." (Jeremiah 3:12) "He is wise in heart." (Job 9:4) He is "a God merciful and gracious, slow to anger

---

8. Why can it be said that the Bible itself is evidence of Jehovah's love for us?

9. What are some examples of direct statements in the Bible that identify God's qualities?

and abundant in loving-kindness and truth." (Exodus 34:6) "You, O Jehovah, are good and ready to forgive." (Psalm 86:5) And, as mentioned in the preceding chapter, one quality is predominant: "God is love." (1 John 4:8) As you reflect on these pleasing attributes, are you not drawn to this incomparable God?

¹⁰ In addition to telling us what his qualities are, Jehovah has lovingly included in his Word concrete examples of these qualities in action. Such accounts paint vivid mental pictures that help us see the various facets of his personality more clearly. That, in turn, helps us draw close to him. Consider an example.

¹¹ It is one thing to read that God is "vigorous in power." (Isaiah 40:26) It is quite another to read about how he delivered Israel through the Red Sea and then sustained the nation in the wilderness for 40 years. You can visualize the surging waters splitting apart. You can picture the nation—perhaps 3,000,000 in all—walking over the dry seabed, the congealed waters standing like massive walls on either side. (Exodus 14:21; 15:8) You can see the evidence of God's protective care in the wilderness. Water flowed out of rock. Food, resembling white seeds, appeared on the ground. (Exodus 16:31; Numbers 20:11) Jehovah here reveals not only that he has power but that he uses it in

10, 11. (a) To help us see his personality more clearly, what has Jehovah included in his Word? (b) What Bible example helps us visualize God's power in action?

behalf of his people. Is it not reassuring to know that our prayers go up to a powerful God who "is for us a refuge and strength, a help that is readily to be found during distresses"?—Psalm 46:1.

¹² Jehovah, who is a spirit, has done even more to help us know him. As humans we are bound by visible realities and therefore cannot see into the spirit realm. For God to describe himself to us in spirit terms would be like trying to explain details of your appearance, such as your eye color or freckles, to someone born blind. Rather, Jehovah kindly helps us to "see" him in terms we can understand. At times, he employs metaphors and similes, likening himself to things that are known to us. He even describes himself as having certain human features.*

¹³ Notice the description of Jehovah found at Isaiah 40: 11: "Like a shepherd he will shepherd his own drove. With his arm he will collect together the lambs; and in his bosom he will carry them." Jehovah is here compared to a shepherd who picks up lambs with "his arm." This denotes God's ability to protect and support his people, even the more vulnerable ones. We can feel safe in his strong arms, for if we are loyal to him, he will never forsake us. (Romans 8:38, 39) The Great Shepherd carries the lambs "in his bosom"—an expression referring to

---

* For example, the Bible speaks of God's face, eyes, ears, nostrils, mouth, arms, and feet. (Psalm 18:15; 27:8; 44:3; Isaiah 60:13; Matthew 4:4; 1 Peter 3:12) Such figurative expressions are not to be taken literally, any more than are such references to Jehovah as "the Rock" or "a shield."—Deuteronomy 32:4; Psalm 84:11.

---

12. How does Jehovah help us to "see" him in terms we can understand?

13. What mental picture does Isaiah 40:11 create, and how does it affect you?

the loose folds of the upper garment, in which a shepherd would at times carry a newborn lamb. We are thus assured that Jehovah cherishes and tenderly cares for us. It is only natural to want to be close to him.

"The Son Is Willing to Reveal Him"

14 In his Word, Jehovah provides the most intimate revelation of himself through his beloved Son, Jesus. No one could reflect God's thinking and feelings more closely or explain Him more vividly than Jesus did. After all, that firstborn Son existed alongside his Father before other spirit creatures and the physical universe were created. (Colossians 1:15) Jesus was intimately acquainted with Jehovah. That is why he could say: "Who the Son is no one knows but the Father; and who the Father is, no one knows but the Son, and he to whom the Son is willing to reveal him." (Luke 10:22)

---

14. Why can it be said that Jehovah provides the most intimate revelation of himself through Jesus?

Jehovah has revealed himself through his creative works and his written Word

When on earth as a man, Jesus revealed his Father in two important ways.

¹⁵ First, Jesus' *teachings* help us to know his Father. Jesus described Jehovah in terms that touch our heart. For example, to explain the merciful God who welcomes back repentant sinners, Jesus likened Jehovah to a forgiving father who is so deeply moved at the sight of his returning prodigal son that he runs and falls upon his son's neck and tenderly kisses him. (Luke 15:11-24) Jesus also portrayed Jehovah as a God who "draws" righthearted people because he loves them as individuals. (John 6:44) He even knows when a tiny sparrow falls to the earth. "Have no fear," Jesus explained, "you are worth more than many sparrows." (Matthew 10:29, 31) We cannot help but feel drawn to such a caring God.

¹⁶ Second, Jesus' *example* shows us what Jehovah is like. Jesus so perfectly reflected his Father that he could say: "He that has seen me has seen the Father also." (John 14:9) Thus, when we read in the Gospels about Jesus—the feelings he displayed and the way he dealt with others—we are in a sense seeing a living portrait of his Father. Jehovah could hardly have given us a clearer revelation of his qualities than that. Why?

¹⁷ To illustrate: Imagine trying to explain what kindness is. You might define it with words. But if you can point to someone actually performing a kind deed and say, "That is an example of kindness," the word "kindness" takes on added meaning and becomes easier to understand. Jehovah has done something similar to help us grasp what he is like. As well as describing himself in words, he has provided us with the living example of his Son. In Jesus,

15, 16. In what two ways did Jesus reveal his Father?
17. Illustrate what Jehovah has done to help us grasp what he is like.

the qualities of God are seen in action. Through the Gospel accounts describing Jesus, Jehovah is, in effect, saying: "That is what I am like." How does the inspired record describe Jesus when on earth?

¹⁸ The four main attributes of God found beautiful expression in Jesus. He had *power* over disease, hunger, even death. Yet, unlike selfish men who abuse their power, he never used miraculous power in his own behalf or to hurt others. (Matthew 4:2-4) He loved *justice*. His heart was filled with righteous indignation at seeing unfair merchants exploiting the people. (Matthew 21:12, 13) He treated the poor and downtrodden with impartiality, helping such ones to "find refreshment" for their souls. (Matthew 11:4, 5, 28-30) There was matchless *wisdom* in the teachings of Jesus, who was "more than Solomon." (Matthew 12:42) But Jesus never made a showy display of his wisdom. His words reached the hearts of common people, for his teachings were clear, simple, and practical.

¹⁹ Jesus was an outstanding example of *love*. Throughout his ministry, he displayed love in its many facets, including empathy and compassion. He could not see the suffering of others without feeling pity. Over and over again, that sympathetic regard moved him to action. (Matthew 14:14) Although he healed the sick and fed the hungry, Jesus expressed compassion in a far more vital way. He helped others to know, accept, and love the truth about God's Kingdom, which will bring

_____

18. How did Jesus express the attributes of power, justice, and wisdom?

19, 20. (a) How was Jesus an outstanding example of love? (b) As we read and reflect on the example of Jesus, what should we keep in mind?

Questions for Meditation

Psalm 15:1-5 What does Jehovah expect of those who want to be his friends?

Psalm 34:1-18 Jehovah is near to whom, and such ones can have what confidence in him?

Psalm 145:18-21 What activity on our part will bring us close to Jehovah?

2 Corinthians 6:14—7:1 What conduct is essential if we are to maintain a close relationship with Jehovah?

permanent blessings to mankind. (Mark 6:34; Luke 4:43) Above all, Jesus showed self-sacrificing love by willingly surrendering his soul in behalf of others.—John 15:13.

[20] Is it any wonder that people of all ages and backgrounds felt drawn to this man of tender warmth and deep feelings? (Mark 10:13-16) However, as we read about and reflect on the living example of Jesus, let us keep ever in mind that in this Son we are seeing a clear reflection of his Father.—Hebrews 1:3.

A Study Aid to Help Us

[21] By revealing himself so clearly in his Word, Jehovah leaves no doubt that he wants us to be close to him. At the same time, he does not force us to seek an approved relationship with him. It is up to us to search for Jehovah "while he may be found." (Isaiah 55:6) Searching for Jehovah involves coming to know his qualities and ways as revealed in the Bible. The study aid that you are now reading is designed to help you in this endeavor.

[22] You will notice that this book is divided into sections

21, 22. What is involved in searching for Jehovah, and what does this study aid contain to help us in this endeavor?

corresponding to Jehovah's four cardinal attributes: power, justice, wisdom, and love. Each section opens with an overview of the quality. The next few chapters discuss how Jehovah manifests that quality in its various aspects. Each section also contains a chapter showing how Jesus exemplified the quality, as well as a chapter examining how we can reflect it in our lives.

23 Starting with this chapter, there is a special feature entitled "Questions for Meditation." For example, look at the box on page 24. The scriptures and questions are not designed as a review of the chapter. Rather, their purpose is to help you reflect on other important aspects of the subject. How can you make effective use of this feature? Look up each of the cited texts, and read the verses carefully. Then consider the question accompanying each citation. Ponder over the answers. You might do some research. Ask yourself some additional questions: 'What does this information tell me about Jehovah? How does it affect my life? How can I use it to help others?'

24 Such meditation can help us draw ever closer to Jehovah. Why? The Bible associates meditation with the heart. (Psalm 19:14) When we reflect appreciatively on what we learn about God, the information filters into our figurative heart, where it affects our thinking, stirs our feelings, and ultimately moves us to action. Our love for God deepens, and that love, in turn, moves us to want to please him as our dearest Friend. (1 John 5:3) To come into such a relationship, we must get to know Jehovah's qualities and ways. First, though, let us discuss an aspect of God's nature that provides a compelling reason for drawing close to him—his holiness.

23, 24. (a) Explain the special feature "Questions for Meditation." (b) How does meditation help us draw ever closer to God?

CHAPTER 3

"Holy, Holy, Holy Is Jehovah"

ISAIAH was overcome with awe at the scene before him —a vision from God. It seemed so real! Isaiah later wrote that he actually "got to see Jehovah" on His lofty throne. Jehovah's flowing raiment filled the huge temple in Jerusalem.—Isaiah 6:1, 2.

2 Isaiah was also awed by what he heard—singing so powerful that it shook the temple to its very foundations. The song was coming from seraphs, spirit creatures of very high rank. Their mighty harmony rang out in words of simple majesty: "Holy, holy, holy is Jehovah of armies. The fullness of all the earth is his glory." (Isaiah 6:3, 4) Singing the word "holy" three times gave it special emphasis, and rightly so, for Jehovah is holy to the superlative degree. (Revelation 4:8) Jehovah's holiness is emphasized throughout the Bible. Hundreds of verses associate his name with the words "holy" and "holiness."

3 Clearly, then, one of the primary things that Jehovah wants us to grasp about him is that he is holy. Yet, many today are put off by the very idea. Some mistakenly associate holiness with self-righteousness or false piety. People who struggle with a negative view of themselves may find God's holiness more daunting than appealing. They may fear that they could never be worthy of drawing close to this holy God. Hence, many turn away from God because of his holiness. That is sad, for God's holiness is really a compelling reason for drawing close to him.

1, 2. What vision did the prophet Isaiah receive, and what does it teach us about Jehovah?

3. How do mistaken views of Jehovah's holiness lead many to turn away from God instead of drawing close to him?

Why? Before we answer that question, let us discuss what true holiness is.

What Is Holiness?

4 That God is holy does not mean that he is smug, haughty, or disdainful of others. On the contrary, he hates such qualities. (Proverbs 16:5; James 4:6) So, what does the word "holy" really mean? In Biblical Hebrew, the word is derived from a term meaning "separate." In worship, "holy" applies to that which is separated from common use, or held sacred. Holiness also strongly conveys the idea of cleanness and purity. How does this word apply to Jehovah? Does it mean that he is "separate" from imperfect humans, far removed from us?

5 Not at all. As "the Holy One of Israel," Jehovah described himself as dwelling "in the midst of" his people, sinful though they were. (Isaiah 12:6; Hosea 11:9) So his holiness does not make him distant. How, then, is he "separate"? In two important ways. First, he is separate from all creation in that he alone is the Most High. His purity, his cleanness, is absolute and infinite. (Psalm 40:5; 83:18) Second, Jehovah is entirely separated from all sinfulness, and that is a comforting thought. Why?

6 We live in a world where true holiness is a rarity. Everything about human society alienated from God is polluted in some way, tainted with sin and imperfection. We all have to war against the sin within us. And all of us are in danger of being overcome by sin if we let down our guard. (Romans 7:15-25; 1 Corinthians 10:12) Jehovah is in no such danger. Completely removed from sinfulness,

---

4, 5. (a) What does holiness mean, and what does it not mean?
(b) In what two important ways is Jehovah "separate"?
6. Why can we find comfort in Jehovah's absolute separation from sinfulness?

he will never be tainted by the slightest trace of sin. This reaffirms our impression of Jehovah as the ideal Father, for it means that he is completely reliable. Unlike many sinful human fathers, Jehovah will never turn corrupt, dissolute, or abusive. His holiness makes any such thing quite impossible. Jehovah has on occasion even sworn oaths by his own holiness, for nothing could be more trustworthy. (Amos 4:2) Is that not reassuring?

[7] Holiness is intrinsic to Jehovah's very nature. What does that mean? To illustrate: Consider the words "man" and "imperfect." You cannot describe the former without invoking the latter. Imperfection pervades us and colors everything we do. Now consider two very different words—"Jehovah" and "holy." Holiness pervades Jehovah. Everything about him is clean, pure, and upright. We cannot get to know Jehovah as he really is without coming to grips with this profound word—"holy."

"Holiness Belongs to Jehovah"

[8] Since Jehovah embodies the quality of holiness, it may rightly be said that he is the source of all holiness. He does not selfishly hoard this precious quality; he imparts it to others, and he does so generously. Why, when God spoke to Moses through an angel at the burning bush, even the surrounding ground became holy as a result of its connection with Jehovah!—Exodus 3:5.

[9] Can imperfect humans become holy with Jehovah's help? Yes, in a relative sense. God gave his people Israel the prospect of becoming "a holy nation." (Exodus 19:6) He blessed that nation with a system of worship that was holy, clean, pure. Holiness is thus a recurring theme of

---

7. Why can it be said that holiness is intrinsic to Jehovah's nature?
8, 9. What shows that Jehovah helps imperfect humans to become holy in a relative sense?

the Mosaic Law. In fact, the high priest wore a golden plate across the front of his turban, where all could see it glittering in the light. Engraved upon it were the words: "Holiness belongs to Jehovah." (Exodus 28:36) So a high standard of cleanness and purity was to distinguish their worship and, indeed, their way of life. Jehovah told them: "You should prove yourselves holy, because I Jehovah your God am holy." (Leviticus 19:2) As long as the Israelites lived by God's counsel to the extent possible for imperfect humans, they were holy in a relative sense.

10 This emphasis on holiness was in stark contrast with the worship of the nations surrounding Israel. Those pagan nations worshiped gods whose very existence was a lie and a sham, gods who were portrayed as violent, greedy, and promiscuous. They were unholy in every possible sense. The worship of such gods made people unholy. Thus, Jehovah warned his servants to keep separate from pagan worshipers and their polluted religious practices.—Leviticus 18:24-28; 1 Kings 11:1, 2.

11 At its best, Jehovah's chosen nation of ancient Israel could provide only a dim reflection of the holiness of God's heavenly organization. The millions of spirit creatures who loyally serve God are referred to as his "holy myriads." (Deuteronomy 33:2; Jude 14) They perfectly reflect the bright, pure beauty of God's holiness. And remember the seraphs that Isaiah saw in his vision. The content of their song suggests that these mighty spirit creatures play an important role in making Jehovah's holiness known throughout the universe. One spirit creature, though, is above all of these—the only-begotten

10. When it came to holiness, what contrast existed between ancient Israel and the surrounding nations?
11. How is the holiness of Jehovah's heavenly organization evident in (a) the angels? (b) the seraphs? (c) Jesus?

Son of God. Jesus is the highest reflection of Jehovah's holiness. Rightly, he is known as "the Holy One of God." —John 6:68, 69.

Holy Name, Holy Spirit

12 What about God's own name? As we saw in Chapter 1, that name is no mere title or label. It represents Jehovah God, embracing all his qualities. Hence, the Bible tells us that his "name is holy." (Isaiah 57:15) The Mosaic Law made it a capital offense to profane God's name. (Leviticus 24:16) And note what Jesus made the first priority in prayer: "Our Father in the heavens, let your name be sanctified." (Matthew 6:9) To sanctify something means to set it apart as sacred and to revere it, to uphold it as holy. But why would something as intrinsically pure as God's own name need to be sanctified?

13 God's holy name has been impugned, besmirched with lies and slander. In Eden, Satan lied about Jehovah and implied that He is an unjust Sovereign. (Genesis 3:1-5) Since then, Satan—the ruler of this unholy world—has made sure that lies about God have proliferated. (John 8:44; 12:31; Revelation 12:9) Religions have painted God as arbitrary, remote, or cruel. They have claimed to have his backing in their bloodthirsty wars. The credit for God's marvelous acts of creation has often been given to blind chance, or evolution. Yes, God's name has been viciously maligned. It must be sanctified; its rightful glory must be restored. We long for the sanctification of his name and the vindication of his sovereignty, and we delight to play any part in that grand purpose.

12, 13. (a) Why is God's name aptly described as holy? (b) Why must God's name be sanctified?

14 There is something else intimately associated with Jehovah that is almost invariably called holy—his spirit, or active force. (Genesis 1:2) Jehovah uses this irresistible force to accomplish his purposes. All that God does, he carries out in a holy, pure, and clean way, so his active force is well named holy spirit, or spirit of holiness. (Luke 11:13; Romans 1:4) Blaspheming the holy spirit, which involves deliberately working against Jehovah's purposes, constitutes an unforgivable sin.—Mark 3:29.

Why Jehovah's Holiness Draws Us to Him

15 It is not hard to see, then, why the Bible makes a connection between the holiness of God and godly fear on the part of man. For example, Psalm 99:3 reads: "Let them laud your name. Great and fear-inspiring, holy it is." This fear, though, is not a morbid dread. Rather, it is a profound sense of reverential awe, respect in its most ennobling form. It is fitting to feel that way, since God's holiness is so far above us. It is brilliantly clean, glorious. Still, it should not repel us. On the contrary, a proper view of God's holiness will draw us closer to him. Why?

16 For one thing, the Bible associates holiness with beauty. At Isaiah 63:15, heaven is described as God's "lofty abode of holiness and beauty." Beauty attracts us. For example, look at the picture on page 33. Are you not drawn to that scene? What makes it so appealing? Note how pure the water looks. Even the air must be clean,

---

14. Why is God's spirit called holy, and why is blaspheming the holy spirit so serious?
15. Why is having godly fear a fitting response to Jehovah's holiness, and what does such fear involve?
16. (a) How is holiness associated with beauty? Give an example. (b) How do visionary descriptions of Jehovah emphasize cleanness, purity, and light?

for the sky is blue and the light seems to sparkle. Now, if that same scene was altered—the stream clogged with garbage, the trees and rocks defaced with graffiti, the air befouled with smog—we would no longer be attracted to it; we would be repelled. We naturally associate beauty with cleanness, purity, and light. These same words can be used to describe Jehovah's holiness. No wonder that visionary descriptions of Jehovah enthrall us! Beaming with light, dazzling as gemstones, glowing like fire or the purest and brightest precious metals—such is the beauty of our holy God.—Ezekiel 1:25-28; Revelation 4:2, 3.

¹⁷ However, should God's holiness make us feel inferior by comparison? The answer, of course, is yes. After all, we *are* inferior to Jehovah—and that is an understatement of epic proportions. Should knowing that alienate us from him? Consider Isaiah's reaction upon hearing the seraphs proclaim Jehovah's holiness. "I proceeded to say: 'Woe to me! For I am as good as brought to silence, because a man unclean in lips I am, and in among a people unclean in lips I am dwelling; for my eyes have seen the King, Jehovah of armies, himself!' " (Isaiah 6:5) Yes, Jehovah's infinite holiness reminded Isaiah of how sinful and imperfect he was. Initially, that faithful man was devastated. But Jehovah did not leave him in that state.

¹⁸ A seraph promptly consoled the prophet. How? The mighty spirit flew to the altar, took a coal from it, and touched the coal to Isaiah's lips. That may sound more painful than comforting. Remember, though, that this was a vision, rich in symbolic meaning. Isaiah, a faithful Jew, well knew that sacrifices were offered daily at the

---

17, 18. (a) How was Isaiah initially affected by his vision? (b) How did Jehovah use a seraph to comfort Isaiah, and what was the significance of the seraph's action?

As beauty attracts us, so should holiness

Questions for Meditation

Leviticus 19:1-18 If our conduct is to be holy, what are some principles we must apply?

Deuteronomy 23:9-14 How does personal cleanness relate to holiness? How should this affect our dress and grooming and our home?

Romans 6:12-23; 12:1-3 As we strive to be holy, how do we need to view sin and the influences of this world?

Hebrews 12:12-17 How may we pursue sanctification, or holiness?

temple altar to make atonement for sins. And the seraph lovingly reminded the prophet that although he was indeed imperfect, "unclean in lips," he could still come into a clean standing before God.* Jehovah was willing to view an imperfect, sinful man as holy—at least in a relative sense.—Isaiah 6:6, 7.

¹⁹ The same holds true today. All those sacrifices offered on the altar in Jerusalem were only shadows of something greater—the one perfect sacrifice, offered up by Jesus Christ in 33 C.E. (Hebrews 9:11-14) If we truly repent of our sins, correct our wrong course, and exercise faith in that sacrifice, we are forgiven. (1 John 2:2) We too can enjoy a clean standing before God. Thus, the apostle Peter reminds us: "It is written: 'You must be holy, because I am holy.'" (1 Peter 1:16) Note that Jehovah did *not* say

---

* The expression "unclean in lips" is apt, for lips are often used in the Bible figuratively to represent speech or language. In all imperfect humans, a high proportion of sins can be traced to the way we use the faculty of speech.—Proverbs 10:19; James 3:2, 6.

19. How is it possible for us to be holy in a relative sense, imperfect though we are?

that we must be *as* holy as he is. He never expects the impossible from us. (Psalm 103:13, 14) Rather, Jehovah tells us to be holy *because* he is holy. "As beloved children," we seek to imitate him to the best of our ability as imperfect humans. (Ephesians 5:1) So achieving holiness is an ongoing process. As we grow spiritually, we work at "perfecting holiness" day by day.—2 Corinthians 7:1.

20 Jehovah loves what is upright and pure. He hates sin. (Habakkuk 1:13) But he does not hate us. As long as we view sin as he does—hating what is bad, loving what is good—and strive to follow in Christ Jesus' perfect footsteps, Jehovah forgives our sins. (Amos 5:15; 1 Peter 2:21) When we understand that we can be clean in the eyes of our holy God, the effects are profound. Remember, Jehovah's holiness at first reminded Isaiah of his own uncleanness. He cried out: "Woe to me!" But once he understood that his sins had been atoned for, his outlook changed. When Jehovah asked for a volunteer to carry out an assignment, Isaiah promptly responded, although he did not even know what would be involved. He exclaimed: "Here I am! Send me."—Isaiah 6:5-8.

21 We are made in the image of the holy God, endowed with moral qualities and the capacity for spirituality. (Genesis 1:26) There is a potential for holiness within us all. As we continue to cultivate holiness, Jehovah is happy to help. In the process, we will draw ever closer to our holy God. Further, as we consider Jehovah's qualities in the chapters to come, we will see that there are many powerful reasons for drawing close to him!

---

20. (a) Why is it important to understand that we can be clean in the eyes of our holy God? (b) How was Isaiah affected when he learned that his sins had been atoned for?
21. What basis do we have for confidence that we can cultivate the quality of holiness?

"VIGOROUS IN POWER"

*In this section we will examine Bible accounts
that testify to Jehovah's power to create,
to destroy, to protect, and to restore.
Understanding how Jehovah God, who is
"vigorous in power," uses his "dynamic energy"
will fill our hearts with awe.*
—Isaiah 40:26.

CHAPTER 4

"Jehovah Is . . . Great in Power"

ELIJAH had seen amazing things before. He had seen ravens carrying food to him twice a day while he lived in hiding. He had seen two containers supplying flour and oil throughout a long famine and never emptying. He had even seen fire falling from the sky in response to his prayer. (1 Kings, chapters 17, 18) Still, Elijah had never seen *anything* like this.

² As he huddled near the mouth of a cave on Mount Horeb, he witnessed a series of spectacular events. First there was a wind. It must have made a howling, deafening roar, for it was so powerful that it sundered mountains and shattered crags. Next there was an earthquake, unleashing immense forces pent up in the earth's crust. Then came a fire. As it swept through the region, Elijah likely felt the blast of its searing heat.—1 Kings 19:8-12.

³ All these diverse events that Elijah witnessed had one thing in common—they were demonstrations of Jehovah God's great power. Of course, we do not need to witness a miracle to discern that God possesses this attribute. It is readily apparent. The Bible tells us that creation gives proof of Jehovah's "eternal power and Godship." (Romans 1:20) Just think of the blinding flashes and rumbling booms of a thunderstorm, the glorious cascade of a mighty waterfall, the overwhelming vastness of a starry sky! Do you not see the power of God in such displays? Yet, few in today's world truly recognize God's power.

1, 2. What amazing things had Elijah seen in his life, but what spectacular events did he witness from the cave on Mount Horeb?
3. Elijah witnessed evidence of what divine attribute, and where can we see evidence of this same quality?

Still fewer view it properly. Understanding this divine attribute, though, gives us many reasons for drawing closer to Jehovah. In this section, we embark upon a detailed study of Jehovah's matchless power.

An Essential Attribute of Jehovah

[4] Jehovah is unique in power. Jeremiah 10:6 says: "In no way is there anyone like you, O Jehovah. You are great, and your name is great in mightiness." Note that mightiness, or power, is linked with Jehovah's name. Remember, this name means "He Causes to Become." What enables Jehovah to cause himself to become whatever he chooses? Power, for one thing. Yes, Jehovah's ability to act, to carry out his will, is unlimited. Such power is one of his essential attributes.

[5] Because we could never grasp the full extent of his power, Jehovah uses illustrations to help us. As we have seen, he uses the bull to symbolize his power. (Ezekiel 1:4-10) That choice is apt, for even the domesticated bull is a huge and powerful creature. People in the Palestine of Bible times rarely, if ever, faced anything stronger. But they did know of a more fearsome sort of bull—the wild bull, or aurochs, which has since become extinct. (Job 39:9-12) Roman Emperor Julius Caesar once observed that these bulls were scarcely smaller than elephants. "Great is their strength," he wrote, "and great their speed." Imagine how tiny and weak you would feel standing in the shadow of such a creature!

4, 5. (a) What link is there between Jehovah's name and his mightiness, or power? (b) Why is it fitting that Jehovah chose the bull to symbolize his power?

"Look! Jehovah was passing by"

⁶ Similarly, man is puny and powerless when compared with the God of power, Jehovah. To him, even mighty nations are like a mere film of dust on a pair of scales. (Isaiah 40:15) Unlike any creature, Jehovah has *unlimited* power, for he alone is called "the Almighty."* (Revelation 15:3) Jehovah is "vigorous in power" and possesses an "abundance of dynamic energy." (Isaiah 40:26) He is the ever-plentiful, inexhaustible source of power. He depends upon no outside source for energy, for "strength *belongs* to God." (Psalm 62:11) By what means, though, does Jehovah exert his power?

How Jehovah Exerts His Power

⁷ Holy spirit pours forth from Jehovah in limitless supply. It is God's power *in action*. In fact, at Genesis 1:2, the Bible refers to it as God's "active force." The original Hebrew and Greek words that are rendered "spirit" may, in other contexts, be translated "wind," "breath," and "blast." According to lexicographers, the original-language words suggest an invisible force in action. Like wind, God's spirit is invisible to our eyes, but its effects are real and discernible.

⁸ God's holy spirit is endlessly versatile. Jehovah can use it to carry out any purpose that he has in mind. Aptly, then, in the Bible, God's spirit is figuratively called his "finger," his "strong hand," or his "outstretched arm." (Luke 11:20; Deuteronomy 5:15; Psalm 8:3) Just as a man

---

* The Greek word rendered "Almighty" literally means "Ruler Over All; One Who Has All Power."

---

6. Why is Jehovah alone called "the Almighty"?
7. What is Jehovah's holy spirit, and what is suggested by the original-language words used in the Bible?
8. In the Bible, what is God's spirit figuratively called, and why are these comparisons fitting?

might apply his hand to a wide range of tasks requiring varying degrees of strength or finesse, so God can use his spirit to accomplish any purpose—such as creating the infinitesimal atom or parting the Red Sea or enabling first-century Christians to speak in foreign tongues.

⁹ Jehovah also exerts power through his authority as Universal Sovereign. Can you imagine having millions upon millions of intelligent, able subjects eager to do your bidding? Jehovah wields such ruling power. He has human servants, in Scripture often likened to an army. (Psalm 68:11; 110:3) A human is a weak creature, though, compared with an angel. Why, when the Assyrian army attacked God's people, a single angel killed 185,000 of those soldiers in one night! (2 Kings 19:35) God's angels are "mighty in power."—Psalm 103:19, 20.

¹⁰ How many angels are there? The prophet Daniel had a vision of heaven in which he saw well over 100 million spirit creatures before Jehovah's throne, but there is no indication that he saw the entire angelic creation. (Daniel 7:10) So there may be hundreds of millions of angels. God is thus called Jehovah of armies. This title describes his powerful position as Commander of a vast, organized array of mighty angels. Above all these spirit creatures, he has placed one in charge, his own beloved Son, "the firstborn of all creation." (Colossians 1:15) As the archangel —chief over all the angels, seraphs, and cherubs—Jesus is the mightiest of all of Jehovah's creations.

¹¹ Jehovah has yet another means of exerting power. Hebrews 4:12 says: "The word of God is alive and exerts

---

9. How extensive is Jehovah's ruling power?
10. (a) Why is the Almighty called Jehovah of armies? (b) Who is the mightiest of all of Jehovah's creations?
11, 12. (a) In what ways does God's word exert power? (b) How did Jesus attest to the extent of Jehovah's power?

power." Have you observed the phenomenal power of God's word, or spirit-inspired message, now preserved in the Bible? It can strengthen us, build up our faith, and help us make profound changes in ourselves. The apostle Paul warned fellow believers against people engaged in grossly immoral life-styles. Then he added: "Yet that is what some of you were." (1 Corinthians 6:9-11) Yes, "the word of God" had exerted its power in them and helped them to change.

12 Jehovah's power is so immense and his means of exerting it are so effective that nothing can stand in his way. Jesus said: "With God all things are possible." (Matthew 19:26) To what purposes does Jehovah direct his power?

Power Guided by Purpose

13 Jehovah's spirit is something far greater than any physical force; and Jehovah is no impersonal force, a mere source of power. He is a personal God in full control of his own power. What, though, moves him to use it?

14 As we shall see, God uses power to create, to destroy, to protect, to restore—in short, to do whatever suits his perfect purposes. (Isaiah 46:10) In some instances, Jehovah uses his power to reveal important aspects of his personality and standards. Above all, he directs his power to fulfill his will—to vindicate his sovereignty and sanctify his holy name by means of the Messianic Kingdom. Nothing can ever thwart that purpose.

15 Jehovah also uses his power to benefit us as individuals. Note what 2 Chronicles 16:9 says: "As regards Jehovah, his eyes are roving about through all the earth to show

---

13, 14. (a) Why can we say that Jehovah is no impersonal source of power? (b) In what ways does Jehovah use his power?
15. Jehovah uses his power for what purpose in connection with his servants, and how was this demonstrated in Elijah's case?

his strength in behalf of those whose heart is complete toward him." Elijah's experience, mentioned at the outset, is a case in point. Why did Jehovah give him that awesome demonstration of divine power? Well, wicked Queen Jezebel had vowed to have Elijah executed. The prophet was on the run, fleeing for his life. He felt alone, frightened, and discouraged—as if all his hard work had been in vain. To comfort the troubled man, Jehovah vividly reminded Elijah of divine power. The wind, the earthquake, and the fire showed that the most powerful Being in the universe was there with Elijah. What had he to fear from Jezebel, with the almighty God on his side?—1 Kings 19:1-12.*

¹⁶ Although now is not his time for performing miracles, Jehovah has not changed since Elijah's day. (1 Corinthians 13:8) He is just as eager today to use his power in behalf of those who love him. True, he dwells in a lofty spirit realm, but he is not far off from us. His power is limitless, so distance is no barrier. Rather, "Jehovah is near to all those calling upon him." (Psalm 145:18) Once when the prophet Daniel called upon Jehovah for help, an angel appeared before he had even finished praying! (Daniel 9:20-23) Nothing can prevent Jehovah from helping and strengthening those whom he loves.—Psalm 118:6.

Does God's Power Make Him Unapproachable?

¹⁷ Should God's power cause us to fear him? We must

---

* The Bible states that "Jehovah was not *in* the wind . . . , the quaking . . . , the fire." Unlike worshipers of mythical nature gods, Jehovah's servants do not look for him within the forces of nature. He is far too great to be contained within anything that he has created. —1 Kings 8:27.

---

16. Why can we take comfort in contemplating Jehovah's great power?
17. In what sense does Jehovah's power promote fear in us, but what kind of fear does it not promote?

answer both yes and no. Yes, in that this attribute gives us ample reason for godly fear, the profound awe and respect we discussed briefly in the preceding chapter. Such fear, the Bible tells us, is "the beginning of wisdom." (Psalm 111:10) We also answer no, however, in that God's power gives us no reason to feel a morbid dread of him or to shy away from approaching him.

18 "Power tends to corrupt; absolute power corrupts absolutely." So wrote English nobleman Lord Acton in 1887. His statement has often been repeated, perhaps because so many people see it as undeniably true. Imperfect humans often abuse power, as history has confirmed again and again. (Ecclesiastes 4:1; 8:9) For this reason, many mistrust the powerful and withdraw from them. Now, Jehovah has absolute power. Has it corrupted him in any way? Certainly not! As we have seen, he is holy, utterly incorruptible. Jehovah is unlike the imperfect men and women of power in this corrupt world. He has never abused his power, and he never will.

19 Remember, power is not Jehovah's sole attribute. We have yet to study his justice, his wisdom, and his love. But we should not assume that Jehovah's attributes come to the fore in a rigid, mechanical manner, as if he exercised only one quality at a time. On the contrary, we will see in the ensuing chapters that Jehovah *always* exercises his power in harmony with his justice, his wisdom, and his love. Think about another quality that God possesses, one that is rarely present in worldly rulers—self-restraint.

18. (a) Why do many mistrust powerful people? (b) How do we know that Jehovah cannot be corrupted by his power?
19, 20. (a) In harmony with what other qualities does Jehovah always exercise his power, and why is this reassuring? (b) How might you illustrate Jehovah's self-restraint, and why is it appealing to you?

Questions for Meditation

2 Chronicles 16:7-13 How does the example of King Asa show the seriousness of failing to trust in Jehovah's power?

Psalm 89:6-18 What effect does Jehovah's power have upon his worshipers?

Isaiah 40:10-31 How is Jehovah's power here described, how extensive is it, and how can it benefit us individually?

Revelation 11:16-18 What does Jehovah promise to do with his power in the future, and why is this reassuring to true Christians?

---

20 Imagine meeting a man so huge and powerful that you feel intimidated by him. However, in time you notice that he seems gentle. He is ever ready and eager to use his power to help and protect people, especially the defenseless and vulnerable. He never abuses his strength. You see him slandered without cause, yet his demeanor is firm but calm, dignified, even kind. You find yourself wondering if you would be able to show the same gentleness and restraint, especially if you were that strong! As you come to know such a man, would you not begin to feel drawn to him? We have far more reason for drawing close to the almighty Jehovah. Consider the full sentence that is the basis for the title of this chapter: "Jehovah is *slow to anger* and great in power." (Nahum 1:3) Jehovah is not quick to use his power against people, not even the wicked. He is mild-tempered and kind. He has proved to be "slow to anger" in the face of many provocations.—Psalm 78:37-41.

21 Consider Jehovah's self-restraint from a different

---

21. Why does Jehovah refrain from forcing people to do his will, and what does this teach us about him?

angle. If you had unlimited power, do you think you might, at times, be tempted to make people do things your way? Jehovah, with all his power, does not coerce people to serve him. Even though serving God is the only way to everlasting life, Jehovah does not force us into such service. Rather, he kindly dignifies each individual with freedom to choose. He warns of the consequences of bad choices and tells of the rewards of good choices. But the choice itself, he leaves to us. (Deuteronomy 30:19, 20) Jehovah simply has no interest in service performed out of coercion or out of morbid fear of his awesome power. He seeks those who will serve him willingly, out of love. —2 Corinthians 9:7.

²² Let us look at a final reason why we need not live in dread of Almighty God. Powerful humans tend to be fearful of sharing power with others. Jehovah, however, delights in empowering his loyal worshipers. He delegates considerable authority to others, such as his Son. (Matthew 28:18) Jehovah also empowers his servants in another way. The Bible explains: "Yours, O Jehovah, are the greatness and the mightiness and the beauty and the excellency and the dignity; for everything in the heavens and in the earth is yours. . . . In your hand there are power and mightiness, and in your hand is ability to make great and to give strength to all."—1 Chronicles 29:11, 12.

²³ Yes, Jehovah will be pleased to give you strength. He even imparts "power beyond what is normal" to those who want to serve him. (2 Corinthians 4:7) Do you not feel drawn to this dynamic God, who uses his power in such kind and principled ways? In the next chapter, we will focus on how Jehovah uses his power to create.

22, 23. (a) What shows that Jehovah delights in empowering others? (b) What will we consider in the next chapter?

CHAPTER 5

Creative Power—"The Maker of Heaven and Earth"

HAVE you ever stood near a fire on a cold night? Perhaps you held out your hands at just the right distance from the flames to enjoy the radiating warmth. If you leaned in too close, the heat became unbearable. If you stepped back too far, the cool night air closed in, and you felt chilled.

2 There is a "fire" that warms our skin by day. That "fire" is burning some 93 million miles away!* What power the sun must have for you to be able to feel its heat from such a distance! Yet, the earth orbits that awesome thermonuclear furnace at just the right distance. Too close, and earth's water would vaporize; too far, and it would all freeze. Either extreme would render our planet lifeless. Essential to life on earth, sunlight is also clean and efficient, not to mention delightful.—Ecclesiastes 11:7.

3 Nevertheless, most people take the sun for granted, even though their lives depend on it. Thus, they miss what the sun can teach us. The Bible says of Jehovah: "You . . . prepared the luminary, even the sun." (Psalm 74:16) Yes, the sun brings honor to Jehovah, "the Maker of heaven and earth." (Psalm 19:1; 146:6) It is just one of countless heavenly bodies that teach us about Jehovah's immense creative power. Let us examine some of these

---

* To put that giant number in perspective, think about this: To drive that distance by car—even speeding along at 100 miles per hour, 24 hours a day—would take you over a hundred years!

1, 2. How does the sun demonstrate Jehovah's creative power?
3. The sun testifies to what important truth?

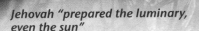

Jehovah "prepared the luminary, even the sun"

more closely and then turn our attention to the earth and the life that thrives upon it.

"Raise Your Eyes High Up and See"

⁴ As you may know, our sun is a star. It appears larger than the stars we see at night because, compared with them, it is quite close. How powerful is it? At its core, the sun is about 27,000,000 degrees Fahrenheit. If you could take a pinhead-sized piece of the sun's core and put it here on the earth, you could not safely stand within 90 miles of that tiny heat source! Every second, the sun emits energy equivalent to the explosion of many hundreds of millions of nuclear bombs.

⁵ The sun is so huge that over 1,300,000 of our earths could fit inside it. Is the sun an unusually large star? No, astronomers call it a yellow dwarf. The apostle Paul wrote that "star differs from star in glory." (1 Corinthians 15:41)

4, 5. How powerful and how large is the sun, yet how does it compare with other stars?

He could not have known how true those inspired words are. There is a star so huge that if it were placed right where the sun is, our earth would be *inside* it. Another giant star so placed would reach all the way out to Saturn —although that planet is so far from the earth that it took a spacecraft four years to get there, traveling over 40 times faster than a bullet fired from a powerful handgun!

⁶ Even more awesome than the size of the stars is their number. In fact, the Bible suggests that the stars are virtually innumerable, as difficult to count as "the sand of the sea." (Jeremiah 33:22) This statement implies that there are far more stars than the naked eye can see. After

---

6. How does the Bible show that the number of the stars is vast from a human standpoint?

"All of [them] he calls even by name"

all, if a Bible writer, such as Jeremiah, had looked up at the night sky and had tried to count the visible stars, he would have counted only three thousand or so, for that is how many the unaided human eye can detect on a clear night. That number might be comparable to the number of grains in a mere *handful* of sand. In reality, though, the number of stars is overwhelming, like the sand of the sea.* Who could count such a number?

7 Isaiah 40:26 answers: "Raise your eyes high up and see. Who has created these things? It is the One who is bringing forth the army of them even by number, all of whom he calls even by name." Psalm 147:4 says: "He is counting the number of the stars." What is "the number of the stars"? That is not a simple question. Astronomers estimate that there are over 100 billion stars in our Milky Way galaxy alone.# But ours is just one of many galaxies, and many of those swarm with even more stars. How many galaxies are there? Some astronomers have estimated 50 billion. Others have calculated that there may be as many as 125 billion. So man cannot even determine the number of galaxies, let alone the exact sum of all the billions of stars they contain. Yet, Jehovah knows that number. Moreover, he gives each star its own *name!*

---

* Some think that ancients in Bible times must have used a rudimentary form of telescope. How else, the reasoning goes, could men of those times have known that the number of stars is so vast, innumerable, from a human standpoint? Such unfounded speculation leaves Jehovah, the Author of the Bible, out of the picture.—2 Timothy 3:16.

Consider how long it would take you just to *count* 100 billion stars. If you were able to count a new one each second—and keep at it 24 hours a day—it would take you 3,171 years!

---

7. (a) About how many stars does our Milky Way galaxy contain, and how large a number is that? (b) Why is it significant that astronomers find it difficult to number the galaxies, and what does this teach us about Jehovah's creative power?

[8] Our awe can only increase when we contemplate the size of galaxies. The Milky Way galaxy has been estimated to measure some 100,000 light-years across. Picture a beam of light traveling at the tremendous speed of 186,000 miles each second. It would take that beam 100,000 years to traverse our galaxy! And some galaxies are many times the size of ours. The Bible says that Jehovah is "stretching out" these vast heavens as if they were mere fabric. (Psalm 104:2) He also orders the movements of these creations. From the smallest speck of interstellar dust to the mightiest galaxy, everything moves according to physical laws that God has formulated and put into effect. (Job 38:31-33) Thus, scientists have likened the precise movements of the celestial bodies to the choreography of an elaborate ballet! Think, then, of the One who has created these things. Do you not stand in awe of the God having such immense creative power?

"The Maker of the Earth by His Power"

[9] Jehovah's creative power is evident in our home, the earth. He has placed the earth very carefully in this vast universe. Some scientists believe that many galaxies might prove inhospitable to a life-bearing planet like ours. Much of our Milky Way galaxy was evidently not designed to accommodate life. The galactic center is packed with stars. Radiation is high, and close encounters between stars are common. The fringes of the galaxy lack many of the elements essential to life. Our solar system is ideally situated between such extremes.

---

8. (a) How would you explain the size of the Milky Way galaxy? (b) By what means does Jehovah order the movements of celestial bodies?
9, 10. How is Jehovah's power evident in connection with the positioning of our solar system, Jupiter, the earth, and the moon?

¹⁰ Earth benefits from a distant but giant protector—the planet Jupiter. More than a thousand times the size of Earth, Jupiter exerts a tremendous gravitational influence. The result? It absorbs or deflects objects that speed through space. Scientists figure that if not for Jupiter, the rain of massive projectiles striking the earth would be 10,000 times more severe than at present. Closer to home, our earth is blessed with an unusual satellite—the moon. More than an object of beauty and a "night-light," the moon holds the earth at a constant, steady tilt. That tilt gives the earth its stable, predictable seasons—another important boon to life here.

¹¹ Jehovah's creative power is evident in every facet of the earth's design. Consider the atmosphere, which serves as a protective shield. The sun emits healthful rays and deadly ones. When the lethal rays strike the earth's upper atmosphere, they cause ordinary oxygen to turn into ozone. The resulting ozone layer, in turn, absorbs most of those rays. In effect, our planet is designed with its own protective umbrella!

¹² That is just one aspect of our atmosphere, a complex mix of gases ideally suited to supporting the creatures living on or near the earth's surface. Among wonders of the atmosphere is the water cycle. Every year the sun lifts up by evaporation over 100,000 cubic miles of water from the earth's oceans and seas. The water forms clouds, which are circulated far and wide by atmospheric winds. This water, now filtered and purified, falls as rain, snow, and ice, replenishing water supplies. It is just as Ecclesiastes 1:7 says: "All the winter torrents are going forth

11. How is earth's atmosphere designed to serve as a protective shield?
12. How does the atmospheric water cycle illustrate Jehovah's creative power?

to the sea, yet the sea itself is not full. To the place where the winter torrents are going forth, there they are returning so as to go forth." Only Jehovah could set such a cycle in motion.

[13] Wherever we see life, we see evidence of the Creator's power. From the mighty redwoods that tower higher than 30-story buildings to the microscopic plant life that teems in the oceans and provides much of the oxygen we breathe, Jehovah's creative power is evident. The very soil is packed with living things—worms, fungi, and microbes, all working together in complex ways that help plants to grow. Fittingly, the Bible speaks of the soil as having power.—Genesis 4:12.

[14] Without a doubt, Jehovah is "the Maker of the earth by his power." (Jeremiah 10:12) God's power is evident even in his smallest creations. For instance, a million atoms laid side by side would not span the thickness of a human hair. And even if an atom were expanded until it was as tall as a 14-story building, its nucleus would be the size of a mere grain of salt located on the seventh floor. Yet, that infinitesimal nucleus is the source of the awesome power unleashed in a nuclear explosion!

"Every Breathing Thing"

[15] Another vivid proof of Jehovah's creative power lies in the abundance of animal life on the earth. Psalm 148 lists many of the things that praise Jehovah, and verse 10 includes "you wild animals and all you domestic animals." To show why man should be in awe of the Creator,

---

13. What evidence of the Creator's power do we see in the earth's vegetation and its soil?
14. What latent power exists even in the tiny atom?
15. By discussing various wild animals, what lesson did Jehovah teach Job?

Jehovah once spoke to Job about such animals as the lion, the zebra, the wild bull, Behemoth (or, hippopotamus), and Leviathan (evidently the crocodile). The point? If man stands in awe of these mighty, fearsome, and untamable creatures, how should he feel about their Creator? —Job, chapters 38-41.

[16] Psalm 148:10 also mentions "winged birds." Just think of the varieties! Jehovah told Job of the ostrich, which "laughs at the horse and at its rider." Indeed, this eight-foot-tall bird may be flightless, but it can run 40 miles per hour, covering up to 15 feet in a single stride! (Job 39:13, 18) On the other hand, the albatross spends most of its life in the air over the seas. A natural glider, this bird has a wingspan of some 11 feet. It may soar for hours at a stretch without flapping its wings. By way of contrast, at only two inches in length, the bee hummingbird is the smallest bird in the world. It may flap its wings up to 80 times in a second! Hummingbirds, glittering like little winged gems, can hover like helicopters and even fly backward.

[17] Psalm 148:7 says that even the "sea monsters" praise Jehovah. Consider what is often thought to be the largest animal ever to live on this planet, the blue whale. This "monster" of the deep may reach a length of 100 feet or more. It may weigh as much as a herd of 30 adult elephants. Its tongue alone weighs as much as one elephant. Its heart is the size of a small car. This huge organ beats only 9 times per minute—in contrast with the hummingbird's heart, which may beat some 1,200 times per minute. At least one of the blue whale's blood vessels is so large that a child could crawl inside it. Surely our hearts move us to echo the exhortation that concludes the

16. What impresses you about some of the birds that Jehovah has created?
17. How large is the blue whale, and what conclusion should we naturally reach after contemplating Jehovah's animal creations?

Questions for Meditation

Psalm 8:3-9 How can Jehovah's creation teach us humility?

Psalm 19:1-6 Jehovah's creative power may incite us to do what, and why?

Matthew 6:25-34 How can contemplating Jehovah's creative power help us to fight anxiety and set proper priorities in life?

Acts 17:22-31 How does Jehovah's use of creative power teach us that idolatry is wrong and that God is not far off from us?

---

book of Psalms: "Every breathing thing—let it praise Jah." —Psalm 150:6.

Learning From Jehovah's Creative Power

¹⁸ What do we learn from Jehovah's use of his creative power? We are awestruck by the diversity of creation. One psalmist exclaimed: "How many your works are, O Jehovah! . . . The earth is full of your productions." (Psalm 104: 24) How true! Biologists have identified well over a million species of living things on earth; yet, opinions vary as to whether there may be as many as 10 million, 30 million, or more. A human artist may find that his creativity runs dry at times. In contrast, Jehovah's creativity—his power to invent and create new and diverse things—is obviously inexhaustible.

¹⁹ Jehovah's use of his creative power teaches us about his sovereignty. The very word "Creator" separates Jehovah from everything else in the universe, all of which is "creation." Even Jehovah's only-begotten Son, who served as "a master worker" during creation, is never called Creator or co-Creator in the Bible. (Proverbs 8:30; Matthew 19:4)

18, 19. How diverse are the living things that Jehovah has made on this earth, and what does creation teach us about his sovereignty?

Rather, he is "the firstborn of all *creation.*" (Colossians 1: 15) Jehovah's position as the Creator gives him the intrinsic right to wield exclusive sovereign power over all the universe.—Romans 1:20; Revelation 4:11.

[20] Has Jehovah stopped exercising his creative power? Well, the Bible does say that when Jehovah finished his creative work on the sixth creative day, "he proceeded to rest on the seventh day from all his work that he had made." (Genesis 2:2) The apostle Paul indicated that this seventh "day" is thousands of years long, for it was still ongoing in his day. (Hebrews 4:3-6) But does "rest" mean that Jehovah has stopped working altogether? No, Jehovah never stops working. (Psalm 92:4; John 5:17) His rest, then, must simply refer to the cessation of his work of physical creation respecting the earth. His work of bringing his purposes to fulfillment, however, has continued uninterrupted. Such work has included the inspiration of the Holy Scriptures. His work has even involved the bringing forth of "a new creation," which will be discussed in Chapter 19.—2 Corinthians 5:17.

[21] When Jehovah's rest day finally comes to an end, he will be able to pronounce all of his work on the earth "very good," much as he did at the end of the six creative days. (Genesis 1:31) How he may choose to exercise his limitless creative power thereafter remains to be seen. In any event, we may be assured that we will continue to be fascinated by Jehovah's use of creative power. Throughout all eternity, we will learn more about Jehovah through his creation. (Ecclesiastes 3:11) The more we learn about him, the more profound our awe will become—and the closer we will draw to our Grand Creator.

----

20. In what sense has Jehovah rested since completing his earthly creation?
21. How will Jehovah's creative power affect faithful humans throughout eternity?

CHAPTER 6

Destructive Power—"Jehovah Is a Manly Person of War"

THE Israelites were trapped—wedged between forbidding mountain cliffs and an impassable sea. The Egyptian army, a ruthless killing machine, was in hot pursuit, determined to annihilate them.* Still, Moses urged God's people not to lose hope. "Jehovah will himself fight for you," he assured them.—Exodus 14:14.

² Even so, Moses apparently called out to Jehovah, and God responded: "Why do you keep crying out to me? . . . Lift up your rod and stretch your hand out over the sea and split it apart." (Exodus 14:15, 16) Just picture the unfolding of events. Jehovah immediately commands his angel, and the pillar of cloud moves to Israel's rear, perhaps spreading out like a wall and blocking the Egyptian line of attack. (Exodus 14:19, 20; Psalm 105:39) Moses stretches out his hand. Driven by a strong wind, the sea splits apart. The waters somehow congeal and stand up like walls, opening up a path wide enough to accommodate the entire nation!—Exodus 14:21; 15:8.

³ Faced with this display of might, Pharaoh should order his troops home. Instead, prideful Pharaoh orders an attack. (Exodus 14:23) The Egyptians rush into the seabed in pursuit, but their charge soon dissolves into chaos as the wheels of their chariots begin falling off. Once the

---

* According to Jewish historian Josephus, the Hebrews were "pursued by 600 chariots along with 50,000 horsemen and heavy infantry to the number of 200,000."—*Jewish Antiquities*, II, 324 [xv, 3].

1-3. (a) What threat did the Israelites face at the hands of the Egyptians? (b) How did Jehovah fight for his people?

Israelites are safe on the other side, Jehovah commands Moses: "Stretch your hand out over the sea, that the waters may come back over the Egyptians, their war chariots and their cavalrymen." The watery walls collapse, burying Pharaoh and his forces!—Exodus 14:24-28; Psalm 136:15.

[4] The deliverance of the nation of Israel at the Red Sea was a momentous event in the history of God's dealings with mankind. There Jehovah proved himself to be "a manly person of war." (Exodus 15:3) How, though, do you react to this portrayal of Jehovah? To be honest, war has brought much pain and misery to humankind. Could it be that God's use of destructive power seems more like a deterrent than an incentive to your drawing close to him?

Divine War Versus Human Conflicts

[5] Nearly three hundred times in the Hebrew Scriptures and twice in the Christian Greek Scriptures, God is given the title "Jehovah of armies." (1 Samuel 1:11) As Sovereign Ruler, Jehovah commands a vast army of angelic forces. (Joshua 5:13-15; 1 Kings 22:19) The destructive potential of this army is awesome. (Isaiah 37:36) The destruction of humans is not pleasant to contemplate. However, we must remember that God's wars are unlike petty human conflicts. Military and political leaders may try to attribute noble motives to their aggression. But human war invariably involves greed and selfishness.

[6] In contrast, Jehovah is not driven by blind emotion.

---

4. (a) What did Jehovah prove to be at the Red Sea? (b) How might some react to this portrayal of Jehovah?
5, 6. (a) Why is God appropriately called "Jehovah of armies"? (b) How does divine warfare differ from human warfare?

At the Red Sea, Jehovah proved himself to be "a manly person of war"

Deuteronomy 32:4 declares: "The Rock, perfect is his activity, for all his ways are justice. A God of faithfulness, with whom there is no injustice; righteous and upright is he." God's Word condemns unbridled rage, cruelty, and violence. (Genesis 49:7; Psalm 11:5) So Jehovah never acts without reason. He uses his destructive power sparingly and as a last resort. It is as he stated through his prophet Ezekiel: " 'Do I take any delight at all in the death of someone wicked,' is the utterance of the Sovereign Lord Jehovah, 'and not in that he should turn back from his ways and actually keep living?' "—Ezekiel 18:23.

7 Why, then, does Jehovah use destructive power? Before answering, we might call to mind the righteous man Job. Satan challenged whether Job—really, any human—would keep his integrity under trial. Jehovah answered that challenge by allowing Satan to test Job's integrity. As a result, Job suffered illness, loss of wealth, and loss of his children. (Job 1:1–2:8) Unaware of the issues involved, Job mistakenly concluded that his suffering was unjust punishment from God. He asked God why He had made him a "target," "an enemy."—Job 7:20; 13:24.

8 A young man named Elihu exposed the flaw in Job's reasoning, saying: "You have said, 'My righteousness is more than God's.' " (Job 35:2) Yes, it is unwise to think that we know better than God or to assume that he has behaved unfairly. "Far be it from the true God to act wickedly, and the Almighty to act unjustly," Elihu declared. Later, he said: "As for the Almighty, we have not found him out; he is exalted in power, and justice and abundance of righteousness he will not belittle." (Job 34:10; 36:22, 23; 37:23) We can be sure that when God fights,

7, 8. (a) What did Job mistakenly conclude about his sufferings? (b) How did Elihu correct Job's thinking in this regard? (c) What lesson can we learn from Job's experience?

he has good cause for doing so. With that in mind, let us explore some of the reasons why the God of peace sometimes assumes the mantle of a warrior.—1 Corinthians 14:33.

Why the God of Peace Is Compelled to Fight

9 After praising God as "a manly person of war," Moses declared: "Who among the gods is like you, O Jehovah? Who is like you, proving yourself mighty in holiness?" (Exodus 15:11) The prophet Habakkuk similarly wrote: "You are too pure in eyes to see what is bad; and to look on trouble you are not able." (Habakkuk 1:13) Although Jehovah is a God of love, he is also a God of holiness, righteousness, and justice. At times, such qualities compel him to use his destructive power. (Isaiah 59:15-19; Luke 18:7) So God does not blemish his holiness when he fights. Rather, he fights *because* he is holy.—Exodus 39:30.

10 Consider the situation that arose after the first human couple, Adam and Eve, rebelled against God. (Genesis 3:1-6) Had he tolerated their unrighteousness, Jehovah would have undermined his own position as Universal Sovereign. As a righteous God, he was obliged to sentence them to death. (Romans 6:23) In the first Bible prophecy, he foretold that enmity would exist between his own servants and the followers of the "serpent," Satan. (Revelation 12:9; Genesis 3:15) Ultimately, this enmity could only be resolved by the crushing of Satan. (Romans 16: 20) But that judgment act would result in great blessings for righteous mankind, ridding the earth of Satan's influence and opening the way to a global paradise.

---

9. Why does the God of peace fight?
10. (a) When and how did the need for God to wage war first arise? (b) How only could the enmity foretold at Genesis 3:15 be resolved, and with what benefits to righteous mankind?

(Matthew 19:28) Until then, those who sided with Satan would constitute an ongoing threat to the physical and spiritual well-being of God's people. On occasion, Jehovah would have to intervene.

God Acts to Remove Wickedness

¹¹ The Deluge of Noah's day was a case of such intervention. Says Genesis 6:11, 12: "The earth came to be ruined in the sight of the true God and the earth became filled with violence. So God saw the earth and, look! it was ruined, because all flesh had ruined its way on the earth." Would God allow the wicked to snuff out the last vestige of morality left on earth? No. Jehovah felt obliged to bring a global deluge to rid the earth of those who were bent on violence and immorality.

¹² It was similar with God's judgment against the Canaanites. Jehovah revealed that out of Abraham would come a "seed" through which all the families of the earth would bless themselves. In harmony with that purpose, God decreed that Abraham's offspring would be given the land of Canaan, a land inhabited by a people called the Amorites. How could God be justified in forcibly evicting these people from their land? Jehovah foretold that the eviction would not come for some 400 years—until "the error of the Amorites" had "come to completion."* (Genesis 12:1-3; 13:14, 15; 15:13, 16; 22:18) During that period of time, the Amorites sank deeper and deeper into moral corruption. Canaan became a land of idolatry, bloodshed,

---

* Evidently, the term "Amorites" here includes all the peoples of Canaan.—Deuteronomy 1:6-8, 19-21, 27; Joshua 24:15, 18.

---

11. Why did God feel obliged to bring a global flood?
12. (a) What did Jehovah foretell regarding Abraham's "seed"? (b) Why were the Amorites to be exterminated?

and degraded sexual practices. (Exodus 23:24; 34:12, 13; Numbers 33:52) The inhabitants of the land even killed children in sacrificial fires. Could a holy God expose his people to such wickedness? No! He declared: "The land is unclean, and I shall bring punishment for its error upon it, and the land will vomit its inhabitants out." (Leviticus 18:21-25) Jehovah did not kill the people indiscriminately, however. Rightly disposed Canaanites, such as Rahab and the Gibeonites, were spared.—Joshua 6:25; 9:3-27.

Fighting in Behalf of His Name

[13] Because Jehovah is holy, his name is holy. (Leviticus 22:32) Jesus taught his disciples to pray: "Let your name be sanctified." (Matthew 6:9) The rebellion in Eden profaned God's name, calling into question God's reputation and way of ruling. Jehovah could never condone such slander and rebellion. He was obliged to clear his name of reproach.—Isaiah 48:11.

[14] Consider, again, the Israelites. As long as they were slaves in Egypt, God's promise to Abraham that by means of his Seed all the families of the earth would bless themselves seemed empty. But by delivering them and establishing them as a nation, Jehovah cleared his name of reproach. The prophet Daniel thus recalled in prayer: "O Jehovah our God, you . . . brought your people out from the land of Egypt by a strong hand and proceeded to make a name for yourself."—Daniel 9:15.

[15] Interestingly, Daniel prayed this way at a time when the Jews needed Jehovah to act once again for the sake of His name. The disobedient Jews found themselves in captivity, this time in Babylon. Their own capital city,

13, 14. (a) Why was Jehovah obliged to sanctify his name? (b) How did Jehovah clear his name of reproach?
15. Why did Jehovah rescue the Jews from captivity in Babylon?

Jerusalem, lay in ruins. Daniel knew that restoring the Jews to their homeland would magnify Jehovah's name. Daniel thus prayed: "O Jehovah, do forgive. O Jehovah, do pay attention and act. Do not delay, for your own sake, O my God, *for your own name* has been called upon your city and upon your people."—Daniel 9:18, 19.

Fighting in Behalf of His People

16 Does Jehovah's interest in defending his name mean that he is cold and self-centered? No, for by acting in accord with his holiness and love of justice, he protects his people. Consider Genesis chapter 14. There we read of four invading kings who kidnapped Abraham's nephew Lot, along with Lot's family. With God's help, Abraham executed a stunning defeat of vastly superior forces! The account of this victory was likely the first entry in "the book of the Wars of Jehovah," evidently a book that also documented some military encounters that are not recorded in the Bible. (Numbers 21:14) Many more victories were to follow.

17 Shortly before the Israelites entered the land of Canaan, Moses assured them: "Jehovah your God is the one going before you. He will fight for you according to all that he did with you in Egypt." (Deuteronomy 1:30; 20:1) Starting with Moses' successor, Joshua, and continuing on through the period of the Judges and the reigns of the faithful kings of Judah, Jehovah indeed fought for his people, giving them many dramatic victories over their enemies.—Joshua 10:1-14; Judges 4:12-17; 2 Samuel 5:17-21.

---

16. Explain why Jehovah's interest in defending his name does not mean that he is cold and self-centered.
17. What shows that Jehovah fought for the Israelites after their entry into the land of Canaan? Give examples.

Questions for Meditation

2 Kings 6:8-17 How can God's role as "Jehovah of armies" prove encouraging to us during times of distress?

Ezekiel 33:10-20 Before Jehovah resorts to destructive power, what opportunity does he mercifully extend to those who transgress his law?

2 Thessalonians 1:6-10 How will the coming destruction of wicked people bring relief to faithful servants of God?

2 Peter 2:4-13 What moves Jehovah to wield his destructive power, providing what lessons for all mankind?

[18] Jehovah has not changed; nor has his purpose to make this planet a peaceful paradise changed. (Genesis 1: 27, 28) God still hates wickedness. At the same time, he dearly loves his people and will soon act in their behalf. (Psalm 11:7) In fact, the enmity described at Genesis 3:15 is expected to reach a dramatic and violent turning point in the near future. To sanctify his name and protect his people, Jehovah will once again become "a manly person of war"!—Zechariah 14:3; Revelation 16:14, 16.

[19] Consider an illustration: Suppose that a man's family was being attacked by a vicious animal and that the man jumped into the fray and killed the violent beast. Would you expect his wife and children to be repelled by this act? On the contrary, you would expect them to be moved by his selfless love for them. In a similar way, we

---

18. (a) Why can we be thankful that Jehovah has not changed? (b) What will happen when the enmity described at Genesis 3:15 reaches its climax?
19. (a) Illustrate why God's use of destructive power can draw us close to him. (b) What effect should God's willingness to fight have upon us?

should not be repelled by God's use of destructive power. His willingness to fight to protect us should increase our love for him. Our respect for his unlimited power should deepen as well. Thus, we can "render God sacred service with godly fear and awe."—Hebrews 12:28.

Draw Close to the "Manly Person of War"

20 Of course, the Bible does not in each case explain all the details of Jehovah's decisions regarding divine warfare. But of this we can always be certain: Jehovah never wields destructive power in an unjust, wanton, or cruel manner. Oftentimes, considering the context of a Bible account or some background information can help us to put things into perspective. (Proverbs 18:13) Even when we do not have all the details, simply learning more about Jehovah and meditating upon his precious qualities can help us to resolve any doubts that might arise. When we do this, we come to see that we have ample reason to trust our God, Jehovah.—Job 34:12.

21 Although Jehovah is "a manly person of war" when the situation demands it, this does not mean that he is warlike at heart. In Ezekiel's vision of the celestial chariot, Jehovah is pictured as being prepared to fight against his enemies. Yet, Ezekiel saw God surrounded by a rainbow —a symbol of peace. (Genesis 9:13; Ezekiel 1:28; Revelation 4:3) Clearly, Jehovah is calm and peaceable. "God is love," wrote the apostle John. (1 John 4:8) All of Jehovah's qualities exist in perfect balance. How privileged we are, then, to be able to draw close to such a powerful yet loving God!

---

20. When we read Bible accounts of divine warfare that we may not fully understand, how should we respond, and why?
21. While he is "a manly person of war" at times, what is Jehovah like at heart?

CHAPTER 7

Protective Power—"God Is for Us a Refuge"

THE Israelites were in danger as they entered the region of Sinai early in 1513 B.C.E. A fear-inspiring trek lay before them, a journey through a "vast and terrible wilderness infested with poisonous snakes and scorpions." (Deuteronomy 8:15, *The New English Bible*) They also faced the threat of attack by hostile nations. Jehovah had brought his people into this situation. As their God, would he be able to protect them?

² Jehovah's words were most reassuring: "You yourselves have seen what I did to the Egyptians, that I might carry you on wings of eagles and bring you to myself." (Exodus 19:4) Jehovah reminded his people that he had delivered them from the Egyptians, using eagles, as it were, to carry them to safety. But there are other reasons why "wings of eagles" fittingly illustrate divine protection.

³ The eagle uses its broad, strong wings for more than just soaring aloft. In the heat of the day, a mother eagle will arch her wings—which may span over seven feet—to form a protective umbrella, shielding her tender nestlings from the scorching sun. At other times, she wraps her wings around her offspring to protect them from the cold wind. Just as the eagle safeguards its young, so Jehovah had shielded and protected the fledgling nation of Israel. Now in the wilderness, his people would continue to find refuge in the shadow of his mighty wings as long

---

1, 2. The Israelites were in what danger as they entered the region of Sinai in 1513 B.C.E., and how did Jehovah reassure them?
3. Why do "wings of eagles" fittingly illustrate divine protection?

as they remained faithful. (Deuteronomy 32:9-11; Psalm 36:7) But can we today rightly expect God's protection?

The Promise of Divine Protection

⁴ Jehovah is certainly capable of protecting his servants. He is "God Almighty"—a title indicating that he possesses irresistible power. (Genesis 17:1) Like an unstoppable tide, Jehovah's applied power cannot be thwarted. Since he is able to do anything his will directs, we may ask, 'Is it Jehovah's will to use his power to protect his people?'

⁵ The answer, in a word, is yes! Jehovah assures us that he will protect his people. "God is for us a refuge and strength, a help that is readily to be found during distresses," says Psalm 46:1. Since God "cannot lie," we can have absolute confidence in his promise of protection. (Titus 1:2) Let us consider some of the vivid word pictures that Jehovah uses to describe his protective care.

⁶ Jehovah is a Shepherd, and "we are his people and the sheep of his pasturage." (Psalm 23:1; 100:3) Few animals are as helpless as domestic sheep. The shepherd of Bible times had to be courageous to protect his sheep from lions, wolves, and bears, as well as from thieves. (1 Samuel 17:34, 35; John 10:12, 13) But there were times when protecting the sheep called for tenderness. When a sheep gave birth far from the fold, the caring shepherd would guard the mother during her helpless moments and then pick up the defenseless lamb and carry it to the fold.

4, 5. Why can we have absolute confidence in God's promise of protection?
6, 7. (a) The shepherd of Bible times provided what protection for his sheep? (b) How does the Bible illustrate Jehovah's heartfelt desire to protect and care for his sheep?

"In his bosom he will carry them"

⁷ By comparing himself to a shepherd, Jehovah assures us of his heartfelt desire to protect us. (Ezekiel 34:11-16) Recall the description of Jehovah found at Isaiah 40: 11, discussed in Chapter 2 of this book: "Like a shepherd he will shepherd his own drove. With his arm he will collect together the lambs; and in his bosom he will carry them." How does the little lamb come to be in the shepherd's "bosom"—the folds of his upper garment? The lamb might approach the shepherd, even nudge his leg. However, it is the shepherd who must bend over, pick up the lamb, and gently place it in the security of his bosom. What a tender picture of the willingness of our Great Shepherd to shield and protect us!

⁸ God's promise of protection is conditional—it is realized only by those who draw close to him. Proverbs 18: 10 states: "The name of Jehovah is a strong tower. Into it the righteous runs and is given protection." In Bible times, towers were sometimes built in the wilderness as safe places of refuge. But it was up to the one in danger to flee to such a tower to find safety. It is similar with finding refuge in God's name. This involves more than just repeating God's name; the divine name itself is no magic charm. Rather, we need to know and trust the Bearer of that name and live in harmony with his righteous standards. How kind of Jehovah to reassure us that if we turn to him in faith, he will be a tower of protection for us!

"Our God . . . Is Able to Rescue Us"

⁹ Jehovah has done more than just *promise* protection. In Bible times, he demonstrated in miraculous ways that

───────────

8. (a) God's promise of protection is extended to whom, and how is this indicated at Proverbs 18:10? (b) What is involved in finding refuge in God's name?

9. How has Jehovah done more than just promise protection?

he is able to protect his people. During Israel's history, Jehovah's mighty "hand" often kept powerful enemies at bay. (Exodus 7:4) However, Jehovah also used his protective power in behalf of individuals.

[10] When three young Hebrews—Shadrach, Meshach, and Abednego—refused to bow down to King Nebuchadnezzar's image of gold, the furious king threatened to throw them into a superheated furnace. "Who is that god that can rescue you out of my hands?" taunted Nebuchadnezzar, the most powerful monarch on earth. (Daniel 3:15) The three young men had complete confidence in the power of their God to protect them, but they did not presume that he would do so. Hence, they answered: "If it is to be, our God whom we are serving is able to rescue us." (Daniel 3:17) Indeed, that fiery furnace, even when heated seven times hotter than normal, presented no challenge to their all-powerful God. He did protect them, and the king was forced to acknowledge: "There does not exist another god that is able to deliver like this one."—Daniel 3:29.

[11] Jehovah also provided a truly remarkable demonstration of his protective power when he transferred the life of his only-begotten Son to the womb of the Jewish virgin Mary. An angel told Mary that she would "conceive in [her] womb and give birth to a son." The angel explained: "Holy spirit will come upon you, and power of the Most High will overshadow you." (Luke 1:31, 35) Seemingly, God's Son had never been so vulnerable. Would the sin and imperfection of the human mother blemish the embryo? Would Satan be able to injure or kill that Son before He was born? Impossible! Jehovah formed, in effect,

---

10, 11. What Bible examples show how Jehovah used his protective power in behalf of individuals?

a protective wall around Mary so that nothing—no imperfection, no hurtful force, no murderous human, nor any demon—could damage the growing embryo, from the moment of conception on. Jehovah continued to protect Jesus during his youth. (Matthew 2:1-15) Until God's appointed time, his dear Son was unassailable.

[12] Why did Jehovah protect certain individuals in such miraculous ways? In many cases Jehovah protected individuals in order to protect something far more important: the outworking of his purpose. For example, the survival of the infant Jesus was essential to the fulfillment of God's purpose, which will ultimately benefit all mankind. The record of the many displays of protective power is part of the inspired Scriptures, which "were written for our instruction, that through our endurance and through the comfort from the Scriptures we might have hope." (Romans 15:4) Yes, these examples strengthen our faith in our all-powerful God. But what protection can we expect from God today?

What Divine Protection Does Not Mean

[13] The promise of divine protection does not mean that Jehovah is obligated to work miracles in our behalf. No, our God does not guarantee us a problem-free life in this old system. Many faithful servants of Jehovah face severe adversities, including poverty, war, sickness, and death. Jesus plainly told his disciples that as individuals they might be put to death because of their faith. That is why Jesus stressed the need for endurance to the end. (Matthew 24:9, 13) If Jehovah were to use his power to effect miraculous deliverance in all cases, there might be a basis

---

12. Why did Jehovah miraculously protect certain individuals in Bible times?
13. Is Jehovah obligated to work miracles in our behalf? Explain.

for Satan to taunt Jehovah and to call into question the genuineness of our devotion to our God.—Job 1:9, 10.

[14] Even in Bible times, Jehovah did not use his protective power to shield each of his servants from untimely death. For example, the apostle James was executed by Herod in about 44 C.E.; yet, shortly afterward, Peter was delivered "out of Herod's hand." (Acts 12:1-11) And John, the brother of James, outlived both Peter and James. Clearly, we cannot expect our God to protect all his servants in identical ways. Besides, "time and unforeseen occurrence" befall us all. (Ecclesiastes 9:11) How, then, does Jehovah protect us today?

Jehovah Provides Physical Protection

[15] Consider, first, the matter of physical protection. As Jehovah's worshipers, we can expect such protection *as a group.* Otherwise, we would be easy prey for Satan. Think about this: Satan, "the ruler of this world," would like nothing more than to eliminate true worship. (John 12: 31; Revelation 12:17) Some of the most powerful governments on earth have banned our preaching work and have tried to wipe us out completely. Yet, Jehovah's people have remained firm and have continued to preach without letup! Why have mighty nations been unable to put a stop to the activity of this relatively small and seemingly defenseless group of Christians? Because Jehovah has shielded us with his powerful wings!—Psalm 17:7, 8.

[16] What about physical protection during the coming "great tribulation"? We need not fear the execution of

---

14. What examples show that Jehovah does not always protect all his servants in identical ways?
15, 16. (a) What evidence is there that Jehovah has provided physical protection for his worshipers as a group? (b) Why can we be confident that Jehovah will protect his servants now and during "the great tribulation"?

God's judgments. After all, "Jehovah knows how to deliver people of godly devotion out of trial, but to reserve unrighteous people for the day of judgment to be cut off." (Revelation 7:14; 2 Peter 2:9) In the meantime, we can always be certain of two things. First, Jehovah will never allow his loyal servants to be effaced from the earth. Second, he will reward integrity keepers with everlasting life in his righteous new world—if necessary, by means of a resurrection. For those who die, there is no safer place to be than in God's memory.—John 5:28, 29.

17 Even now, Jehovah safeguards us through his living "word," which has the motivating power to heal hearts and reform lives. (Hebrews 4:12) By applying its principles, we can in some respects be protected from physical harm. "I, Jehovah, am . . . teaching you to benefit yourself," says Isaiah 48:17. Without question, living in harmony with God's Word can improve our health and extend our life. For example, because we apply the Bible's counsel to abstain from fornication and to cleanse ourselves of defilement, we avoid the unclean practices and hurtful habits that wreak havoc in the lives of many ungodly ones. (Acts 15:29; 2 Corinthians 7:1) How thankful we are for the protection of God's Word!

Jehovah Protects Us Spiritually

18 Most important, Jehovah provides spiritual protection. Our loving God protects us from spiritual harm by equipping us with what we need in order to endure trials and to safeguard our relationship with him. Jehovah thus works to preserve our life, not just for a few short years but for eternity. Consider some of God's provisions that can protect us spiritually.

---

17. How does Jehovah safeguard us through his Word?
18. What spiritual protection does Jehovah provide for us?

Questions for Meditation

Psalm 23:1-6 As the Great Shepherd, how does Jehovah protect and care for his sheeplike people?

Psalm 91:1-16 How does Jehovah protect us from spiritual calamity, and what must we do to come under his protection?

Daniel 6:16-22, 25-27 How did Jehovah teach an ancient king about His protective power, and what can we learn from this example?

Matthew 10:16-22, 28-31 What opposition can we expect, but why should we not fear opposers?

---

¹⁹ Jehovah is the "Hearer of prayer." (Psalm 65:2) When life's pressures seem overwhelming, pouring out our heart to him can bring us much relief. (Philippians 4:6, 7) He may not miraculously remove our trials, but in response to our heartfelt prayers, he can grant us the wisdom to deal with them. (James 1:5, 6) More than that, Jehovah gives holy spirit to those asking him. (Luke 11:13) That powerful spirit can make us equal to any trial or problem we may face. It can infuse us with "power beyond what is normal" to endure until Jehovah removes all painful problems in the new world so near at hand. —2 Corinthians 4:7.

²⁰ At times, Jehovah's protective power may be expressed through our fellow worshipers. Jehovah has drawn his people into a worldwide "association of brothers." (1 Peter 2:17; John 6:44) In the warmth of that brotherhood, we see living testimony to the power of God's holy spirit to influence people for good. That spirit produces in

---

19. How can Jehovah's spirit make us equal to any trial we may face?
20. How may Jehovah's protective power be expressed through our fellow worshipers?

us fruitage—beautiful, precious qualities including love, kindness, and goodness. (Galatians 5:22, 23) Hence, when we are in distress and a fellow believer is moved to offer helpful counsel or share much-needed words of encouragement, we can thank Jehovah for such expressions of his protective care.

²¹ Jehovah provides something else to protect us: timely spiritual food. To help us draw strength from his Word, Jehovah has commissioned "the faithful and discreet slave" to dispense spiritual food. That faithful slave class uses printed publications, including the journals *The Watchtower* and *Awake!,* as well as meetings, assemblies, and conventions to provide us with "food at the proper time" —what we need, when we need it. (Matthew 24:45) Have you ever heard something at a Christian meeting—in a comment, in a talk, or even in a prayer—that provided just the needed strength and encouragement? Has your life ever been touched by a specific article published in one of our journals? Remember, Jehovah makes all such provisions in order to protect us spiritually.

²² Jehovah is certainly a shield "to all those taking refuge in him." (Psalm 18:30) We understand that he does not use his power to protect us from all calamity now. He does, however, always use his protective power to ensure the outworking of his purpose. In the long run, his doing so is in the best interests of his people. If we draw close to him and remain in his love, Jehovah will give us an eternity of perfect life. With that prospect in mind, we may indeed view any suffering in this system as "momentary and light."—2 Corinthians 4:17.

---

21. (a) What timely spiritual food does Jehovah provide through "the faithful and discreet slave"? (b) How have you personally benefited from Jehovah's provisions to protect us spiritually?
22. Jehovah always uses his power in what way, and why is his doing so in our best interests?

CHAPTER 8

Restorative Power—Jehovah Is "Making All Things New"

A CHILD loses or breaks a beloved toy and lets out a plaintive cry. The sound is heartrending! Have you ever seen, though, how a child's face lights up when a parent restores what was lost? To the parent, it may be a simple matter to find the toy or even to fix it. But the child is all smiles and full of wonder. What seemed to be gone forever has been restored!

² Jehovah, the ultimate Parent, has the power to restore what his earthly children may view as hopelessly lost. Of course, we do not mean mere toys. In these "critical times hard to deal with," we have to face losses that are far more serious. (2 Timothy 3:1-5) Much of what people hold dear seems ever at risk—home, possessions, employment, even health. We may also feel dismayed when we contemplate the destruction of the environment and the resulting loss, by extinction, of many species of living things. However, nothing hits us as hard as the death of someone we love. The feelings of loss and powerlessness can be overwhelming.—2 Samuel 18:33.

³ How comforting, then, to learn about Jehovah's restorative power! As we will see, there is an amazing scope to what God can and will restore to his earthly children. In fact, the Bible shows that Jehovah purposes the "restoration of *all things*." (Acts 3:21) To accomplish this, Jehovah will use the Messianic Kingdom, ruled by his Son,

---

1, 2. What losses afflict the human family today, and how do these affect us?

3. What comforting prospect is outlined at Acts 3:21, and by what means will Jehovah fulfill it?

Jesus Christ. The evidence shows that this Kingdom began ruling in heaven in 1914.* (Matthew 24:3-14) What will be restored? Let us consider some of Jehovah's grand acts of restoration. One of these we can already see and experience. Others will occur on a large scale in the future.

The Restoration of Pure Worship

⁴ One thing that Jehovah has already restored is pure worship. In order to grasp what this means, let us briefly examine the history of the kingdom of Judah. Doing so will give us thrilling insight into Jehovah's restorative power at work.—Romans 15:4.

⁵ Just imagine how faithful Jews felt in 607 B.C.E. when Jerusalem was destroyed. Their beloved city was shattered, its walls torn down. Worse still, the glorious temple that Solomon had built, the one center for pure worship of Jehovah in all the earth, was left in ruins. (Psalm 79:1) The survivors were taken into exile in Babylon, leaving their homeland a desolate haunt of wild animals. (Jeremiah 9:11) From a human standpoint, all seemed lost. (Psalm 137:1) But Jehovah, who had long foretold this destruction, provided hope that a time of restoration lay ahead.

⁶ In fact, restoration was a recurring theme in the writ-

---

* "The times of restoration of all things" began when the Messianic Kingdom was established with an heir of faithful King David on the throne. Jehovah had promised David that an heir of his would rule forever. (Psalm 89:35-37) But after Babylon destroyed Jerusalem in 607 B.C.E., no human descendant of David sat on God's throne. Jesus, who was born on earth as an heir of David, became the long-promised King when he was enthroned in heaven.

4, 5. What happened to God's people in 607 B.C.E., and what hope did Jehovah offer them?

6-8. (a) What recurring theme is found in the writings of the Hebrew prophets, and how did such prophecies see an initial fulfillment? (b) In modern times, how have God's people experienced a fulfillment of the restoration prophecies?

ings of the Hebrew prophets.* Through them, Jehovah promised a land restored and repopulated, fertile, protected from wild beasts and enemy attack. He described their restored land as a veritable paradise! (Isaiah 65:25; Ezekiel 34:25; 36:35) Above all, pure worship would be re-established, and the temple would be rebuilt. (Micah 4:1-5) These prophecies gave the exiled Jews hope, helping them to endure their 70-year captivity in Babylon.

⁷ At last, the time of restoration came. Freed from Babylon, the Jews returned to Jerusalem and rebuilt Jehovah's temple there. (Ezra 1:1, 2) As long as they adhered to pure worship, Jehovah blessed them and made their land fertile and prosperous. He protected them from enemies and from the wild beasts that had overrun their land for decades. How they must have rejoiced in Jehovah's restorative power! But those events represented only an initial, limited fulfillment of the restoration prophecies. A greater fulfillment was to come "in the final part of the days," our own time, when the long-promised Heir of King David would be enthroned.—Isaiah 2:2-4; 9:6, 7.

⁸ Shortly after Jesus was enthroned in the heavenly Kingdom in 1914, he addressed the spiritual needs of God's faithful people on earth. Just as the Persian conqueror Cyrus freed a remnant of Jews from Babylon in 537 B.C.E., Jesus freed a remnant of spiritual Jews—his own footstep followers—from the influence of a modern-day Babylon, the world empire of false religion. (Romans 2:29; Revelation 18:1-5) From 1919 onward, pure worship has been restored to its proper place in the lives of genuine Christians. (Malachi 3:1-5) Ever since then, Jehovah's people have worshiped him in his spiritual temple—God's arrangement for pure worship. Why is this important to us today?

---

* For example, Moses, Isaiah, Jeremiah, Ezekiel, Hosea, Joel, Amos, Obadiah, Micah, and Zephaniah all developed this theme.

Spiritual Restoration—Why It Matters

9 Consider the historical perspective. Christians back in the first century enjoyed many spiritual blessings. But Jesus and the apostles foretold that true worship would be corrupted and lost. (Matthew 13:24-30; Acts 20:29, 30) After the apostolic age, Christendom arose. Her clergymen adopted pagan teachings and practices. They also made approach to God all but impossible, painting him as an incomprehensible Trinity and teaching people to confess to priests and to pray to Mary and various "saints" instead of to Jehovah. Now, after many centuries of such corruption, what has Jehovah done? In the midst of today's world —a world that is choked with religious falsehood and befouled with ungodly practices—he has stepped in and restored pure worship! Without exaggerating, we can say that this restoration is one of the most important developments in modern times.

10 True Christians today therefore enjoy a spiritual paradise. What does this paradise involve? Primarily, two elements. The first is the pure worship of the true God, Jehovah. He has blessed us with a way of worship that is free of lies and distortions. He has blessed us with spiritual food. This enables us to learn about our heavenly Father, to please him, and to draw close to him. (John 4:24) The second aspect of the spiritual paradise involves people. As Isaiah foretold, "in the final part of the days," Jehovah has taught his worshipers the ways of peace. He has abolished warfare among us. Despite our imperfections, he helps us

9. After the apostolic age, what did the churches of Christendom do to the worship of God, but what has Jehovah done in our day?

10, 11. (a) What two elements does the spiritual paradise involve, and how are you affected? (b) Jehovah has gathered into the spiritual paradise what type of people, and what will they be privileged to witness?

to put on "the new personality." He blesses our efforts with his holy spirit, which produces beautiful fruitage in us. (Ephesians 4:22-24; Galatians 5:22, 23) When you work in harmony with God's spirit, you are truly part of the spiritual paradise.

¹¹ Jehovah has gathered into this spiritual paradise the type of people that he loves—those who love him, who love peace, and who are "conscious of their spiritual need." (Matthew 5:3) Such are the people who will be privileged to witness an even more spectacular restoration —that of mankind and of the entire earth.

"Look! I Am Making All Things New"

¹² Many of the restoration prophecies call for more than a spiritual restoration. Isaiah, for example, wrote of a time when the sick, the lame, the blind, and the deaf would be healed and even death itself would be swallowed up forever. (Isaiah 25:8; 35:1-7) Such promises did not see a literal fulfillment in ancient Israel. And while we have seen a spiritual fulfillment of these promises in our day, there is every reason to believe that in the future, there will be a literal, full-scale fulfillment. How do we know that?

¹³ Back in Eden, Jehovah made clear his purpose for the earth: It was to be inhabited by a happy, healthy, united family of mankind. Man and woman were to care for the earth and all of its creatures, to turn the entire planet into a paradise. (Genesis 1:28) That is a far cry from the present state of affairs. Rest assured, though, that Jehovah's purposes are never thwarted. (Isaiah 55:10, 11) Jesus, as the Messianic King appointed by Jehovah, will bring about this global Paradise.—Luke 23:43.

12, 13. (a) Why must the restoration prophecies see still another fulfillment? (b) What is Jehovah's purpose for the earth as stated in Eden, and why does this give us hope for the future?

14 Imagine seeing the whole earth turned into Paradise! Jehovah says of that time: "Look! I am making all things new." (Revelation 21:5) Consider what that will mean. When Jehovah has finished wielding his destructive power against this wicked old system, there will remain "new heavens and a new earth." This means that a new government will reign from heaven over a new earthly society composed of those who love Jehovah and who do his will. (2 Peter 3:13) Satan, along with his demons, will be put out of commission. (Revelation 20:3) For the first time in thousands of years, mankind will be free of that corrupt, hateful, negative influence. The sense of relief will no doubt be overwhelming.

15 At last, we will be able to take care of this beautiful planet as we were originally meant to do. The earth has natural restorative powers. Polluted lakes and rivers can cleanse themselves if the source of the pollution is eliminated; battle-scarred landscapes can heal if the wars cease. What a pleasure it will be to work in harmony with the earth, helping to turn it into a gardenlike park, a global Eden of endless variety! Instead of wantonly wiping out animal and plant species, man will be at peace with all creation on earth. Even children will have nothing to fear from wild animals.—Isaiah 9:6, 7; 11:1-9.

16 We will also experience restoration on a personal level. After Armageddon, the survivors will see miraculous healings on a global scale. As he did while on earth, Jesus will use his God-given power to restore sight to the blind, hearing to the deaf, soundness of body to the lame and infirm. (Matthew 15:30) The aged will delight in renewed youthful strength, health, and vigor. (Job 33:25) Wrinkles will

14, 15. (a) How will Jehovah make "all things new"? (b) What will life be like in Paradise, and which aspect is most appealing to you?
16. In Paradise, what restoration will affect each faithful individual?

vanish, limbs will straighten, and muscles will flex with renewed power. All of faithful mankind will sense that the effects of sin and imperfection are gradually diminishing, dropping away. How we will thank Jehovah God for his marvelous restorative power! Let us now focus on one especially heartwarming aspect of this thrilling time of restoration.

Restoring Life to the Dead

[17] In the first century C.E., some religious leaders, called Sadducees, did not believe in the resurrection. Jesus reprimanded them with the words: "You are mistaken, because you know neither the Scriptures nor the power of God." (Matthew 22:29) Yes, the Scriptures reveal that Jehovah has such restorative power. How so?

[18] Picture what happened in Elijah's day. A widow was holding the limp body of her only child in her arms. The boy was dead. The prophet Elijah, who had been the widow's guest for some time, must have been shocked. Earlier, he helped rescue this child from starvation. Elijah may well have grown attached to the little fellow. The mother was just heartbroken. This boy had been her only living reminder of her dead husband. She may have hoped that her son would care for her in her old age. Distraught, the widow feared that she was being punished for some past error. Elijah could not bear to see this tragedy thus compounded. He gently took the corpse from the mother's bosom, carried it up to his room, and asked Jehovah God to restore the child's soul, or life.—1 Kings 17:8-21.

[19] Elijah was not the first person to believe in the

17, 18. (a) Why did Jesus reprimand the Sadducees? (b) What circumstances led Elijah to ask Jehovah to perform a resurrection?
19, 20. (a) How did Abraham show that he had faith in Jehovah's restorative power, and what was the basis for such faith? (b) How did Jehovah reward Elijah's faith?

resurrection. Centuries earlier, Abraham believed that Jehovah has such restorative power—and for good reason. When Abraham was 100 years old and Sarah was 90, Jehovah restored their deadened reproductive powers, miraculously enabling Sarah to bear a son. (Genesis 17:17; 21:2, 3) Later, when the boy was fully grown, Jehovah asked Abraham to sacrifice his son. Abraham showed faith, reckoning that Jehovah could restore his beloved Isaac to life. (Hebrews 11:17-19) Such intense faith may explain why Abraham, before ascending the mountain to offer up his son, assured his servants that he and Isaac would return together.—Genesis 22:5.

²⁰ Jehovah spared Isaac, so there was no need for a resurrection at that time. In Elijah's case, however, the widow's son was already dead—but not for long. Jehovah rewarded the prophet's faith by resurrecting the child! Elijah then handed the boy over to his mother, with these unforgettable words: "See, your son is alive"!—1 Kings 17:22-24.

²¹ Thus for the first time in the Bible record, we see Jehovah using his power to restore a human life. Later, Jehovah also empowered Elisha, Jesus, Paul, and Peter to restore the dead to life. Of course, those who were resurrected eventually died again. Nonetheless, such Bible accounts give us a wonderful preview of things to come.

²² In Paradise, Jesus will fulfill his role as "the resurrection and the life." (John 11:25) He will resurrect countless millions, giving them an opportunity to live forever in Paradise on earth. (John 5:28, 29) Imagine the reunions as beloved friends and relatives, long separated by death,

---

21, 22. (a) What was the purpose of the resurrections recorded in the Scriptures? (b) In Paradise, how extensive will the resurrection be, and who will carry it out?

"See, your son is alive"!

Questions for Meditation

2 Kings 5:1-15 Because he cultivated humility, how did one man in Bible times benefit from Jehovah's restorative power?

Job 14:12-15 What confidence did Job have, and how might these verses affect our own hope for the future?

Psalm 126:1-6 How might Christians today feel about the restoration of pure worship and their share in it?

Romans 4:16-25 Why is it important to put faith in Jehovah's restorative power?

---

embrace one another, quite beside themselves with joy! All mankind will praise Jehovah for his restorative power.

²³ Jehovah has furnished a rock-solid guarantee that such hopes are secure. In the greatest of all demonstrations of his power, he resurrected his Son, Jesus, as a mighty spirit creature, making him second only to Jehovah. The resurrected Jesus appeared to hundreds of eyewitnesses. (1 Corinthians 15:5, 6) Even for skeptics, such evidence should be ample. Jehovah has the power to restore life.

²⁴ Not only does Jehovah have the power to restore the dead but he also has the desire to do so. The faithful man Job was inspired to say that Jehovah actually *yearns* to bring back the dead. (Job 14:15) Are you not drawn to our God, who is eager to use his restorative power in such a loving way? Remember, though, that the resurrection is but one aspect of Jehovah's great restoration work ahead. As you draw ever closer to him, always cherish the precious hope that you can be there to see Jehovah "making all things new."—Revelation 21:5.

---

23. What was the greatest of all demonstrations of Jehovah's power, and how does this guarantee our hope for the future?
24. Why can we be confident that Jehovah will resurrect the dead, and what hope may each of us cherish?

CHAPTER 9

"Christ the Power of God"

THE disciples were terrified. They were sailing across the Sea of Galilee when a storm suddenly descended upon them. No doubt they had seen storms on this lake before —after all, some of the men were experienced fishermen.* (Matthew 4:18, 19) But this was "a great violent windstorm," and it quickly churned the sea into a wet fury. The men worked frantically to steer the vessel, but the storm was overpowering. Surging waves were "dashing into the boat," which began filling with water. Despite the commotion, Jesus was fast asleep in the stern, exhausted after a day of teaching the crowds. Fearing for their lives, the disciples woke him up, pleading: "Lord, save us, we are about to perish!"—Mark 4:35-38; Matthew 8:23-25.

² Jesus was not afraid. With complete confidence, he rebuked the wind and the sea: "Hush! Be quiet!" Immediately, the wind and the sea obeyed—the tempest ceased, the waves disappeared into stillness, and "a great calm set in." An unusual fear now gripped the disciples. "Who really is this?" they murmured to one another. Indeed, what kind of man could rebuke the wind and the sea as if correcting an unruly child?—Mark 4:39-41; Matthew 8:26, 27.

³ But Jesus was no ordinary man. Jehovah's power was

---

* Sudden storms are common to the Sea of Galilee. Because of the sea's low elevation (some 700 feet below sea level), the air is much warmer there than in the surrounding area, and this creates atmospheric disturbances. Strong winds rush down the Jordan Valley from Mount Hermon, situated to the north. The calm of one moment may well yield to the raging storm of the next.

1-3. (a) What terrifying experience did the disciples have on the Sea of Galilee, and what did Jesus do? (b) Why is Jesus rightly called "Christ the power of God"?

displayed toward him and through him in extraordinary ways. The inspired apostle Paul could rightly refer to him as "Christ the power of God." (1 Corinthians 1:24) In what ways is God's power manifested in Jesus? And what bearing can Jesus' use of power have on our life?

The Power of God's Only-Begotten Son

⁴ Consider the power that Jesus had during his prehuman existence. Jehovah exercised his own "eternal power" when he created his only-begotten Son, who came to be known as Jesus Christ. (Romans 1:20; Colossians 1:15) Thereafter, Jehovah delegated tremendous power and authority to this Son, assigning him to carry out His creative purposes. Concerning the Son, the Bible says: "All things came into existence through him, and apart from him not even one thing came into existence."—John 1:3.

⁵ We can but barely perceive the magnitude of that assignment. Imagine the power needed to bring into existence millions of mighty angels, the physical universe with its billions of galaxies, and the earth with its abundant variety of life. To accomplish those tasks, the only-begotten Son had at his disposal the most powerful force in the universe—God's holy spirit. This Son found great pleasure in being the Master Worker, whom Jehovah used in creating all other things.—Proverbs 8:22-31.

⁶ Could the only-begotten Son receive even more power and authority? Following Jesus' death on earth and his resurrection, he said: "All authority has been given me in heaven and on the earth." (Matthew 28:18) Yes, Jesus has been granted the ability and the right to exercise power

4, 5. (a) Jehovah delegated what power and authority to his only-begotten Son? (b) How was this Son equipped to carry out his Father's creative purposes?
6. Following his death on earth and his resurrection, Jesus was granted what power and authority?

universally. As "King of kings and Lord of lords," he has been authorized to bring to "nothing all government and all authority and power"—visible and invisible—that stand in opposition to his Father. (Revelation 19:16; 1 Corinthians 15:24-26) God has "left nothing that is not subject to" Jesus—that is, with the exception of Jehovah himself.—Hebrews 2:8; 1 Corinthians 15:27.

⁷ Do we need to worry that Jesus might misuse his power? Absolutely not! Jesus really loves his Father and would never do anything to displease him. (John 8:29; 14:31) Jesus well knows that Jehovah never misuses his almighty power. Jesus has observed firsthand that Jehovah searches for opportunities "to show his strength in behalf of those whose heart is complete toward him." (2 Chronicles 16:9) Indeed, Jesus shares his Father's love for mankind, so we can trust that Jesus will always use his power for good. (John 13:1) Jesus has established a flawless record in this regard. Let us consider the power he had while on earth and how he was moved to use it.

"Powerful in . . . Word"

⁸ Evidently, Jesus performed no miracles when he was a boy growing up in Nazareth. But that changed after he was baptized in 29 C.E., at about 30 years of age. (Luke 3:21-23) The Bible tells us: "God anointed him with holy spirit and power, and he went through the land doing good and healing all those oppressed by the Devil." (Acts 10:38) "Doing good"—does that not indicate that Jesus used his power aright? After his anointing, he "became a prophet powerful in work and word."—Luke 24:19.

---

7. Why can we be sure that Jesus will never misuse the power that Jehovah has placed in his hands?
8. Following his anointing, what was Jesus empowered to do, and how did he use his power?

⁹ How was Jesus powerful in word? He often taught in the open air—on lakeshores and hillsides as well as on the streets and in marketplaces. (Mark 6:53-56; Luke 5:1-3; 13: 26) His listeners could simply walk away if his words did not hold their interest. In the era before printed books, appreciative listeners had to carry his words in their mind and heart. So Jesus' teaching needed to be thoroughly arresting, plainly understood, and easily remembered. But this challenge posed no problem for Jesus. Consider, for example, his Sermon on the Mount.

¹⁰ One morning early in 31 C.E., a crowd gathered on a hillside near the Sea of Galilee. Some had come from Judea and Jerusalem, 60 to 70 miles away. Others had come from the seacoast area of Tyre and Sidon, to the north. Many sick people drew close to Jesus to touch him, and he healed them all. When there was not even one seriously ill person left among them, he began to teach. (Luke 6:17-19) When he finished speaking some time later, they were amazed by what they had heard. Why?

¹¹ Years later, one who had heard that sermon wrote: "The crowds were astounded at his way of teaching; for he was teaching them as a person having authority." (Matthew 7:28, 29) Jesus spoke with a power they could feel. He spoke for God and backed up his teaching with the authority of God's Word. (John 7:16) Jesus' statements were clear, his exhortations persuasive, and his arguments irrefutable. His words got to the heart of issues as well as to the hearts of his listeners. He taught them how to find happiness, how to pray, how to seek God's Kingdom, and how to build for a secure future. (Matthew 5:3–7:27) His words

9-11. (a) Where did Jesus do much of his teaching, and what challenge did he face? (b) Why were the crowds astounded at Jesus' way of teaching?

"They beheld Jesus walking upon the sea"

awakened the hearts of those hungering for truth and righteousness. Such ones were willing to "disown" themselves and abandon everything in order to follow him. (Matthew 16:24; Luke 5:10, 11) What a testimony to the power of Jesus' words!

"Powerful in Work"

¹² Jesus was also "powerful in work." (Luke 24:19) The Gospels report over 30 specific miracles performed by him—all in "Jehovah's power."* (Luke 5:17) Jesus' miracles touched the lives of thousands. Just two miracles—the feeding of 5,000 men and later 4,000 men "besides women and young children"—involved crowds probably totaling some 20,000 people!—Matthew 14:13-21; 15:32-38.

¹³ There was great diversity in Jesus' miracles. He had authority over demons, expelling them with ease. (Luke 9: 37-43) He had power over physical elements, turning water into wine. (John 2:1-11) To the amazement of his disciples, he walked on the windswept Sea of Galilee. (John 6:18, 19) He had mastery over disease, curing organic defects, chronic illness, and life-threatening sickness. (Mark 3:1-5; John 4:46-54) He performed such healings in various ways. Some were healed from a distance, whereas others felt Jesus' personal touch. (Matthew 8:2, 3, 5-13) Some were healed instantly, others gradually.—Mark 8:22-25; Luke 8:43, 44.

¹⁴ Outstandingly, Jesus had the power to undo death.

---

* In addition, the Gospels at times group many miracles under a single, general description. For example, on one occasion a "whole city" came to see him, and he cured "many" sick ones.—Mark 1: 32-34.

12, 13. In what sense was Jesus "powerful in work," and what diversity was there in his miracles?
14. Under what circumstances did Jesus demonstrate that he had the power to undo death?

On three recorded occasions, he raised the dead, giving a 12-year-old daughter back to her parents, an only child to his widowed mother, and a beloved brother to his sisters. (Luke 7:11-15; 8:49-56; John 11:38-44) No circumstance proved too formidable. He raised the 12-year-old girl from her deathbed shortly after she died. He resurrected the widow's son from the funeral bier, no doubt on the day of his death. And he raised Lazarus from the burial tomb after he had been dead for four days.

Unselfish, Responsible, and Considerate Use of Power

15 Can you imagine the potential for abuse if Jesus' power were placed in the hands of an imperfect ruler? But Jesus was sinless. (1 Peter 2:22) He refused to be tainted by the selfishness, ambition, and greed that drive imperfect men to use their power to hurt others.

16 Jesus was unselfish in the use of his power, never employing it for personal gain. When he was hungry, he refused to turn stones into bread for himself. (Matthew 4: 1-4) His meager possessions were evidence that he did not profit materially from the use of his power. (Matthew 8: 20) There is further proof that his powerful works sprang from unselfish motives. When he performed miracles, he did so at some cost to himself. When he cured the sick, power went out of him. He was sensitive to this outflow of power, even in the case of just one cure. (Mark 5:25-34) Yet, he let *crowds* of people touch him, and they were healed. (Luke 6:19) What a selfless spirit!

17 Jesus was responsible in the use of his power. Never

15, 16. What evidence is there that Jesus was unselfish in the use of his power?

17. How did Jesus demonstrate that he was responsible in the use of his power?

did he perform powerful works for mere showy display or purposeless theatrics. (Matthew 4:5-7) He was unwilling to perform signs merely to satisfy Herod's wrongly motivated curiosity. (Luke 23:8, 9) Far from advertising his power, Jesus often instructed those whom he healed not to tell anyone. (Mark 5:43; 7:36) He did not want people to reach conclusions about him on the basis of sensational reports.—Matthew 12:15-19.

[18] This powerful man, Jesus, was nothing like those rulers who have wielded power in callous disregard for the needs and suffering of others. Jesus cared about people. The mere sight of the afflicted touched him so deeply that he was motivated to relieve their suffering. (Matthew 14: 14) He was considerate of their feelings and needs, and this tender concern influenced the way he used his power. A moving example is found at Mark 7:31-37.

[19] On this occasion, great crowds found Jesus and brought to him many who were sick, and he cured them all. (Matthew 15:29, 30) But Jesus singled out one man for special consideration. The man was deaf and hardly able to talk. Jesus may have sensed this man's particular nervousness or embarrassment. Thoughtfully, Jesus took the man aside—away from the crowd—to a private place. Then Jesus used some signs to convey to the man what he was about to do. He "put his fingers into the man's ears and, after spitting, he touched his tongue."* (Mark 7:33) Next,

---

* Spitting was a means or sign of healing accepted by both Jews and Gentiles, and the use of saliva in cures is reported in rabbinic writings. Jesus may have spit simply to convey to the man that he was about to be healed. Whatever the case, Jesus was not using his saliva as a natural healing agent.

18-20. (a) What influenced the way in which Jesus used his power? (b) How do you feel about the manner in which Jesus healed a certain deaf man?

Jesus looked up to heaven and uttered a prayerful sigh. These actions would say to the man, 'What I am about to do for you is due to power from God.' Finally, Jesus said: "Be opened." (Mark 7:34) At that, the man's hearing was restored, and he was able to speak normally.

20 How touching to think that even when using his God-given power to heal the afflicted, Jesus showed a sympathetic regard for their feelings! Is it not reassuring to know that Jehovah has placed the Messianic Kingdom in the hands of such a caring, considerate Ruler?

A Portent of Things to Come

21 The powerful works that Jesus performed on earth were just foregleams of even grander blessings to come under his kingly rule. In God's new world, Jesus will once again work miracles—but on a global scale! Consider some of the thrilling prospects ahead.

22 Jesus will restore the earth's ecology to perfect balance. Recall that he demonstrated control of natural forces by calming a windstorm. Surely, then, under Christ's Kingdom rule, mankind will have no need to fear being harmed by typhoons, earthquakes, volcanoes, or other natural disasters. Since Jesus is the Master Worker, whom Jehovah used to create the earth and all life on it, he fully understands the makeup of the earth. He knows how to use its resources properly. Under his rule, this entire earth will be turned into Paradise.—Luke 23:43.

23 What about mankind's needs? Jesus' ability to feed thousands bountifully, using only a few meager provisions, assures us that his rule will bring freedom from

---

21, 22. (a) What did the miracles of Jesus portend? (b) Because Jesus has control of natural forces, what can we expect under his Kingdom rule?

23. As King, how will Jesus satisfy mankind's needs?

Questions for Meditation

Isaiah 11:1-5 How does Jesus manifest "the spirit of . . . mightiness," and what confidence can we thus have in his rule?

Mark 2:1-12 Jesus' miraculous healings demonstrate that he has been granted what authority?

John 6:25-27 Although Jesus miraculously satisfied people's physical needs, what was the primary thrust of his ministry?

John 12:37-43 Why did some eyewitnesses of Jesus' miracles not put faith in him, and what can we learn from this?

hunger. Indeed, an abundance of food, distributed fairly, will end hunger forever. (Psalm 72:16) His mastery over sickness and disease tells us that sick, blind, deaf, maimed, and lame people will be healed—completely and permanently. (Isaiah 33:24; 35:5, 6) His ability to resurrect the dead ensures that his mightiness as a heavenly King includes the power to resurrect the countless millions whom his Father is pleased to remember.—John 5: 28, 29.

24 As we reflect on the power of Jesus, let us keep in mind that this Son perfectly imitates his Father. (John 14:9) Jesus' use of power thus gives us a clear picture of how Jehovah uses power. For example, think about the tender way that Jesus healed a certain leper. Moved with pity, Jesus touched the man and said: "I want to." (Mark 1:40-42) By means of accounts such as this, Jehovah is, in effect, saying, 'That is how I use my power!' Are you not moved to praise our almighty God and give thanks that he uses his power in such a loving way?

24. As we reflect on the power of Jesus, what should we keep in mind, and why?

"Become Imitators of God" in Your Use of Power

"NEVER a power without the lurk of a subtle snare." Those words of a 19th-century poet call attention to an insidious danger: the misuse of power. Sadly, imperfect humans all too easily fall prey to this snare. Indeed, throughout history "man has dominated man to his injury." (Ecclesiastes 8:9) The exercise of power without love has resulted in untold human suffering.

2 Is it not remarkable, though, that Jehovah God, who has unlimited power, *never* misuses that power? As we have noted in the preceding chapters, he always uses his power—whether creative, destructive, protective, or restorative—in harmony with his loving purposes. When we contemplate the way he exerts his power, we are moved to draw close to him. That, in turn, can motivate us to "become imitators of God" in our own use of power. (Ephesians 5:1) But what power do we puny humans possess?

3 Remember that man was created "in God's image" and likeness. (Genesis 1:26, 27) Hence, we too have power—at least a measure of it. Our power may include the capacity to accomplish things, to work; the possession of control or authority over others; the ability to influence others, particularly those who love us; physical strength (might); or material resources. Concerning Jehovah, the psalmist said: "With you is the source of life." (Psalm 36:9) Therefore, directly or indirectly, God is the source of any

1. To what insidious snare do imperfect humans easily fall prey?
2, 3. (a) What is remarkable about Jehovah's use of power? (b) What may our power include, and how should we use all such power?

legitimate power we might have. We therefore want to use it in ways that please him. How can we do so?

Love Is the Key

⁴ The key to using power aright is love. Does not God's own example demonstrate this? Recall the discussion of God's four cardinal attributes—power, justice, wisdom, and love—in Chapter 1. Of the four qualities, which one predominates? Love. "God is love," says 1 John 4:8. Yes, Jehovah's very essence is love; it influences all that he does. So every expression of his power is motivated by love and is ultimately for the good of those who love him.

⁵ Love will also help us to use our power aright. After all, the Bible tells us that love is "kind" and "does not look for its own interests." (1 Corinthians 13:4, 5) Hence, love will not allow us to act in a harsh or cruel manner toward those over whom we have a measure of authority. Instead, we will treat others with dignity and put their needs and feelings ahead of our own.—Philippians 2:3, 4.

⁶ Love is related to another quality that can help us to avoid misusing power: godly fear. What is the value of this quality? "In the fear of Jehovah one turns away from bad," says Proverbs 16:6. The misuse of power is certainly among the bad ways from which we should turn away. Fear of God will restrain us from mistreating those over whom we have power. Why? For one thing, we know that we are accountable to God for the way we treat such ones. (Nehemiah 5:1-7, 15) But godly fear involves more

---

4, 5. (a) What is the key to using power aright, and how does God's own example demonstrate this? (b) How will love help us to use our power aright?

6, 7. (a) What is godly fear, and why will this quality help us to avoid misusing power? (b) Illustrate the connection between fear of displeasing God and love for God.

than that. The original-language terms used for "fear" often refer to a profound reverence and awe of God. The Bible thus associates fear with love for God. (Deuteronomy 10:12, 13) This reverential awe includes a healthy fear of displeasing God—not simply because we fear the consequences but because we truly love him.

7 To illustrate: Think about the wholesome relationship between a little boy and his father. The boy senses his father's warm, loving interest in him. But the boy is also aware of what his father requires of him, and he knows that his father will discipline him if he misbehaves. The boy does not live in morbid fear of his father. On the contrary, he dearly loves his father. The youngster delights in doing what will bring his father's smile of approval. So it is with godly fear. Because we love Jehovah, our heavenly Father, we dread doing anything that would make him feel "hurt at his heart." (Genesis 6:6) Rather, we long to make his heart rejoice. (Proverbs 27:11) That is why we want to use our power aright. Let us take a closer look at how we may do so.

Within the Family

8 Consider first the family circle. "A husband is head of his wife," says Ephesians 5:23. How is a husband to exercise this God-given authority? The Bible tells husbands to dwell with their wives "according to knowledge, assigning them honor as to a weaker vessel." (1 Peter 3:7) The Greek noun rendered "honor" means "price, value, . . . respect." Forms of this word are translated "gifts" and "precious." (Acts 28:10; 1 Peter 2:7) A husband who honors his wife would never assault her physically; neither would

8. (a) What authority do husbands have in the family, and how is it to be exercised? (b) How can a husband demonstrate that he honors his wife?

he humiliate or disparage her, causing her to feel worthless. Rather, he recognizes her value and treats her with respect. He shows by his words and deeds—in private and in public—that she is precious to him. (Proverbs 31:28) Such a husband gains not only his wife's love and respect but, more important, God's approval.

⁹ Wives too have a measure of power in the family. The Bible tells of godly women who, within the framework of proper headship, took the initiative to influence their husbands in a positive way or to help them avoid errors in judgment. (Genesis 21:9-12; 27:46–28:2) A wife may have a keener mind than her husband has, or she may have other abilities that he does not have. Yet, she is to have "deep respect" for her husband and to "be in subjection" to him "as to the Lord." (Ephesians 5:22, 33) Thinking in terms of pleasing God can help a wife to use her abilities to support her husband rather than belittling him or trying to dominate him. Such a "truly wise woman" cooperates closely with her husband to build up the family. She thereby maintains peace with God.—Proverbs 14:1.

¹⁰ Parents also have authority granted them by God. The Bible admonishes: "Fathers, do not be irritating your children, but go on bringing them up in the discipline and mental-regulating of Jehovah." (Ephesians 6:4) In the Bible, the word "discipline" can mean "upbringing, training, instruction." Children need discipline; they thrive under clear-cut guidelines, boundaries, and limits. The Bible associates such discipline, or instruction, with love. (Proverbs 13:24) Therefore, "the rod of discipline" should

---

9. (a) Wives have what power in the family? (b) What can help a wife to use her abilities to support her husband, and with what result?
10. (a) God has granted what authority to parents? (b) What is the meaning of the word "discipline," and how should it be administered? (See also footnote.)

never be abusive—emotionally or physically.* (Proverbs 22:15; 29:15) Discipline that is rigid or harsh with no sense of love is an abuse of parental authority and can crush a child's spirit. (Colossians 3:21) On the other hand, balanced discipline that is properly administered conveys to children that their parents love them and care about the kind of person they are becoming.

¹¹ What about children? How can they use their power aright? "The beauty of young men is their power," says Proverbs 20:29. Surely there is no finer way for young people to use their strength and vigor than in serving our "Grand Creator." (Ecclesiastes 12:1) Young ones do well to remember that their actions can affect the feelings of their parents. (Proverbs 23:24, 25) When children obey their God-fearing parents and hold to a right course, they bring joy to their parents' hearts. (Ephesians 6:1) Such conduct is "well-pleasing in the Lord."—Colossians 3:20.

Within the Congregation

¹² Jehovah has provided overseers to take the lead in the Christian congregation. (Hebrews 13:17) These qualified men are to use their God-given authority to provide needed assistance and to contribute to the welfare of the flock. Does their position entitle elders to lord it over their fellow believers? Not at all! Elders need to have a balanced, humble view of their role in the congregation. (1 Peter 5: 2, 3) The Bible tells overseers: "Shepherd the congregation

---

* In Bible times, the Hebrew word for "rod" meant a stick or a staff, such as the one a shepherd used to guide his sheep. (Psalm 23:4) Similarly, "the rod" of parental authority suggests loving guidance, not harsh or brutal punishment.

---

11. How can children use their power aright?
12, 13. (a) What view should elders have of their authority in the congregation? (b) Illustrate why elders should treat the flock with tenderness.

of God, which he purchased with the blood of his own Son." (Acts 20:28) Therein lies a powerful reason for treating each member of the flock with tenderness.

¹³ We might illustrate it this way. A close friend asks you to care for a cherished possession. You know that your friend paid a high price for the item. Would you not treat it delicately, with great care? Similarly, God has entrusted elders with the responsibility to care for a truly valued possession: the congregation, whose members are likened to sheep. (John 21:16, 17) Jehovah's sheep are dear to him —so dear, in fact, that he purchased them with the precious blood of his only-begotten Son, Jesus Christ. Jehovah could not have paid a higher price for his sheep. Humble elders keep that in mind and treat Jehovah's sheep accordingly.

"The Power of the Tongue"

¹⁴ "Death and life are in the power of the tongue," says the Bible. (Proverbs 18:21) Indeed, the tongue can do much damage. Who of us has never felt the sting of a thoughtless or even disparaging remark? But the tongue also has the power to mend. "The tongue of the wise ones is a healing," says Proverbs 12:18. Yes, positive, wholesome words can be like an application of soothing, healing balm to the heart. Consider some examples.

¹⁵ "Speak consolingly to the depressed souls," urges 1 Thessalonians 5:14. Yes, even faithful servants of Jehovah may at times struggle with depression. How can we help such ones? Offer specific, genuine commendation to help them see their own value in Jehovah's eyes. Share with them the powerful words of Bible texts showing that Jehovah truly cares about and loves those who

14. The tongue has what power?
15, 16. In what ways may we use the tongue to encourage others?

are "broken at heart" and "crushed in spirit." (Psalm 34:18) When we use the power of our tongue to console others, we show that we are imitating our compassionate God, "who comforts the depressed."—2 Corinthians 7:6, *New American Standard Bible.*

¹⁶ We can also use the power of our tongue to provide much-needed encouragement to others. Has a fellow believer lost a loved one in death? Sympathetic words expressing our care and concern can comfort a grieving heart. Is an elderly brother or sister feeling unneeded? A thoughtful tongue can reassure older ones that they are valued and appreciated. Is someone struggling with a chronic illness? Kind words shared on the phone or in person can do much to lift the spirits of one who is sick. How pleased our Creator must be when we use the power of speech to utter sayings that are "good for building up"!—Ephesians 4:29.

Husbands and wives use their power aright by treating each other with love and respect

¹⁷ There is no more important way to use the power of

17. In what important way can we use our tongue to benefit others, and why should we do so?

the tongue than by our sharing the good news of God's Kingdom with others. "Do not hold back good from those to whom it is owing, when it happens to be in the power of your hand to do it," says Proverbs 3:27. We owe it to others to share with them the lifesaving good news. It would not be right to keep to ourselves the urgent message that Jehovah has so generously granted us. (1 Corinthians 9:16, 22) But to what extent does Jehovah expect us to share in this work?

Serving Jehovah With Our "Whole Strength"

¹⁸ Our love for Jehovah moves us to have a full share in

18. What does Jehovah expect of us?

*Sharing the good news
—an excellent way to use our power*

the Christian ministry. What does Jehovah expect of us in this regard? Something that all of us, no matter what our situation in life, can give: "Whatever you are doing, work at it whole-souled as to Jehovah, and not to men." (Colossians 3:23) In stating the greatest commandment, Jesus said: "You must love Jehovah your God with your whole heart and with your whole soul and with your whole mind and with your whole strength." (Mark 12:30) Yes, Jehovah expects each one of us to love and serve him in a whole-souled way.

[19] What does it mean to serve God whole-souled? The soul refers to the entire person, with all his physical and mental abilities. Since the soul embraces the heart, the mind, and the strength, why are these other faculties mentioned at Mark 12:30? Consider an illustration. In Bible times, a person might sell himself (his soul) into slavery. Yet, the slave might not serve his master wholeheartedly; he might not use his full strength or his full mental abilities to advance his master's interests. (Colossians 3:22) Hence, Jesus evidently mentioned these other faculties in order to emphasize that we must not hold anything back in our service to God. Serving God whole-souled means giving of ourselves, using our strength and energies to the fullest extent possible in his service.

[20] Does serving whole-souled mean that we must all spend the same amount of time and energy in the ministry? That could hardly be possible, for circumstances and abilities differ from one person to another. For example, a young person with good health and physical stamina may be able to spend more time in preaching than can

---

19, 20. (a) Since the soul includes the heart, the mind, and the strength, why are these other faculties mentioned at Mark 12:30? (b) What does it mean to serve Jehovah whole-souled?

Questions for Meditation

Proverbs 3:9, 10 What "valuable things" do we possess, and how can we use these to honor Jehovah?

Ecclesiastes 9:5-10 Why should you use your strength now in a manner that God will approve?

Acts 8:9-24 What abuse of power is described here, and how can we avoid giving in to such wrongdoing?

Acts 20:29-38 What might those with responsible positions in the congregation learn from Paul's example?

---

one whose strength is sapped by advancing age. A single person who is free from family obligations may be able to do more than can one who has to care for a family. If we have the strength and circumstances that enable us to do much in the ministry, how thankful we should be! Of course, we would never want to have a critical spirit, comparing ourselves with others in this regard. (Romans 14:10-12) Rather, we want to use our power to encourage others.

21 Jehovah has set the perfect example in using his power aright. We want to imitate him to the best of our ability as imperfect humans. We can use our power aright by treating with dignity those over whom we have a measure of authority. In addition, we want to be whole-souled in carrying out the lifesaving preaching work that Jehovah has given us to accomplish. (Romans 10:13, 14) Remember, Jehovah is pleased when you give the best that you—your soul—can give. Does not your heart move you to want to do all you can in serving such an understanding and loving God? There is no better or more important way to use your power.

---

21. What is the best and most important way to use our power?

"A LOVER OF JUSTICE"

Injustice is rampant in today's world, and much blame is wrongly placed on God. Yet, the Bible teaches a heartwarming truth—that "Jehovah is a lover of justice." (Psalm 37:28) In this section we will learn how he has proved those words true, offering hope to all mankind.

CHAPTER 11

"All His Ways Are Justice"

IT WAS a gross injustice. The handsome young man had committed no crime, yet he found himself confined in a dungeon, falsely accused of attempted rape. But this was not his first encounter with injustice. Years earlier, at the age of 17, this young man, Joseph, had been betrayed by his own brothers, who had nearly murdered him. He had then been sold into slavery in a foreign land. There he had refused the advances of his master's wife. The spurned woman framed the false accusation, and that was how he came to be in custody. Sadly, there seemed to be no one to intercede for Joseph.

2 However, the God who is "a lover of righteousness and justice" was watching. (Psalm 33:5) Jehovah acted to correct the injustices, maneuvering events so that Joseph was finally released. More than that, Joseph—the man who had been cast into a "prison hole"—was eventually placed in a position of great responsibility and extraordinary honor. (Genesis 40:15; 41:41-43; Psalm 105:17, 18) In the end, Joseph was vindicated, and he used his lofty position to further God's purpose.—Genesis 45:5-8.

3 Such an account speaks to our heart, does it not? Who of us has not seen injustice or been a victim of it? Indeed, we all yearn to be treated in a just, fair manner. This is not surprising, since Jehovah bestowed upon us qualities that reflect his own personality, and justice is one of

---

1, 2. (a) What gross injustices did Joseph experience? (b) How did Jehovah correct the injustices?
3. Why is it not surprising that we all want to be treated in a just manner?

his principal attributes. (Genesis 1:27) To know Jehovah well, we need to understand his sense of justice. We can thus come to appreciate his wonderful ways even more and be moved to draw closer to him.

What Is Justice?

[4] From a human standpoint, justice is often understood to be nothing more than the fair application of the rules of law. The book *Right and Reason—Ethics in Theory and Practice* says that "justice is connected with law, obligation, rights, and duties, and measures out its awards according to equality or merit." Jehovah's justice, however, involves more than the cold application of regulations out of a sense of duty or obligation.

[5] The breadth and depth of Jehovah's justice can better be understood by considering the original-language words used in the Bible. In the Hebrew Scriptures, three principal words are involved. The word most often rendered "justice" may also be rendered "what is right." (Genesis 18:25) The other two words are usually rendered "righteousness." In the Christian Greek Scriptures, the word translated "righteousness" is defined as the "quality of being right or just." Basically, then, there is no distinction between righteousness and justice.—Amos 5:24.

[6] Hence, when the Bible says that God is just, it is telling us that he does what is right and fair and that he does so consistently, without partiality. (Romans 2:11) Really, it is inconceivable that he would act otherwise. Faithful

---

4. From a human standpoint, how is justice often understood?

5, 6. (a) What is the meaning of the original-language words rendered "justice"? (b) What does it mean that God is just?

Elihu stated: "Far be it from the true God to act wickedly, and the Almighty to act unjustly!" (Job 34:10) Indeed, it is impossible for Jehovah "to act unjustly." Why? For two important reasons.

⁷ First, he is holy. As we noted in Chapter 3, Jehovah is infinitely pure and upright. Therefore, he is incapable of acting unrighteously, or unjustly. Consider what that means. The holiness of our heavenly Father gives us every reason to trust that he will never mistreat his children. Jesus had such confidence. On the final night of his earthly life, he prayed: "Holy Father, watch over them [the disciples] on account of your own name." (John 17: 11) "Holy Father"—in the Scriptures, that form of address applies to Jehovah alone. This is fitting, for no human father can compare with Him in holiness. Jesus had complete faith that his disciples would be safe in the hands of the Father, who is absolutely pure and clean and entirely separated from all sinfulness.—Matthew 23:9.

⁸ Second, unselfish love is intrinsic to God's very nature. Such love moves him to be righteous, or just, in his dealings with others. But injustice in its many forms —including racism, discrimination, and partiality—often springs from greed and selfishness, the opposites of love. Regarding the God of love, the Bible assures us: "Jehovah is righteous; he does love righteous acts." (Psalm 11:7) Jehovah says of himself: "I, Jehovah, am loving justice." (Isaiah 61:8) Is it not comforting to know that our God takes delight in doing what is right, or just?—Jeremiah 9:24.

7, 8. (a) Why is Jehovah incapable of acting unjustly? (b) What moves Jehovah to be righteous, or just, in his dealings?

Joseph suffered unjustly in "the prison hole"

Mercy and Jehovah's Perfect Justice

⁹ Jehovah's justice, like every other facet of his matchless personality, is perfect, not lacking in anything. Extolling Jehovah, Moses wrote: "The Rock, perfect is his activity, for all his ways are justice. A God of faithfulness, with whom there is no injustice; righteous and upright is he." (Deuteronomy 32:3, 4) Every expression of Jehovah's justice is flawless—never too lenient, never too harsh.

¹⁰ There is a close connection between Jehovah's justice and his mercy. Psalm 116:5 says: "Jehovah is gracious and righteous ["just," *The New American Bible*]; and our God is One showing mercy." Yes, Jehovah is both just and merciful. The two traits are not at odds. His exercising of mercy is not a watering down of his justice, as if his justice would otherwise be too severe. Rather, the two qualities are often expressed by him at the same time, even in the same act. Consider an example.

¹¹ All humans are by inheritance sinful and thus deserving of sin's penalty—death. (Romans 5:12) But Jehovah finds no pleasure in the death of sinners. He is "a God of acts of forgiveness, gracious and merciful." (Nehemiah 9:17) Still, because he is holy, he cannot condone unrighteousness. How, then, could he show mercy to inherently sinful humans? The answer is found in one of the most precious truths of God's Word: Jehovah's provision of a ransom for mankind's salvation. In Chapter 14 we will learn more about this loving arrangement. It is at once profoundly just and supremely merciful. By means of it, Jehovah can express tender mercy toward repentant sin-

---

9-11. (a) What connection is there between Jehovah's justice and his mercy? (b) How is Jehovah's justice as well as his mercy evident in the way he deals with sinful humans?

ners while maintaining his standards of perfect justice.
—Romans 3:21-26.

Jehovah's Justice Is Heartwarming

¹² Jehovah's justice is, not a cold quality that repels us,
but an endearing quality that draws us to him. The Bible clearly describes the compassionate nature of Jehovah's justice, or righteousness. Let us consider some of
the heartwarming ways that Jehovah exercises his justice.

¹³ Jehovah's perfect justice moves him to show faithfulness and loyalty toward his servants. The psalmist David came to appreciate firsthand this facet of Jehovah's
justice. From his own experience and from his study of
God's ways, what conclusion did David reach? He declared: "Jehovah is a lover of justice, and he will not
leave his loyal ones. To time indefinite they will certainly
be guarded." (Psalm 37:28) What comforting assurance!
Our God will never for one moment abandon those who
are loyal to him. We can therefore count on his closeness
and his loving care. His justice guarantees this!—Proverbs
2:7, 8.

¹⁴ Divine justice is sensitive to the needs of the afflicted. Jehovah's concern for disadvantaged ones is evident in the Law he gave to Israel. For example, the Law
made special provisions to ensure that orphans and widows were cared for. (Deuteronomy 24:17-21) Recogniz-
ing how difficult life could be for such families, Jehovah himself became their fatherly Judge and Protector,

---

12, 13. (a) Why does Jehovah's justice draw us to him? (b) What
conclusion did David reach regarding Jehovah's justice, and how can
this comfort us?

14. How is Jehovah's concern for disadvantaged ones evident in the
Law he gave to Israel?

the one "executing judgment for the fatherless boy and the widow."* (Deuteronomy 10:18; Psalm 68:5) Jehovah warned the Israelites that if they victimized defenseless women and children, he would unfailingly hear the outcry of such ones. He stated: "My anger will indeed blaze." (Exodus 22:22-24) While anger is not one of Jehovah's dominant qualities, he is provoked to righteous indignation by deliberate acts of injustice, especially when the victims are the lowly and the helpless.—Psalm 103:6.

¹⁵ Jehovah also assures us that he "treats none with partiality nor accepts a bribe." (Deuteronomy 10:17) Unlike many humans with power or influence, Jehovah is not swayed by material wealth or outward appearance. He is completely free from bias or favoritism. Consider a truly remarkable evidence of Jehovah's impartiality. The opportunity of becoming his true worshipers, with endless life in view, is not restricted to an elite few. Rather, "in every nation the man that fears him and works righteousness is acceptable to him." (Acts 10:34, 35) This marvelous prospect is open to all regardless of their social standing, the color of their skin, or the country in which they live. Is that not true justice at its very best?

¹⁶ There is another aspect of Jehovah's perfect justice that merits our consideration and respect: the way he deals with transgressors of his righteous standards.

---

* Although the Hebrew word for "fatherless boy" is in the masculine gender, this in no way suggests a lack of concern for girls. Jehovah included in the Law an account about a judicial decision that guaranteed an inheritance for the fatherless daughters of Zelophehad. That ruling established a precedent, thus upholding the rights of fatherless girls.—Numbers 27:1-8.

15, 16. What is a truly remarkable evidence of Jehovah's impartiality?

No Exemption From Punishment

[17] Some may wonder: 'Since Jehovah does not condone unrighteousness, how can we account for the unjust suffering and the corrupt practices that are all too common in today's world?' Such inequities in no way impugn Jehovah's justice. The many injustices in this wicked world are a consequence of the sin that humans have inherited from Adam. In a world where imperfect humans have chosen their own sinful ways, injustices abound—but not for long.—Deuteronomy 32:5.

[18] While Jehovah shows great mercy toward those who draw near to him in sincerity, he will not forever tolerate a situation that brings reproach upon his holy name. (Psalm 74:10, 22, 23) The God of justice is not one to be mocked; he will not shield willful sinners from the adverse judgment their course deserves. Jehovah is "a God merciful and gracious, slow to anger and abundant in lovingkindness and truth, . . . but by no means will he give exemption from punishment." (Exodus 34:6, 7) True to these words, Jehovah has at times found it necessary to execute judgment upon those who deliberately violate his righteous laws.

[19] Take, for example, God's dealings with ancient Israel. Even when settled in the Promised Land, the Israelites repeatedly lapsed into unfaithfulness. Though their corrupt ways made Jehovah "feel hurt," he did not immediately cast them off. (Psalm 78:38-41) Rather, he mercifully extended opportunities for them to change their course. He pleaded: "I take delight, not in the death of the wicked one, but in that someone wicked turns back from his

---

17. Explain why the inequities in this world in no way impugn Jehovah's justice.
18, 19. What shows that Jehovah will not forever tolerate those who deliberately violate his righteous laws?

Questions for Meditation

Jeremiah 18:1-11 How did Jehovah teach Jeremiah that He is not quick to express adverse judgment?

Habakkuk 1:1-4, 13; 2:2-4 How did Jehovah reassure Habakkuk that He will not forever tolerate injustice?

Zechariah 7:8-14 How does Jehovah feel about those who trample upon the rights of others?

Romans 2:3-11 On what basis does Jehovah judge individuals as well as nations?

---

way and actually keeps living. Turn back, turn back from your bad ways, for why is it that you should die, O house of Israel?" (Ezekiel 33:11) Viewing life as precious, Jehovah repeatedly sent his prophets so that the Israelites might turn back from their bad ways. But, by and large, the hard-hearted people refused to listen and repent. Finally, for the sake of his holy name and all that it stands for, Jehovah gave them into the hands of their enemies.—Nehemiah 9: 26-30.

[20] Jehovah's dealings with Israel teach us much about him. We learn that his all-seeing eyes take note of unrighteousness and that he is deeply affected by what he sees. (Proverbs 15:3) It is also reassuring to know that he seeks to show mercy if there is a basis for doing so. In addition, we learn that his justice is never hasty. Because of Jehovah's patience and long-suffering, many people wrongly conclude that he will never execute judgment against the wicked. But that is far from the truth, for God's dealings with Israel also teach us that divine patience has limits. Jehovah is firm for righteousness. Unlike humans, who of-

---

20. (a) Jehovah's dealings with Israel teach us what about him? (b) Why is the lion a fitting symbol of Jehovah's justice?

ten shrink back from exercising justice, he never lacks the courage to stand up for what is right. Fittingly, the lion as a symbol of courageous justice is associated with God's presence and throne.* (Ezekiel 1:10; Revelation 4:7) We can thus be sure that he will fulfill his promise to rid this earth of injustice. Yes, his way of judging can be summed up as follows: firmness where necessary, mercy wherever possible.—2 Peter 3:9.

Drawing Close to the God of Justice

21 When we meditate on how Jehovah exercises justice, we should not think of him as a cold, stern judge concerned only with passing judgment on wrongdoers. Instead, we should think of him as a loving but firm Father who always deals with his children in the best possible way. As a just, or righteous, Father, Jehovah balances firmness for what is right with tender compassion toward his earthly children, who need his help and forgiveness. —Psalm 103:10, 13.

22 How thankful we can be that divine justice involves much more than passing sentence on wrongdoers! Guided by his justice, Jehovah has made it possible for us to have a truly thrilling prospect—perfect, endless life in a world where "righteousness is to dwell." (2 Peter 3:13) Our God deals with us in this way because his justice seeks to save rather than to condemn. Truly, a better understanding of the scope of Jehovah's justice draws us to him! In the following chapters, we will take a closer look at how Jehovah expresses this sterling quality.

---

* Interestingly, Jehovah likens himself to a lion in executing judgment on unfaithful Israel.—Jeremiah 25:38; Hosea 5:14.

21. When we meditate on how Jehovah exercises justice, in what way should we think of him, and why?
22. Guided by his justice, Jehovah has made it possible for us to have what prospect, and why does he deal with us in this way?

"Is There Injustice With God?"

AN ELDERLY widow is swindled out of her life savings. A helpless infant is abandoned by a coldhearted parent. A man is imprisoned for a crime he did not commit. How do you react to these scenarios? Likely, each one disturbs you, and understandably so. We humans have a strong sense of right and wrong. When an injustice is committed, we are incensed. We want the victim to be compensated and the offender brought to justice. If this does not happen, we may wonder: 'Does God see what is happening? Why does he not act?'

2 Throughout history, faithful servants of Jehovah have asked similar questions. For example, the prophet Habakkuk prayed to God: "Why do you make me watch such terrible injustice? Why do you allow violence, lawlessness, crime, and cruelty to spread everywhere?" (Habakkuk 1:3, *Contemporary English Version*) Jehovah did not censure Habakkuk for his candid inquiry, for He is the one who instilled in humans the very concept of justice. Yes, Jehovah has blessed us with a small measure of his profound sense of justice.

Jehovah Hates Injustice

3 Jehovah is not oblivious to injustice. He sees what is going on. Regarding Noah's day, the Bible tells us: "Jehovah saw that the badness of man was abundant in the earth and every inclination of the thoughts of his heart

1. How may we be affected by instances of injustice?
2. How did Habakkuk react to injustice, and why did Jehovah not censure him for this?
3. Why can it be said that Jehovah is more aware of injustice than we are?

was only bad all the time." (Genesis 6:5) Consider the implications of that statement. Often, our perception of injustice is based on a few incidents that we have either heard about or personally encountered. In contrast, Jehovah is aware of injustice on a *global* scale. He sees it all! More than that, he can discern the inclinations of the heart—the debased thinking behind unjust acts.—Jeremiah 17:10.

4 But Jehovah does more than simply take note of injustice. He also cares about those who have been victimized by it. When his people were cruelly treated by enemy nations, Jehovah was distressed "over their groaning because of their oppressors and those who were shoving them around." (Judges 2:18) Perhaps you have observed that the more some people see injustice, the more they become calloused to it. Not so with Jehovah! He has seen injustice in its entire scope for some 6,000 years, yet he has not wavered in his hatred for it. Rather, the Bible assures us that such things as "a false tongue," "hands that are shedding innocent blood," and "a false witness that launches forth lies" are detestable to him.—Proverbs 6:16-19.

5 Consider, too, Jehovah's strong criticism of the unjust leaders in Israel. "Is it not your business to know justice?" he inspired his prophet to ask them. After describing in graphic terms their abuse of power, Jehovah foretold the outcome for these corrupt men: "They will call to Jehovah for aid, but he will not answer them. And he will conceal his face from them in that time, according as they committed badness in their dealings." (Micah 3:1-4) What an aversion Jehovah has to injustice! Why, he himself has experienced it firsthand! For thousands of years, Satan

---

4, 5. (a) How does the Bible show that Jehovah cares for those who have been treated unjustly? (b) How has Jehovah himself been touched by injustice?

has been unjustly taunting him. (Proverbs 27:11) Further-more, Jehovah was touched by the most horrendous act of injustice when his Son, who "committed no sin," was ex-ecuted as a criminal. (1 Peter 2:22; Isaiah 53:9) Clearly, Je-hovah is neither oblivious of nor indifferent to the plight of those who suffer injustice.

⁶ Yet, when we observe injustice—or when we ourselves become victims of unfair treatment—it is only natural for us to react strongly. We are made in God's image, and in-justice is diametrically opposed to all that Jehovah stands for. (Genesis 1:27) Why, then, does God allow injustice?

The Issue of God's Sovereignty

⁷ The answer to this question is related to the issue of sovereignty. As we have seen, the Creator has the right to rule over the earth and all those dwelling in it. (Psalm 24:1; Revelation 4:11) Early in human history, however, Jehovah's sovereignty was challenged. How did this come about? Jehovah commanded the first man, Adam, not to eat from a certain tree in the garden that was his Para-dise home. And if he disobeyed? "You will positively die," God told him. (Genesis 2:17) God's command worked no hardship on Adam or his wife, Eve. Nevertheless, Sa-tan convinced Eve that God was being unduly restrictive. What if she did eat from the tree? Satan told Eve outright: "You positively will *not* die. For God knows that in the very day of your eating from it your eyes are bound to be opened and you are bound to be like God, knowing good and bad."—Genesis 3:1-5.

⁸ In this statement Satan implied not only that Jehovah

---

6. How might we react when faced with injustice, and why?
7. Describe how Jehovah's sovereignty was challenged.
8. (a) What did Satan imply by his statements to Eve? (b) What did Satan challenge with regard to God's sovereignty?

had withheld crucial information from Eve but also that He had lied to her. Satan was careful not to question the *fact* of God's sovereignty. But he did challenge the rightfulness, deservedness, and righteousness of it. In other words, he maintained that Jehovah was not exercising His sovereignty in a righteous way and in the best interests of His subjects.

⁹ Subsequently, both Adam and Eve disobeyed Jehovah by eating from the forbidden tree. Their disobedience put them in line to receive the punishment of death, just as God had decreed. Satan's lie raised some vital questions. Does Jehovah truly have the right to rule mankind, or should man rule himself? Does Jehovah exercise his sovereignty in the best possible way? Jehovah could have used his almighty power to destroy the rebels right then and there. But the questions raised pertained to God's rulership, not his power. So eliminating Adam, Eve, and Satan would not have affirmed the righteousness of God's rule. If anything, it might have called his rulership into question even further. The only way to determine whether humans could successfully rule themselves, independent of God, was to let time pass.

¹⁰ What has the passing of time revealed? Throughout the millenniums, people have experimented with many forms of government, including autocracy, democracy, socialism, and communism. The sum total of them all is epitomized in the Bible's frank comment: "Man has dominated man to his injury." (Ecclesiastes 8:9) With good reason, the prophet Jeremiah stated: "I well know, O Jehovah, that to earthling man his way does not belong. It

9. (a) For Adam and Eve, what was the consequence of disobedience, and what vital questions did this raise? (b) Why did Jehovah not simply destroy the rebels?
10. What has history revealed regarding human rule?

does not belong to man who is walking even to direct his step."—Jeremiah 10:23.

¹¹ Jehovah knew from the beginning that mankind's independence, or self-rule, would result in much suffering. Was it unjust of him, then, to allow the inevitable to run its course? Not at all! To illustrate: Suppose you have a child who needs surgery to cure a life-threatening ailment. You realize that the operation will cause your child a degree of suffering, and this deeply grieves you. At the same time, you know that the procedure will enable your child to enjoy better health later in life. Similarly, God knew—and even foretold—that his allowance of human rule would bring along with it a measure of pain and suffering. (Genesis 3:16-19) But he also knew that lasting and meaningful relief would be possible only if he allowed all mankind to see the bad fruitage produced by rebellion. In this way the issue could be settled *permanently,* for all eternity.

The Issue of Man's Integrity

¹² There is another aspect of this matter. In challenging the rightfulness and righteousness of God's rule, not only has Satan slandered Jehovah with regard to His sovereignty; he has also slandered God's servants concerning their integrity. Note, for example, what Satan said to Jehovah regarding the righteous man Job: "Have not you yourself put up a hedge about him and about his house and about everything that he has all around? The work of his hands you have blessed, and his livestock itself has spread abroad

---

11. Why did Jehovah let the human race be subjected to suffering?
12. As illustrated in Job's case, what accusation has Satan brought against humans?

Jehovah will never "sweep away the righteous with the wicked"

in the earth. But, for a change, thrust out your hand, please, and touch everything he has and see whether he will not curse you to your very face."—Job 1:10, 11.

13 Satan contended that Jehovah was using His protective power to buy Job's devotion. In turn, this implied that Job's integrity was a mere sham, that he worshiped God only for what he could get in return. Satan asserted that if Job was deprived of God's blessing, even that man would curse his Creator. Satan knew that Job was outstanding in being "blameless and upright, fearing God and turning aside from bad."* So if Satan could break Job's integrity, what would that say for the rest of mankind? Thus Satan was really calling into question the loyalty of all of those who want to serve God. Indeed, broadening the issue, Satan said to Jehovah: "Everything that *a man* [not just Job] has he will give in behalf of his soul."—Job 1:8; 2:4.

14 History has shown that many, like Job, have remained loyal to Jehovah in the face of trial—contrary to Satan's claim. They have made Jehovah's heart glad by their faithful course, and this has given Jehovah a reply to Satan's boastful taunt that humans will stop serving God when they are subjected to hardship. (Hebrews 11:4-38) Yes, righthearted ones have refused to turn their backs on God. Even when perplexed by the most distressing situations, they have relied all the more on Jehovah to give them the strength to endure.—2 Corinthians 4:7-10.

---

* Jehovah said regarding Job: "There is no one like him in the earth." (Job 1:8) Likely, then, Job lived after the death of Joseph and before Moses became Israel's appointed leader. Thus, at that time it could be said that no one had integrity like that of Job.

---

13. What did Satan imply by his accusations regarding Job, and how does this involve all humans?
14. What has history shown regarding Satan's accusation against humans?

¹⁵ But Jehovah's exercise of justice involves more than the issues of sovereignty and man's integrity. The Bible provides us with a record of Jehovah's judgments in relation to individuals and even entire nations. It also contains prophecies of judgments he will render in the future. Why can we be confident that Jehovah has been and will be righteous in his judgments?

Why God's Justice Is Superior

¹⁶ Concerning Jehovah, it can rightly be said: "All his ways are justice." (Deuteronomy 32:4) None of us can make such a claim about ourselves, for so often our limited perspective clouds our perception of what is right. For example, consider Abraham. He pleaded with Jehovah concerning the destruction of Sodom—despite the rampant wickedness there. He asked Jehovah: "Will you really sweep away the righteous with the wicked?" (Genesis 18:23-33) Of course, the answer was no. It was only when righteous Lot and his daughters arrived safely at the city of Zoar that Jehovah "made it rain sulphur and fire" upon Sodom. (Genesis 19:22-24) In contrast, Jonah became "hot with anger" when God extended mercy to the people of Nineveh. Since Jonah had already announced their destruction, he would have been content to see them exterminated—regardless of their heartfelt repentance.—Jonah 3:10–4:1.

¹⁷ Jehovah reassured Abraham that His exercise of justice includes not only destroying the wicked but also saving the righteous. On the other hand, Jonah had to learn that Jehovah is merciful. If the wicked change their ways, he is "ready to forgive." (Psalm 86:5) Unlike some insecure

---

15. What question might arise concerning God's past and future judgments?
16, 17. What examples show that humans have a limited perspective when it comes to true justice?

humans, Jehovah does not administer adverse judgment simply to make a statement about his power, nor does he withhold compassion out of fear that he will be viewed as weak. His way is to show mercy whenever there is a basis for it.—Isaiah 55:7; Ezekiel 18:23.

[18] However, Jehovah is not blinded by mere sentiment. When his people became steeped in idolatry, Jehovah firmly declared: "I will judge you according to your ways and bring upon you all your detestable things. And my eye will not feel sorry for you, neither will I feel compassion, for upon you I shall bring your own ways." (Ezekiel 7:3, 4) So when humans are hardened in their course, Jehovah judges accordingly. But his judgment is based on solid evidence. Thus, when a loud "cry of complaint" reached his ears regarding Sodom and Gomorrah, Jehovah stated: "I am quite determined to go down that I may see whether they act altogether according to the outcry over it that has come to me." (Genesis 18:20, 21) How thankful we can be that Jehovah is not like many humans who jump to conclusions before hearing all the facts! Truly, Jehovah is as the Bible depicts him, "a God of faithfulness, with whom there is no injustice."—Deuteronomy 32:4.

Have Confidence in Jehovah's Justice

[19] The Bible does not address every question regarding Jehovah's actions in the past; nor does it provide every detail about how Jehovah will render judgment concerning individuals and groups in the future. When we are puzzled by accounts or prophecies in the Bible where such

---

18. Show from the Bible that Jehovah does not act on mere sentiment.
19. What can we do if we have perplexing questions about Jehovah's exercise of justice?

Questions for Meditation

Deuteronomy 10:17-19 Why can we be confident that Jehovah is impartial in his dealings?

Job 34:1-12 When you are faced with injustice, how can Elihu's words strengthen your confidence in God's righteousness?

Psalm 1:1-6 Why is it reassuring to know that Jehovah carefully weighs the acts of both the righteous and the wicked?

Malachi 2:13-16 How did Jehovah feel about the injustice done to women whose husbands divorced them with no proper basis?

detail is lacking, we can display the same loyalty as did the prophet Micah, who wrote: "I will show a waiting attitude for the God of my salvation."—Micah 7:7.

[20] We can be confident that in every situation, Jehovah will do what is right. Even when injustices are seemingly ignored by man, Jehovah promises: "Vengeance is mine; I will repay." (Romans 12:19) If we show a waiting attitude, we will echo the firm conviction expressed by the apostle Paul: "Is there injustice with God? Never may that become so!"—Romans 9:14.

[21] In the meantime, we live in "critical times hard to deal with." (2 Timothy 3:1) Injustice and "acts of oppression" have resulted in many cruel abuses. (Ecclesiastes 4:1) However, Jehovah has not changed. He still hates injustice, and he cares deeply for those who are victims of it. If we remain loyal to Jehovah and his sovereignty, he will give us the strength to endure until the appointed time when he will correct all injustices under his Kingdom rule.—1 Peter 5:6, 7.

20, 21. Why can we be confident that Jehovah will always do what is right?

CHAPTER 13

"The Law of Jehovah Is Perfect"

"LAW is a bottomless pit, it . . . devours everything." That statement appeared in a book published back in 1712. Its author decried a legal system in which lawsuits sometimes dragged through the courts for years, bankrupting those seeking justice. In many lands, legal and judicial systems are so complex, so rife with injustice, prejudice, and inconsistencies, that contempt for law has become widespread.

² By way of contrast, consider these words written some 2,700 years ago: "How I do love your law!" (Psalm 119:97) Why did the psalmist feel so strongly? Because the law he praised originated, not with any secular government, but with Jehovah God. As you study Jehovah's laws, you may come to feel more and more as the psalmist did. Such a study will give you insight into the greatest judicial mind in the universe.

The Supreme Lawgiver

³ "One there is that is lawgiver and judge," the Bible tells us. (James 4:12) Indeed, Jehovah is the only true Lawgiver. Even the movements of the heavenly bodies are governed by his "celestial laws." (Job 38:33, *The New Jerusalem Bible*) Jehovah's myriads of holy angels are likewise governed by divine law, for they are organized into definite ranks and serve under Jehovah's command as his ministers.—Psalm 104:4; Hebrews 1:7, 14.

⁴ Jehovah has given laws to mankind as well. Each of us

1, 2. Why do many people have little regard for law, yet how may we come to feel about God's laws?
3, 4. In what ways has Jehovah proved to be Lawgiver?

has a conscience, a reflection of Jehovah's sense of justice. A kind of internal law, the conscience can help us to distinguish right from wrong. (Romans 2:14) Our first parents were blessed with a perfect conscience, so they needed but a few laws. (Genesis 2:15-17) Imperfect man, however, needs more laws to guide him in the doing of God's will. Such patriarchs as Noah, Abraham, and Jacob received laws from Jehovah God and transmitted these to their families. (Genesis 6:22; 9:3-6; 18:19; 26:4, 5) Jehovah caused himself to become Lawgiver in an unprecedented way when he gave the nation of Israel a Law code by means of Moses. This legal code offers us extensive insight into Jehovah's sense of justice.

The Mosaic Law—An Overview

⁵ Many seem to think that the Mosaic Law was an unwieldy, complex set of laws. Such a notion is far from the truth. There are over 600 laws in the entire code. That may sound like a lot, but just think: By the end of the 20th century, the federal laws of the United States filled over 150,-000 pages of legal books. Every two years some 600 more laws are added! So in terms of sheer volume, the mountain of human laws dwarfs the Mosaic Law. Yet, God's Law governed the Israelites in areas of life that modern laws do not even begin to touch. Consider an overview.

⁶ *The Law exalted Jehovah's sovereignty.* Thus, the Mosaic Law is beyond comparison with any other law code. The greatest of its laws was this: "Listen, O Israel: Jehovah our God is one Jehovah. And you must love Jehovah

5. Was the Mosaic Law an unwieldy, complex set of laws, and why do you so answer?
6, 7. (a) What differentiates the Mosaic Law from any other law code, and what is that Law's greatest commandment? (b) How could the Israelites show their acceptance of Jehovah's sovereignty?

your God with all your heart and all your soul and all your vital force." How were God's people to express love for him? They were to serve him, submitting to his sovereignty.—Deuteronomy 6:4, 5; 11:13.

7 Each Israelite showed his acceptance of Jehovah's sovereignty by submitting to those placed in authority over him. Parents, chieftains, judges, priests and, eventually, the king all represented divine authority. Jehovah viewed any rebellion against those in authority as rebellion against him. On the other hand, those in authority risked Jehovah's wrath if they dealt unjustly or arrogantly with his people. (Exodus 20:12; 22:28; Deuteronomy 1:16, 17; 17:8-20; 19:16, 17) Both sides were thus responsible for upholding God's sovereignty.

8 *The Law upheld Jehovah's standard of holiness.* The words "holy" and "holiness" occur over 280 times in the Mosaic Law. The Law helped God's people to distinguish between what was clean and unclean, pure and impure, citing about 70 different things that could render an Israelite ceremonially unclean. These laws touched on physical hygiene, diet, and even waste disposal. Such laws provided remarkable health benefits.* But they had a higher purpose—that of keeping the people in Jehovah's favor, separate from the sinful practices of the debased nations surrounding them. Consider an example.

9 Statutes of the Law covenant stated that sexual relations and childbirth—even among married people—brought on

---

* For instance, laws requiring the burying of human waste, the quarantining of the sick, and the washing of anyone who touched a dead body were many centuries ahead of the times.—Leviticus 13:4-8; Numbers 19:11-13, 17-19; Deuteronomy 23:13, 14.

8. How did the Law uphold Jehovah's standard of holiness?
9, 10. The Law covenant included what statutes regarding sexual relations and childbirth, and what benefits did such laws provide?

a period of uncleanness. (Leviticus 12:2-4; 15:16-18) Such statutes did not denigrate these clean gifts from God. (Genesis 1:28; 2:18-25) Rather, those laws upheld Jehovah's holiness, keeping his worshipers free from contamination. It is noteworthy that the nations surrounding Israel tended to mix worship with sex and fertility rites. Canaanite religion included male and female prostitution. Degradation of the worst sort resulted and spread. In contrast, the Law made the worship of Jehovah entirely separate from sexual matters.* There were other benefits too.

¹⁰ Those laws served to teach a vital truth.# How, after all, is the stain of Adam's sin transmitted from one generation to the next? Is it not through sexual relations and childbirth? (Romans 5:12) Yes, God's Law reminded his people of the ever-present reality of sin. All of us, in fact, are born in sin. (Psalm 51:5) We need forgiveness and redemption in order to draw close to our holy God.

¹¹ *The Law upheld Jehovah's perfect justice.* The Mosaic Law advocated the principle of equivalence, or balance, in matters of justice. Thus, the Law stated: "Soul will be for soul, eye for eye, tooth for tooth, hand for hand, foot for foot." (Deuteronomy 19:21) In criminal cases, then, the punishment had to fit the crime. This aspect of divine justice permeated the Law and to this day is essential

---

* Whereas Canaanite temples featured rooms set aside for sexual activity, the Mosaic Law stated that those in an unclean state could not even enter the temple. Thus, since sexual relations brought on a period of uncleanness, no one could lawfully make sex a part of worship at Jehovah's house.

Teaching was a primary purpose of the Law. In fact, the *Encyclopaedia Judaica* notes that the Hebrew word for "law," *toh·rah'*, means "instruction."

11, 12. (a) The Law advocated what vital principle of justice? (b) What safeguards against the perversion of justice did the Law include?

to understanding the ransom sacrifice of Christ Jesus, as Chapter 14 will show.—1 Timothy 2:5, 6.

¹² The Law also included safeguards against the perversion of justice. For instance, at least two witnesses were required in order to establish the validity of an accusation. The penalty for perjury was severe. (Deuteronomy 19:15, 18, 19) Corruption and bribery were also strictly forbidden. (Exodus 23:8; Deuteronomy 27:25) Even in their business practices, God's people had to uphold Jehovah's lofty standard of justice. (Leviticus 19:35, 36; Deuteronomy 23:19, 20) That noble and just legal code was a great blessing to Israel!

Laws That Highlight Judicial Mercy and Fair Treatment

¹³ Was the Mosaic Law a rigid, unmerciful body of rules? Far from it! King David was inspired to write: "The law of Jehovah is perfect." (Psalm 19:7) As he well knew, the Law promoted mercy and fair treatment. How did it do so?

¹⁴ In some lands today, the law seems to show more leniency and favor to the criminals than it does concern for the victims. For instance, thieves may spend time in prison. Meanwhile, the victims may still be without their goods, yet they have to pay the taxes that house and feed such criminals. In ancient Israel, there were no prisons as we know them today. There were strict limits regarding the severity of punishments. (Deuteronomy 25:1-3) A thief had to compensate the victim for what had been stolen. In addition, the thief had to make further payment. How much? It varied. Evidently, the judges were given latitude to weigh a number of factors, such as the sinner's repentance. That would explain why the compensation

---

13, 14. How did the Law promote the fair and just treatment of a thief and his victim?

required from a thief according to Leviticus 6:1-7 is far less than that specified at Exodus 22:7.

¹⁵ The Law mercifully acknowledged that not all wrongs are deliberate. For example, when a man killed someone by accident, he did not have to pay soul for soul if he took the right action by fleeing to one of the cities of refuge scattered throughout Israel. After qualified judges examined his case, he had to reside in the city of refuge until the death of the high priest. Then he would be free to live wherever he chose. Thus he benefited from divine mercy. At the same time, this law emphasized the great value of human life.—Numbers 15:30, 31; 35:12-25.

¹⁶ The Law safeguarded personal rights. Consider the ways in which it protected those in debt. The Law forbade entry into a debtor's home to seize property as security for a loan. Rather, a creditor had to remain outside and allow the debtor to bring the security to him. Thus a man's home was held inviolate. If the creditor took the debtor's outer garment as a pledge, he had to return it by nightfall, for the debtor likely needed it to keep warm at night. —Deuteronomy 24:10-14.

¹⁷ Even warfare was regulated under the Law. God's people were to wage war, not to satisfy a mere lust for power or conquest, but to act as God's agents in "Wars of Jehovah." (Numbers 21:14) In many cases, the Israelites had to offer terms of surrender first. If a city rejected the offer, then Israel could besiege it—but according to God's rules. Unlike many soldiers throughout history, men in Israel's army were not allowed to rape women or engage in

---

15. How did the Law ensure both mercy and justice in the case of one who killed a person by accident?
16. How did the Law safeguard certain personal rights?
17, 18. In matters involving warfare, how were the Israelites different from other nations, and why?

wanton slaughter. They were even to respect the environment, not felling the enemy's fruit trees.* Other armies had no such restrictions.—Deuteronomy 20:10-15, 19, 20; 21:10-13.

[18] Do you shudder to hear that in some lands mere children are being trained as soldiers? In ancient Israel, no man under 20 years of age was inducted into the army. (Numbers 1:2, 3) Even an adult male was exempt if he suffered from undue fear. A newly married man was exempt for a full year so that before embarking upon such hazardous service, he might see an heir born. In this way, the Law explained, the young husband would be able to make his new wife "rejoice."—Deuteronomy 20:5, 6, 8; 24:5.

[19] The Law also protected women, children, and families, providing for them. It commanded parents to give their children constant attention and instruction in spiritual things. (Deuteronomy 6:6, 7) It forbade all forms of incest, under penalty of death. (Leviticus, chapter 18) It likewise forbade adultery, which so often breaks up families and destroys their security and dignity. The Law provided for widows and orphans and in the strongest possible terms forbade the mistreatment of them.—Exodus 20:14; 22:22-24.

[20] In this connection, however, some might wonder, 'Why did the Law allow for polygamy?' (Deuteronomy

---

* The Law pointedly asked: "Is the tree of the field a man to be besieged by you?" (Deuteronomy 20:19) Philo, a Jewish scholar of the first century, cited this law, explaining that God thinks it "unjust that the anger which is excited against men should wreak itself on things which are innocent of all evil."

---

19. What provisions did the Law include for the protection of women, children, families, widows, and orphans?
20, 21. (a) Why did the Mosaic Law allow for polygamy among the Israelites? (b) In the matter of divorce, why did the Law differ from the standard that Jesus later restored?

21:15-17) We need to consider such laws within the context of the times. Those who judge the Mosaic Law from the perspective of modern times and cultures are bound to misunderstand it. (Proverbs 18:13) Jehovah's standard, set way back in Eden, made marriage a lasting union between one husband and one wife. (Genesis 2:18, 20-24) By the time Jehovah gave the Law to Israel, however, such practices as polygamy had been entrenched for centuries. Jehovah well knew that his "stiff-necked people" would frequently fail to obey even the most basic commands, such as those forbidding idolatry. (Exodus 32:9) Wisely, then, he did not choose that era as the time to reform all of their marital practices. Keep in mind, though, that Jehovah did not institute polygamy. He did, however, use the Mosaic Law to *regulate* polygamy among his people and to prevent abuses of the practice.

[21] Similarly, the Mosaic Law allowed a man to divorce his wife on a relatively broad range of serious grounds. (Deuteronomy 24:1-4) Jesus called this a concession that God had made to the Jewish people "out of regard for [their] hardheartedness." However, such concessions were temporary. For his followers, Jesus restored Jehovah's original standard for marriage.—Matthew 19:8.

The Law Promoted Love

[22] Can you imagine a modern-day legal system that encourages love? The Mosaic Law promoted love above all else. Why, in the book of Deuteronomy alone, the word for "love" occurs in various forms over 20 times. "You must love your fellow as yourself" was the second-greatest commandment in all the Law. (Leviticus 19:18; Matthew 22:37-40) God's people were to show such love not only

---

22. In what ways did the Mosaic Law encourage love, and toward whom?

Questions for Meditation

Leviticus 19:9, 10; Deuteronomy 24:19 How do you feel about the God who makes such laws?

Psalm 19:7-14 How did David feel about "the law of Jehovah," and how precious should God's laws be to us?

Micah 6:6-8 How does this passage help us to see that Jehovah's laws cannot rightly be viewed as burdensome?

Matthew 23:23-39 How did the Pharisees show that they had missed the point of the Law, and how is this a warning example for us?

to one another but also to the alien residents in their midst, remembering that the Israelites too had once been alien residents. They were to show love to the poor and afflicted, helping them out materially and refraining from taking advantage of their weaknesses. They were even directed to treat beasts of burden with kindness and consideration.—Exodus 23:6; Leviticus 19:14, 33, 34; Deuteronomy 22:4, 10; 24:17, 18.

²³ What other nation has been blessed with such a legal code? No wonder the psalmist wrote: "How I do love your law!" His love, however, was not merely a feeling. It moved him to action, for he strove to obey that law and to live by it. Further, he continued: "All day long [your law] is my concern." (Psalm 119:11, 97) Yes, he regularly spent time studying Jehovah's laws. There can be no doubt that as he did, his love for them increased. At the same time, his love for the Lawgiver, Jehovah God, grew as well. As you continue to study divine law, may you too grow ever closer to Jehovah, the Great Lawgiver and God of justice.

---

23. What was the writer of Psalm 119 moved to do, and what might we resolve to do?

CHAPTER 14

Jehovah Provides "a Ransom in Exchange for Many"

"ALL creation keeps on groaning together and being in pain together." (Romans 8:22) With those words the apostle Paul describes the pitiful state in which we find ourselves. From a human standpoint, there seems to be no way out of suffering, sin, and death. But Jehovah does not have human limitations. (Numbers 23:19) The God of justice has provided us with a way out of our distress. It is called the ransom.

² The ransom is Jehovah's greatest gift to mankind. It makes possible our deliverance from sin and death. (Ephesians 1:7) It is the foundation of the hope of everlasting life, whether in heaven or on a paradise earth. (Luke 23:43; John 3:16; 1 Peter 1:4) But just what is the ransom? How does it teach us about Jehovah's superlative justice?

How the Need for a Ransom Arose

³ The ransom became necessary because of the sin of Adam. By disobeying God, Adam bequeathed to his offspring a legacy of sickness, sorrow, pain, and death. (Genesis 2:17; Romans 8:20) God could not yield to sentiment and simply commute the death sentence. To do so would be to ignore his own law: "The wages sin pays is death." (Romans 6:23) And were Jehovah to invalidate his own standards of justice, then universal chaos and lawlessness would reign!

1, 2. How does the Bible describe the state of mankind, and what is the only way out?

3. (a) Why did the ransom become necessary? (b) Why could God not simply commute the death sentence on Adam's offspring?

⁴ As we saw in Chapter 12, the rebellion in Eden raised even greater issues. Satan cast a dark shadow across God's good name. In effect, he accused Jehovah of being a liar and a cruel dictator who deprived his creatures of freedom. (Genesis 3:1-5) By seemingly thwarting God's purpose to fill the earth with righteous humans, Satan also labeled God a failure. (Genesis 1:28; Isaiah 55:10, 11) Had Jehovah left these challenges unanswered, many of his intelligent creatures might well have lost a measure of confidence in his rulership.

⁵ Satan also slandered Jehovah's loyal servants, charging that they served Him only out of selfish motives and that if placed under pressure, none would remain faithful to God. (Job 1:9-11) These issues were of far greater importance than the human predicament. Jehovah rightly felt obliged to answer Satan's slanderous charges. But how could God settle these issues and also save mankind?

Ransom—An Equivalent

⁶ Jehovah's solution was both supremely merciful and profoundly just—one that no human could ever have devised. Yet, it was elegantly simple. It is variously referred to as a purchase, a reconciliation, a redemption, a propitiation, and an atonement. (Psalm 49:8; Daniel 9:24; Galatians 3:13; Colossians 1:20; Hebrews 2:17) But the expression that perhaps best describes matters is the one used by Jesus himself. He said: "The Son of man came, not to be ministered to, but to minister and to give his soul a ransom [Greek, *ly′tron*] in exchange for many."—Matthew 20:28.

4, 5. (a) How did Satan slander God, and why was Jehovah obliged to answer those challenges? (b) What charge did Satan make regarding Jehovah's loyal servants?

6. What are some of the expressions used in the Bible to describe God's means of saving mankind?

⁷ What is a ransom? The Greek word used here comes from a verb meaning "to let loose, to release." This term was used to describe money paid in exchange for the release of prisoners of war. Basically, then, a ransom can be defined as something paid to buy something back. In the Hebrew Scriptures, the word for "ransom" (*ko'pher*) comes from a verb meaning "to cover." For example, God told Noah that he must "cover" (a form of the same word) the ark with tar. (Genesis 6:14) This helps us appreciate that to ransom also means to *cover* sins.—Psalm 65:3.

⁸ Significantly, the *Theological Dictionary of the New Testament* observes that this word (*ko'pher*) "always denotes an equivalent," or a correspondency. Thus, the cover of the ark of the covenant had a shape corresponding to the ark itself. Likewise, in order to ransom, or cover, sin, a price must be paid that fully corresponds to, or fully covers, the damage caused by the sin. God's Law to Israel thus stated: "Soul will be for soul, eye for eye, tooth for tooth, hand for hand, foot for foot."—Deuteronomy 19:21.

⁹ Men of faith from Abel onward offered animal sacrifices to God. In so doing, they demonstrated their awareness of sin and of the need for redemption, and they showed their faith in God's promised liberation through his "seed." (Genesis 3:15; 4:1-4; Leviticus 17:11; Hebrews 11:4) Jehovah looked upon such sacrifices with favor and granted these worshipers a good standing. Nevertheless, animal offerings were, at best, a mere token. Animals could not really cover man's sin, for they are inferior to humans. (Psalm

------

7, 8. (a) What does the term "ransom" mean in the Scriptures? (b) In what way does a ransom involve equivalency?

9. Why did men of faith offer up animal sacrifices, and how did Jehovah view such sacrifices?

"A corresponding ransom for all"

8:4-8) Hence, the Bible says: "It is not possible for the blood of bulls and of goats to take sins away." (Hebrews 10:1-4) Such sacrifices were only pictorial, or symbolic, of the true ransom sacrifice that was to come.

"A Corresponding Ransom"

10 "In Adam all are dying," said the apostle Paul. (1 Corinthians 15:22) The ransom thus had to involve the death of the exact equal of Adam—a perfect human. (Romans 5:14) No other kind of creature could balance the scales of justice. Only a perfect human, someone not under the Adamic death sentence, could offer "a corresponding ransom"—one corresponding perfectly to Adam. (1 Timothy 2:6) It would not be necessary for untold millions of individual humans to be sacrificed so as to correspond to each descendant of Adam. The apostle Paul explained: "Through *one man* [Adam] sin entered into the world and death through sin." (Romans 5:12) And "since death is through a man," God provided for the redemption of mankind "through a man." (1 Corinthians 15:21) How?

11 Jehovah arranged to have a perfect man voluntarily sacrifice his life. According to Romans 6:23, "the wages sin pays is death." In sacrificing his life, the ransomer would "taste death for every man." In other words, he would pay the wage for Adam's sin. (Hebrews 2:9; 2 Corinthians 5:21; 1 Peter 2:24) This would have profound legal consequences. By nullifying the death sentence upon Adam's

10. (a) To whom did the ransomer have to correspond, and why? (b) Why was only one human sacrifice necessary?

11. (a) How would the ransomer "taste death for every man"? (b) Why could Adam and Eve not have benefited from the ransom? (See footnote.)

obedient offspring, the ransom would cut off the destructive power of sin right at its source.*—Romans 5:16.

¹² To illustrate: Imagine that you live in a town where most of the residents are employed at a large factory. You and your neighbors are well paid for your labors and lead comfortable lives. That is, until the day the factory closes its doors. The reason? The factory manager turned corrupt, forcing the business into bankruptcy. Suddenly out of work, you and your neighbors are unable to pay the bills. Marriage mates, children, and creditors suffer because of that one man's corruption. Is there a way out? Yes! A wealthy benefactor decides to intervene. He appreciates the value of the company. He also feels for its many employees and their families. So he arranges to pay off the company's debt and reopen the factory. The cancellation of that one debt brings relief to the many employees and their families and to the creditors. Similarly, the cancellation of Adam's debt benefits untold millions.

Who Provides the Ransom?

¹³ Only Jehovah could provide "the Lamb . . . that takes away the sin of the world." (John 1:29) But God did not send just any angel to rescue mankind. Instead, he sent the One who could furnish the ultimate,

---

* Adam and Eve could not have benefited from the ransom. The Mosaic Law stated this principle regarding a willful murderer: "You must take no ransom for the soul of a murderer who is deserving to die." (Numbers 35:31) Clearly, Adam and Eve deserved to die because they willingly and knowingly disobeyed God. They thereby gave up their prospect of everlasting life.

---

12. Illustrate how paying one debt can benefit many people.
13, 14. (a) How did Jehovah provide the ransom for mankind? (b) To whom is the ransom paid, and why is such a payment necessary?

conclusive answer to Satan's charge against Jehovah's servants. Yes, Jehovah made the supreme sacrifice of sending his only-begotten Son, "the one he was specially fond of." (Proverbs 8:30) Willingly, God's Son "emptied himself" of his heavenly nature. (Philippians 2:7) Miraculously, Jehovah transferred the life and the personality pattern of his firstborn heavenly Son to the womb of a Jewish virgin named Mary. (Luke 1:27, 35) As a man, he would be called Jesus. But in a legal sense, he could be called the second Adam, for he corresponded perfectly to Adam. (1 Corinthians 15:45, 47) Jesus could thus offer himself up in sacrifice as a ransom for sinful mankind.

¹⁴ To whom would that ransom be paid? Psalm 49:7 specifically says that the ransom is paid "to God." But is not Jehovah the one who arranges for the ransom in the first place? Yes, but this does not reduce the ransom to a pointless, mechanical exchange—like taking money out of one pocket and putting it into another. It must be appreciated that the ransom is, not a physical exchange, but a legal transaction. By providing for the payment of the ransom, even at enormous cost to himself, Jehovah affirmed his unwavering adherence to his own perfect justice.—Genesis 22:7, 8, 11-13; Hebrews 11:17; James 1:17.

¹⁵ In the spring of 33 C.E., Jesus Christ willingly submitted to an ordeal that led to the payment of the ransom. He allowed himself to be arrested on false charges, judged guilty, and nailed to a stake of execution. Was it really necessary for Jesus to suffer so much? Yes, because the issue of the integrity of God's servants had to be settled. Significantly, God did not allow the infant Jesus to be killed by Herod. (Matthew 2:13-18) But when Jesus was an adult, he was able to withstand the brunt of Satan's attacks with

---

15. Why was it necessary for Jesus to suffer and die?

full comprehension of the issues.* By remaining "loyal, guileless, undefiled, separated from the sinners" in spite of horrific treatment, Jesus proved with dramatic finality that Jehovah does have servants who remain faithful under trial. (Hebrews 7:26) No wonder, then, that at the moment before his death, Jesus cried out triumphantly: "It has been accomplished!"—John 19:30.

Finishing His Redemptive Work

¹⁶ Jesus had yet to finish his redemptive work. On the third day after Jesus' death, Jehovah raised him from the dead. (Acts 3:15; 10:40) By this momentous act, Jehovah not only rewarded his Son for his faithful service but gave him the opportunity to finish his redemptive work as God's High Priest. (Romans 1:4; 1 Corinthians 15:3-8) The apostle Paul explains: "When Christ came as a high priest . . . , he entered, no, not with the blood of goats and of young bulls, but with his own blood, once for all time into the holy place and obtained an everlasting deliverance for us. For Christ entered, not into a holy place made with hands, which is a copy of the reality, but into heaven itself, now to appear before the person of God for us."—Hebrews 9:11, 12, 24.

¹⁷ Christ could not take his literal blood into heaven. (1 Corinthians 15:50) Rather, he took what that blood

---

* In order to counterbalance the sin of Adam, Jesus had to die, not as a perfect child, but as a perfect man. Remember, Adam's sin was willful, carried out with full knowledge of the seriousness of the act and its consequences. So in order to become "the last Adam" and cover that sin, Jesus had to make a mature, knowing choice to keep his integrity to Jehovah. (1 Corinthians 15:45, 47) Thus Jesus' entire faithful life course—including his sacrificial death—served as "one act of justification."—Romans 5:18, 19.

16, 17. (a) How did Jesus continue his redemptive work? (b) Why was it necessary for Jesus to appear "before the person of God for us"?

symbolized: the legal value of his sacrificed perfect human life. Then, before the person of God, he made formal presentation of the value of that life as a ransom in exchange for sinful mankind. Did Jehovah accept that sacrifice? Yes, and this became evident at Pentecost 33 C.E., when the holy spirit was poured out upon about 120 disciples in Jerusalem. (Acts 2:1-4) Thrilling though that was, the ransom was then just beginning to provide marvelous benefits.

Benefits of the Ransom

[18] In his letter to the Colossians, Paul explains that God saw good through Christ to reconcile to Himself all other things by making peace through the blood Jesus shed on the torture stake. Paul also explains that this reconciliation involves two distinct groups of individuals, namely, "the things in the heavens" and "the things upon the earth." (Colossians 1:19, 20; Ephesians 1:10) That first group consists of 144,000 Christians who are given the hope of serving as heavenly priests and ruling as kings over the earth with Christ Jesus. (Revelation 5:9, 10; 7:4; 14:1-3) Through them, the benefits of the ransom will gradually be applied to obedient mankind over a period of a thousand years. —1 Corinthians 15:24-26; Revelation 20:6; 21:3, 4.

[19] "The things upon the earth" are those individuals in line to enjoy perfect life in Paradise on earth. Revelation 7: 9-17 describes them as "a great crowd" who will survive the coming "great tribulation." But they do not have to wait until then to enjoy the benefits of the ransom. They have already "washed their robes and made them white in the blood of the Lamb." Because they exercise faith in

18, 19. (a) What two groups of individuals benefit from the reconciliation made possible by Christ's blood? (b) For those of the "great crowd," what are some of the present and future benefits of the ransom?

Questions for Meditation

Numbers 3:39-51 Why is it essential that the ransom be an exact equivalent?

Psalm 49:7, 8 Why are we indebted to God for providing the ransom?

Isaiah 43:25 How does this scripture help us to see that man's salvation is not the primary reason that Jehovah provided the ransom?

1 Corinthians 6:20 What effect should the ransom have on our conduct and life-style?

---

the ransom, they are even now receiving spiritual benefits from that loving provision. They have been declared righteous as God's friends! (James 2:23) As a result of Jesus' sacrifice, they can "approach with freeness of speech to the throne of undeserved kindness." (Hebrews 4:14-16) When they err, they receive real forgiveness. (Ephesians 1:7) In spite of being imperfect, they enjoy a cleansed conscience. (Hebrews 9:9; 10:22; 1 Peter 3:21) Being reconciled to God is thus, not some hoped-for development, but a present reality! (2 Corinthians 5:19, 20) During the Millennium, they will gradually "be set free from enslavement to corruption" and will finally "have the glorious freedom of the children of God."—Romans 8:21.

[20] "Thanks to God through Jesus Christ" for the ransom! (Romans 7:25) It is simple in principle, yet profound enough to fill us with awe. (Romans 11:33) And by our meditating appreciatively on it, the ransom touches our hearts, drawing us ever closer to the God of justice. Like the psalmist, we have every reason to praise Jehovah as "a lover of righteousness and justice."—Psalm 33:5.

---

20. How does contemplating the ransom affect you personally?

CHAPTER 15

Jesus "Sets Justice in the Earth"

JESUS was visibly angry—and with good reason. You might find it difficult to imagine him that way, for he was such a mild-tempered man. (Matthew 21:5) He remained perfectly controlled, of course, for his was righteous wrath.* But what had so provoked this peace-loving man? A case of gross injustice.

² The temple in Jerusalem was dear to Jesus' heart. In all the world, it was the only sacred place dedicated to the worship of his heavenly Father. Jews from many lands traveled great distances to worship there. Even God-fearing Gentiles came, entering the temple courtyard set aside for their use. But early in his ministry, Jesus entered the temple area and met with an appalling sight. Why, the place was more like a market than a house of worship! It was crowded with merchants and money brokers. Where, though, was the injustice? For these men, God's temple was merely a place to exploit people—even rob them. How so?—John 2:14.

³ The religious leaders had ruled that only one specific type of coin could be used to pay the temple tax. Visitors had to exchange their money to acquire such coins. So money changers set up their tables right inside the temple, charging a fee for each transaction. The business of

---

* In displaying righteous anger, Jesus was like Jehovah, who is "disposed to rage" against all wickedness. (Nahum 1:2) For example, after Jehovah told his wayward people that they had made his house "a mere cave of robbers," he said: "My anger and my rage are being poured forth upon this place."—Jeremiah 7:11, 20.

1, 2. On what occasion did Jesus become angry, and why?
3, 4. What greedy exploitation was taking place at Jehovah's house, and what action did Jesus take to correct matters?

selling animals was also very profitable. Visitors who wanted to offer up sacrifices could buy from any merchant in the city, but the temple officials might well reject their offerings as unfit. However, offerings bought right there in the temple area were sure to be accepted. With the people thus at their mercy, the merchants at times charged exorbitant prices.* This was worse than crass commercialism. It amounted to robbery!

⁴ Jesus could not tolerate such injustice. This was his own Father's house! He made a whip of ropes and drove the herds of cattle and sheep from the temple. Then he strode over to the money changers and overturned their tables. Imagine all those coins skittering across the marble floor! He sternly ordered the men selling doves: "Take these things away from here!" (John 2:15, 16) No one, it seems, dared to oppose this courageous man.

"Like Father, Like Son"

⁵ Of course, the merchants returned. About three years later, Jesus addressed the same injustice, this time quoting Jehovah's own words condemning those who made His house "a cave of robbers." (Matthew 21:13; Jeremiah 7:11) Yes, when Jesus saw the greedy exploitation of the people and the defilement of God's temple, he felt just as his Father did. And no wonder! For countless millions of

---

* According to the Mishnah, a protest arose some years later over the high price of the doves sold at the temple. The price was promptly reduced by some 99 percent! Who profited most from this lucrative trade? Some historians suggest that the temple markets were owned by the house of High Priest Annas, providing much of that priestly family's vast wealth.—John 18:13.

5-7. (a) How did Jesus' prehuman existence influence his sense of justice, and what can we learn by studying his example? (b) How has Christ fought against the injustices involving Jehovah's sovereignty and name?

years, Jesus had been taught by his heavenly Father. As a result, he was imbued with Jehovah's sense of justice. He became a living illustration of the saying, "Like father, like son." So if we want to obtain a clear picture of Jehovah's quality of justice, we can do no better than ponder the example of Jesus Christ.—John 14:9, 10.

⁶ Jehovah's only-begotten Son was present when Satan unjustly called Jehovah God a liar and questioned the righteousness of His rule. What slander! The Son also heard Satan's later challenge that no one would serve Jehovah unselfishly, out of love. These false charges surely pained the Son's righteous heart. How thrilled he must have been to learn that he would play the key role in setting the record straight! (2 Corinthians 1:20) How would he do that?

⁷ As we learned in Chapter 14, Jesus Christ gave the ultimate, conclusive answer to Satan's charge impugning the integrity of Jehovah's creatures. Jesus thereby laid the basis for the final vindication of Jehovah's sovereignty and the sanctification of His name. As Jehovah's Chief Agent, Jesus will establish divine justice throughout the universe. (Acts 5:31) His life course on earth likewise reflected divine justice. Jehovah said of him: "I will put my spirit upon him, and what justice is he will make clear to the nations." (Matthew 12:18) How did Jesus fulfill those words?

Jesus Clarifies "What Justice Is"

⁸ Jesus loved Jehovah's Law and lived by it. But the religious leaders of his day twisted and misapplied that Law.

8-10. (a) How did the oral traditions of the Jewish religious leaders promote contempt for non-Jews and women? (b) In what way did the oral laws turn Jehovah's Sabbath law into a burden?

"Take these things away from here!"

Jesus said to them: "Woe to you, scribes and Pharisees, hypocrites! . . . You have disregarded the weightier matters of the Law, namely, justice and mercy and faithfulness." (Matthew 23:23) Decidedly, those teachers of God's Law were not making clear "what justice is." Rather, they were obscuring divine justice. How so? Consider a few examples.

⁹ Jehovah directed his people to keep separate from the pagan nations surrounding them. (1 Kings 11:1, 2) However, some fanatic religious leaders encouraged the people to hold all non-Jews in contempt. The Mishnah even included this rule: "Cattle may not be left in the inns of the gentiles since they are suspected of bestiality." Such blanket prejudice against all non-Jews was unjust and quite contrary to the spirit of the Mosaic Law. (Leviticus 19:34) Other man-made rules demeaned women. The oral law said that a wife should walk behind, not beside, her husband. A man was warned against conversing with a woman in public, even his own wife. Like slaves, women were not allowed to offer testimony in court. There was even a formal prayer in which men thanked God that they were not women.

¹⁰ The religious leaders buried God's Law under a mass of man-made rules and regulations. The Sabbath law, for instance, simply forbade work on the Sabbath, setting that day aside for worship, spiritual refreshment, and rest. But the Pharisees made a burden of that law. They took it upon themselves to decide just what "work" meant. They labeled as work 39 different activities, such as reaping or hunting. These categories gave rise to endless questions. If a man killed a flea on the Sabbath, was he hunting? If he plucked a handful of grain to eat as he walked along, was he reaping? If he healed someone who was ill, was

he working? Such questions were addressed with rigid, detailed rules.

[11] In such a climate, how was Jesus to help people understand what justice is? In his teachings and in the way he lived, he took a courageous stand against those religious leaders. Consider first some of his teachings. He directly condemned their myriad man-made rules, saying: "You make the word of God invalid by your tradition which you handed down."—Mark 7:13.

[12] Jesus powerfully taught that the Pharisees were wrong about the Sabbath law—that, in fact, they had missed the whole point of that law. The Messiah, he explained, is "Lord of the sabbath" and therefore entitled to cure people on the Sabbath. (Matthew 12:8) To stress the point, he openly performed miraculous cures on the Sabbath. (Luke 6:7-10) Such cures were a preview of the healing that he will perform earth wide during his Thousand Year Reign. That Millennium will itself be the ultimate Sabbath, when all faithful mankind will at last rest from centuries of laboring under the burdens of sin and death.

[13] Jesus also made clear what justice is in that a new law, "the law of the Christ," came into being after he completed his earthly ministry. (Galatians 6:2) Unlike its predecessor, the Mosaic Law, this new law largely depended, not upon a series of written commands, but upon principle. It did include some direct commands, though. One of these Jesus called "a new commandment." Jesus taught all his followers to love one another just as he had loved them. (John 13:34, 35) Yes, self-sacrificing love was to be the hallmark of all those who live by "the law of the Christ."

11, 12. How did Jesus express his opposition to the unscriptural traditions of the Pharisees?

13. What law came into being as a result of Christ's earthly ministry, and how did it differ from its predecessor?

A Living Example of Justice

¹⁴ Jesus did more than teach about love. He *lived* "the law of the Christ." It was embodied in his life course. Consider three ways in which Jesus' example made clear what justice is.

¹⁵ First, Jesus scrupulously avoided committing any injustice. Perhaps you have noticed that many injustices come about when imperfect humans grow arrogant and overstep the proper bounds of their authority. Jesus did not do that. On one occasion, a man approached Jesus and said: "Teacher, tell my brother to divide the inheritance with me." Jesus' response? "Man, who appointed me judge or apportioner over you persons?" (Luke 12:13, 14) Is that not remarkable? Jesus' intellect, his judgment, and even his level of God-given authority exceeded that of anyone on earth; yet, he refused to involve himself in this matter, since he had not been granted the particular authority to do so. Jesus has always been modest in this way, even during the millenniums of his prehuman existence. (Jude 9) It says much for Jesus that he humbly trusts Jehovah to determine what is just.

¹⁶ Second, Jesus displayed justice in the way he preached the good news of God's Kingdom. He showed no bias. Rather, he earnestly endeavored to reach all kinds of people, whether rich or poor. In contrast, the Pharisees dismissed poor, common people with the contemptuous term 'am-ha·'a'rets, or "people of the land." Jesus courageously set that injustice right. When he taught people the good news—or, for that matter, when he ate with people, fed them, cured them, or even resurrected them—he

---

14, 15. How did Jesus show that he recognized the limits of his own authority, and why is this reassuring?
16, 17. (a) How did Jesus display justice in preaching the good news of God's Kingdom? (b) How did Jesus show that his sense of justice was merciful?

upheld the justice of the God who wants to reach "all sorts of men."*—1 Timothy 2:4.

[17] Third, Jesus' sense of justice was profoundly merciful. He reached out to help sinners. (Matthew 9:11-13) He readily came to the aid of people who were powerless to protect themselves. For instance, Jesus did not join the religious leaders in promoting a distrust of all Gentiles. He mercifully helped and taught some of these, even though his primary mission was to the Jewish people. He agreed to perform a miraculous cure for a Roman army officer, saying: "With no one in Israel have I found so great a faith."—Matthew 8:5-13.

[18] Similarly, Jesus did not support the prevailing views toward women. Instead, he courageously did what was just. Samaritan women were held to be as unclean as Gentiles. Yet, Jesus did not hesitate to preach to the Samaritan woman at the well of Sychar. In fact, it was to this woman that Jesus first plainly identified himself as the promised Messiah. (John 4:6, 25, 26) The Pharisees said that women should not be taught God's Law, but Jesus spent much time and energy teaching women. (Luke 10:38-42) And whereas tradition held that women could not be trusted to give reliable testimony, Jesus dignified several women with the privilege of being the first to see him after his resurrection. He even told them to go tell his male disciples about this most important event!—Matthew 28:1-10.

---

* The Pharisees held that lowly people, who were not versed in the Law, were "accursed." (John 7:49) They said that one should neither teach such people nor do business with them nor eat with them nor pray with them. To allow one's daughter to marry one of them would be worse than exposing her to wild beasts. They deemed the resurrection hope to be closed to such lowly ones.

18, 19. (a) In what ways did Jesus promote the dignity of women? (b) How does Jesus' example help us to see the link between courage and justice?

¹⁹ Yes, Jesus made clear to the nations what justice is. In many cases, he did so at great personal risk. Jesus' example helps us to see that upholding true justice requires courage. Fittingly, he was called "the Lion that is of the tribe of Judah." (Revelation 5:5) Recall that the lion is a symbol of courageous justice. In the near future, though, Jesus will effect even greater justice. In the fullest sense, he will set "justice in the earth."—Isaiah 42:4.

The Messianic King "Sets Justice in the Earth"

²⁰ Since becoming the Messianic King in 1914, Jesus has promoted justice in the earth. How so? He has sponsored the fulfillment of his prophecy found at Matthew 24:14. Jesus' followers on earth have taught people of all lands the truth about Jehovah's Kingdom. Like Jesus, they have preached in an impartial and just manner, seeking to give everyone—young or old, rich or poor, male or female—an opportunity to come to know Jehovah, the God of justice.

²¹ Jesus is also promoting justice within the Christian congregation, of which he is the Head. As prophesied, he provides "gifts in men," faithful Christian elders who take the lead in the congregation. (Ephesians 4:8-12) In shepherding the precious flock of God, such men follow the example of Jesus Christ in promoting justice. They keep ever in mind that Jesus wants his sheep to be dealt with justly—regardless of position, prominence, or material circumstances.

²² In the near future, though, Jesus will set justice in the earth in an unprecedented way. Injustice is rampant in this corrupt world. Every child that dies of starvation

---

20, 21. In our own time, how has the Messianic King promoted justice throughout the earth and within the Christian congregation?
22. How does Jehovah feel about the rampant injustices of today's world, and what has he appointed his Son to do about it?

Questions for Meditation

Psalm 45:1-7 Why can we be confident that the Messianic King will promote perfect justice?

Matthew 12:19-21 According to prophecy, how would the Messiah treat lowly ones?

Matthew 18:21-35 How did Jesus teach that genuine justice is merciful?

Mark 5:25-34 How did Jesus demonstrate that divine justice takes into account a person's circumstances?

is a victim of an inexcusable injustice, especially when we think of the money and time that are lavished on producing weapons of war and indulging the selfish whims of pleasure seekers. The millions of needless deaths each year are but one among many forms of injustice, all of which provoke Jehovah's righteous anger. He has appointed his Son to wage a just war against this entire wicked system of things to end all injustice permanently. —Revelation 16:14, 16; 19:11-15.

²³ However, Jehovah's justice calls for more than merely the destruction of the wicked. He has also appointed his Son to rule as the "Prince of Peace." After the war of Armageddon, Jesus' reign will establish peace throughout the earth, and he will rule "by means of justice." (Isaiah 9:6, 7) Jesus will then delight in undoing all the injustices that have caused so much misery and suffering in the world. Throughout all eternity, he will faithfully uphold Jehovah's perfect justice. It is vital, then, that we seek to imitate Jehovah's justice now. Let us see how we can do that.

---

23. After Armageddon, how will Christ promote justice throughout all eternity?

CHAPTER 16

"Exercise Justice" in Walking With God

IMAGINE being trapped on a sinking ship. Just when you think that there is no hope, a rescuer arrives and pulls you to safety. How relieved you feel as your rescuer takes you away from the danger and says: "You are safe now"! Would you not feel indebted to that person? In a very real sense, you would owe him your life.

² In some respects, this illustrates what Jehovah has done for us. Surely we are indebted to him. After all, he has provided the ransom, making it possible for us to be rescued from the clutches of sin and death. We feel safe knowing that as long as we exercise faith in that precious sacrifice, our sins are forgiven, and our eternal future is secure. (1 John 1:7; 4:9) As we saw in Chapter 14, the ransom is a supreme expression of Jehovah's love and justice. How should we respond?

³ It is fitting to consider what our loving Rescuer himself asks back from us. Jehovah says by means of the prophet Micah: "He has told you, O earthling man, what is good. And what is Jehovah asking back from you but to exercise justice and to love kindness and to be modest in walking with your God?" (Micah 6:8) Notice that one of the things Jehovah asks back from us is that we "exercise justice." How can we do so?

Pursuing "True Righteousness"

⁴ Jehovah expects us to live by his standards of right

1-3. (a) Why are we indebted to Jehovah? (b) What does our loving Rescuer ask back from us?
4. How do we know that Jehovah expects us to live in harmony with his righteous standards?

and wrong. Since his standards are just and righteous, we are pursuing justice and righteousness when we conform to them. "Learn to do good; search for justice," says Isaiah 1:17. God's Word exhorts us to "seek righteousness." (Zephaniah 2:3) It also urges us to "put on the new personality which was created according to God's will in true righteousness." (Ephesians 4:24) True righteousness—true justice—shuns violence, uncleanness, and immorality, for these violate what is holy.—Psalm 11:5; Ephesians 5:3-5.

⁵ Is it a burden for us to conform to Jehovah's righteous standards? No. A heart that is drawn to Jehovah does not chafe at his requirements. Because we love our God and all that he stands for, we want to live in a way that pleases him. (1 John 5:3) Recall that Jehovah "does love righteous acts." (Psalm 11:7) If we are truly to imitate divine justice, or righteousness, we must come to love what Jehovah loves and hate what he hates.—Psalm 97:10.

⁶ It is not easy for imperfect humans to pursue righteousness. We must strip off the old personality with its sinful practices and put on the new one. The Bible says that the new personality is "being made new" through accurate knowledge. (Colossians 3:9, 10) The words "being made new" indicate that putting on the new personality is a continuing process, one that requires diligent effort. No matter how hard we try to do what is right, there are times when our sinful nature causes us to stumble in thought, word, or deed.—Romans 7:14-20; James 3:2.

⁷ How should we view setbacks in our efforts to pursue righteousness? Of course, we would not want to minimize

---

5, 6. (a) Why is it not a burden for us to conform to Jehovah's standards? (b) How does the Bible show that pursuing righteousness is a continuing process?
7. In what way should we view setbacks in our efforts to pursue righteousness?

the seriousness of sin. At the same time, we must never give up, feeling that our shortcomings make us unfit to serve Jehovah. Our gracious God has made provision to restore sincerely repentant ones to his favor. Consider the reassuring words of the apostle John: "I am writing you these things that you may not commit a sin." But then he realistically added: "Yet, if anyone does commit a sin [because of inherited imperfection], we have a helper with the Father, Jesus Christ." (1 John 2:1) Yes, Jehovah has provided Jesus' ransom sacrifice so that we might acceptably serve Him in spite of our sinful nature. Does that not move us to want to do our best to please Jehovah?

The Good News and Divine Justice

8 We can exercise justice—in fact, imitate divine justice—by having a full share in preaching the good news of God's Kingdom to others. What connection is there between Jehovah's justice and the good news?

9 Jehovah will not bring an end to this wicked system without first having the warning sounded. In his prophecy about what would take place during the time of the end, Jesus said: "In all the nations the good news has to be preached first." (Mark 13:10; Matthew 24:3) The use of the word "first" implies that other events will follow the worldwide preaching work. Those events include the foretold great tribulation, which will mean destruction for the wicked and will pave the way for a righteous new world. (Matthew 24:14, 21, 22) Certainly, no one can rightly charge Jehovah with being unjust toward the wicked. By having the warning sounded, he is giving such ones ample opportunity to change their ways and therefore escape destruction.—Jonah 3:1-10.

_____

8, 9. How does the proclamation of the good news demonstrate Jehovah's justice?

[10] How does our preaching the good news reflect godly justice? First of all, it is only right that we do what we can to help others gain salvation. Consider again the illustration of being rescued from a sinking ship. Safe in a lifeboat, you would surely want to help others who are still in the water. Similarly, we have an obligation toward those who are still struggling in the "waters" of this wicked world. True, many reject our message. But as long as Jehovah continues to be patient, we have the responsibility to give them the opportunity to "attain to repentance" and thus come in line for salvation.—2 Peter 3:9.

[11] By preaching the good news to all whom we meet, we display justice in another important way: We show impartiality. Recall that "God is not partial, but in every nation the man that fears him and works righteousness is acceptable to him." (Acts 10:34, 35) If we are to imitate His justice, we must not prejudge people. Instead, we should share the good news with others regardless of their race, social status, or financial standing. We thus give all who will listen an opportunity to hear and respond to the good news.—Romans 10:11-13.

How We Treat Others

[12] We can also exercise justice by treating others the way Jehovah treats us. It is all too easy to sit in judgment of others, criticizing their faults and questioning their motives. But who of us would want Jehovah to scrutinize our motives and shortcomings in a merciless manner? That is not how Jehovah deals with us. The psalmist observed: "If

----

10, 11. How does our having a share in preaching the good news reflect godly justice?
12, 13. (a) Why should we not be quick to sit in judgment of others? (b) What is the meaning of Jesus' counsel to "stop judging" and "stop condemning"? (See also footnote.)

errors were what you watch, O Jah, O Jehovah, who could stand?" (Psalm 130:3) Are we not grateful that our just and merciful God chooses not to dwell on our failings? (Psalm 103:8-10) How, then, should we treat others?

¹³ If we appreciate the merciful nature of God's justice, we will not be quick to judge others in matters that really do not concern us or that are of lesser importance. In his Sermon on the Mount, Jesus warned: "Stop judging that you may not be judged." (Matthew 7:1) According to Luke's account, Jesus added: "Stop condemning, and you will by no means be condemned."* (Luke 6:37) Jesus showed his awareness that imperfect humans have a tendency to be judgmental. Any of his listeners who were in the habit of harshly judging others were to stop it.

¹⁴ Why must we "stop judging" others? For one thing, our authority is limited. The disciple James reminds us: "One there is that is lawgiver and judge"—Jehovah. So James pointedly asks: "Who are you to be judging your neighbor?" (James 4:12; Romans 14:1-4) In addition, our sinful nature can so easily render our judgments unfair. Many attitudes and motives—including prejudice, injured pride, jealousy, and self-righteousness—can distort the way we see fellow humans. We have further limitations, and reflecting on these should restrain us from being quick to find fault with others. We cannot read hearts; nor can we know all the personal circumstances of others. Who, then, are we to impute wrong motives to fellow believers or to criticize their efforts in God's service?

---

* Some translations say "do not judge" and "do not condemn." Such renderings imply "do not start judging" and "do not start condemning." However, the Bible writers here use negative commands in the present (continuous) tense. So the actions described were currently going on but had to cease.

---

14. For what reasons must we "stop judging" others?

We display godly justice when we impartially share the good news with others

How much better it is to imitate Jehovah by looking for the good in our brothers and sisters rather than focusing on their failings!

15 What about our family members? Sadly, in today's world some of the harshest judgments are handed down in what should be a haven of peace—the home. It is not uncommon to hear about abusive husbands, wives, or parents who "sentence" their family members to a constant barrage of verbal or physical abuse. But vicious words, bitter sarcasm, and abusive treatment have no place among God's worshipers. (Ephesians 4:29, 31; 5:33; 6:4) Jesus' counsel to "stop judging" and "stop condemning" does not cease to apply when we are at home. Recall

15. What words and treatment have no place among God's worshipers, and why?

that exercising justice involves treating others the way Jehovah treats us. And our God is never harsh or cruel in dealing with us. Rather, he "is very tender in affection" toward those who love him. (James 5:11) What a marvelous example for us to imitate!

Elders Serving "for Justice Itself"

16 All of us have a responsibility to exercise justice, but elders in the Christian congregation especially have a responsibility in this regard. Notice the prophetic description of "princes," or elders, recorded by Isaiah: "Look! A king will reign for righteousness itself; and as respects princes, they will rule as princes for justice itself." (Isaiah 32:1) Yes, Jehovah expects elders to serve in the interests of justice. How can they do this?

17 These spiritually qualified men are well aware that justice, or righteousness, requires that the congregation be kept clean. At times, elders are obliged to judge cases of serious wrongdoing. When doing so, they remember that divine justice seeks to extend mercy if at all possible. They thus try to lead the sinner to repentance. But what if the sinner fails to manifest genuine repentance despite such efforts to help him? In perfect justice, Jehovah's Word directs that a firm step be taken: "Remove the wicked man from among yourselves." That means expelling him from the congregation. (1 Corinthians 5:11-13; 2 John 9-11) It saddens the elders to have to take such action, but they recognize that it is necessary in order to protect the moral and spiritual cleanness of the congregation. Even then, they hope that someday the sinner will come to his senses and return to the congregation.—Luke 15:17, 18.

16, 17. (a) What does Jehovah expect of elders? (b) What has to be done when a sinner fails to manifest genuine repentance, and why?

¹⁸ Serving in the interests of justice also involves offering Bible-based counsel when needed. Of course, elders do not *look* for flaws in others. Nor do they seize every opportunity to offer correction. But a fellow believer may take "some false step before he is aware of it." Remembering that divine justice is neither cruel nor unfeeling will move elders to "try to readjust such a man in a spirit of mildness." (Galatians 6:1) Hence, elders would not scold an erring one or employ harsh words. Instead, counsel that is given lovingly encourages the one receiving it. Even when giving pointed reproof—straightforwardly outlining the consequences of an unwise course—elders keep in mind that a fellow believer who has erred is a sheep in Jehovah's flock.* (Luke 15:7) When counsel or reproof is clearly motivated by and given in love, it is more likely to readjust the erring one.

¹⁹ Elders are often called upon to make decisions that affect their fellow believers. For example, elders periodically meet to consider whether other brothers in the congregation qualify to be recommended as elders or ministerial servants. The elders know the importance of being impartial. They let God's requirements for such appointments guide them in making decisions, not relying on mere personal feelings. They thus act "without prejudgment, doing nothing according to a biased leaning."—1 Timothy 5:21.

---

* At 2 Timothy 4:2, the Bible says that elders must at times "reprove, reprimand, exhort." The Greek word rendered "exhort" (*pa·ra·ka·le′o*) can mean "to encourage." A related Greek word, *pa·ra′kle·tos*, can refer to an advocate in a legal matter. Thus, even when elders give firm reproof, they are to be helpers of those needing spiritual assistance.

---

18. What do elders keep in mind when offering Bible-based counsel to others?
19. What decisions are elders called upon to make, and on what must they base such decisions?

Elders reflect Jehovah's justice when they encourage downhearted ones

²⁰ Elders administer divine justice in other ways as well. After foretelling that elders would serve "for justice itself," Isaiah continued: "Each one must prove to be like a hiding place from the wind and a place of concealment from the rainstorm, like streams of water in a waterless country, like the shadow of a heavy crag in an exhausted land." (Isaiah 32:2) Elders, then, strive to be sources of comfort and refreshment to their fellow worshipers.

²¹ Today, with all the problems that tend to dishearten, many need encouragement. Elders, what can you do to help "depressed souls"? (1 Thessalonians 5:14) Listen to them with empathy. (James 1:19) They may need to share the "anxious care" in their heart with someone they trust.

20, 21. (a) What do elders strive to be, and why? (b) What can elders do to help "depressed souls"?

Questions for Meditation

Deuteronomy 1:16, 17 What did Jehovah require of judges in Israel, and what might elders learn from this?

Jeremiah 22:13-17 Jehovah warns against what unjust practices, and what is essential to imitating his justice?

Matthew 7:2-5 Why should we not be quick to look for the faults in our fellow believers?

James 2:1-9 How does Jehovah view the showing of favoritism, and how can we apply this counsel in our dealings with others?

(Proverbs 12:25) Reassure them that they are wanted, valued, and loved—yes, by Jehovah and also by their brothers and sisters. (1 Peter 1:22; 5:6, 7) In addition, you can pray with and for such ones. Hearing an elder say a heartfelt prayer in their behalf can be most comforting. (James 5:14, 15) Your loving efforts to help depressed ones will not go unnoticed by the God of justice.

²² Truly, we draw ever closer to Jehovah by imitating his justice! When we uphold his righteous standards, when we share the lifesaving good news with others, and when we choose to focus on the good in others rather than looking for their faults, we are displaying godly justice. Elders, when you protect the cleanness of the congregation, when you offer upbuilding Scriptural counsel, when you make impartial decisions, and when you encourage downhearted ones, you are reflecting godly justice. How it must delight Jehovah's heart to look down from the heavens and see his people trying their best to "exercise justice" in walking with their God!

---

22. In what ways can we imitate Jehovah's justice, and with what result?

SECTION 3

"WISE IN HEART"

Genuine wisdom is one of the most precious treasures you can seek. Jehovah alone is its source. In this section we will take a closer look at the limitless wisdom of Jehovah God, the one of whom the faithful man Job said: "He is wise in heart."
—Job 9:4.

CHAPTER 17

"O the Depth of God's . . . Wisdom!"

RUINED! Mankind, the crowning glory of the sixth creative day, suddenly plummeted from the heights to the depths. Jehovah had pronounced "everything he had made," including humankind, "very good." (Genesis 1: 31) But at the start of the seventh day, Adam and Eve chose to follow Satan into rebellion. They plunged into sin, imperfection, and death.

² It might have appeared that Jehovah's purpose for the seventh day had been thrown hopelessly off track. That day, like the six that preceded it, was to be thousands of years long. Jehovah had pronounced it sacred, and it would ultimately see the whole earth made into a paradise filled with a perfect family of mankind. (Genesis 1: 28; 2:3) But after the catastrophic rebellion, how could such a thing ever come about? What would God do? Here was a dramatic test of Jehovah's wisdom—perhaps the ultimate test.

³ Jehovah responded immediately. He pronounced sentence on the rebels in Eden, and at the same time, he provided a glimpse of something wondrous: his purpose to remedy the ills they had just set in motion. (Genesis 3:15) Jehovah's farsighted purpose extends from Eden through all the thousands of years of human history and onward, far into the future. It is elegantly simple yet so profound

1, 2. What was Jehovah's purpose for the seventh day, and how was divine wisdom put to the test at the start of this day?
3, 4. (a) Why is Jehovah's response to the rebellion in Eden an awe-inspiring example of his wisdom? (b) Humility should move us to keep what truth in mind as we study Jehovah's wisdom?

that a Bible reader could spend a rewarding lifetime in studying and contemplating it. Furthermore, Jehovah's purpose is absolutely sure of success. It will put an end to all wickedness, sin, and death. It will bring faithful mankind to perfection. All of this will come about *before* the seventh day ends, so that, despite everything, Jehovah will have fulfilled his purpose for the earth and mankind right on schedule!

⁴ Such wisdom inspires awe, does it not? The apostle Paul was moved to write: "O the depth of God's . . . wisdom!" (Romans 11:33) As we undertake a study of various aspects of this divine quality, humility should move us to keep a vital truth in mind—that, at best, we can only scratch the surface of Jehovah's vast wisdom. (Job 26:14) First, let us define this awe-inspiring quality.

What Is Divine Wisdom?

⁵ Wisdom is not the same as knowledge. Computers can store enormous amounts of knowledge, but it is hard to imagine anyone calling such machines wise. Nonetheless, knowledge and wisdom are related. (Proverbs 10:14) For instance, if you needed wise counsel on treating a serious health problem, would you consult someone with little or no knowledge of medicine? Hardly! So accurate knowledge is essential to true wisdom.

⁶ Jehovah has a boundless store of knowledge. As the "King of eternity," he alone has been alive forever. (Revelation 15:3) And during all those untold ages, he has been aware of everything. The Bible says: "There is not a creation that is not manifest to his sight, but all things are naked and openly exposed to the eyes of him with whom

---

5, 6. What is the relationship between knowledge and wisdom, and how extensive is Jehovah's knowledge?

we have an accounting." (Hebrews 4:13; Proverbs 15:3) As the Creator, Jehovah has full understanding of what he has made, and he has observed all human activity from the start. He examines each human heart, missing nothing. (1 Chronicles 28:9) Having created us as free moral agents, he is pleased when he sees that we are making wise choices in life. As the "Hearer of prayer," he listens to countless expressions at once! (Psalm 65:2) And needless to say, Jehovah has a perfect memory.

7 Jehovah has more than knowledge. He also sees how facts interrelate and discerns the overall picture that is created by myriad details. He evaluates and judges, distinguishing between good and bad, important and trivial. Moreover, he looks beyond the surface and peers right into the heart. (1 Samuel 16:7) Thus, Jehovah has understanding and discernment, qualities that are superior to knowledge. But wisdom is of a still higher order.

8 Wisdom brings knowledge, discernment, and understanding together and puts them to work. In fact, some of the original Bible words translated "wisdom" literally mean "effectual working" or "practical wisdom." So Jehovah's wisdom is not merely theoretical. It is practical, and it works. Drawing upon his breadth of knowledge and his depth of understanding, Jehovah always makes the best decisions possible, carrying them out by means of the best course of action conceivable. That is true wisdom! Jehovah demonstrates the truth of Jesus' statement: "Wisdom is proved righteous by its works." (Matthew 11:19) Jehovah's works throughout the universe give powerful testimony to his wisdom.

―――――

7, 8. How does Jehovah display understanding, discernment, and wisdom?

Evidences of Divine Wisdom

⁹ Have you ever marveled at the ingenuity of a craftsman who makes beautiful things that work well? That is an impressive type of wisdom. (Exodus 31:1-3) Jehovah himself is the source of and the ultimate possessor of such wisdom. King David said of Jehovah: "I shall laud you because in a fear-inspiring way I am wonderfully made. Your works are wonderful, as my soul is very well aware." (Psalm 139:14) Indeed, the more we learn about the human body, the more we find ourselves awed by Jehovah's wisdom.

¹⁰ To illustrate: You started as a single cell—an egg cell from your mother, fertilized by a sperm from your father. Soon, that cell started to divide. You, the end product, are made of some 100 trillion cells. They are tiny. About 10,-000 average-sized cells would fit on the head of a pin. Yet, each one is a creation of mind-boggling complexity. The cell is far more intricate than any man-made machine or factory. Scientists say that a cell is like a walled city—one with controlled entrances and exits, a transportation system, a communications network, power plants, production plants, waste disposal and recycling facilities, defense agencies, and even a sort of central government in its nucleus. Furthermore, the cell can make a complete replica of itself within just a few hours!

¹¹ Not all cells are the same, of course. As the cells of an embryo continue to divide, they assume very different functions. Some will be nerve cells; others bone, muscle,

---

9, 10. (a) Jehovah demonstrates what type of wisdom, and how has he displayed it? (b) How does the cell give evidence of Jehovah's wisdom?

11, 12. (a) What causes the cells in a developing embryo to differentiate, and how does this harmonize with Psalm 139:16? (b) In what ways does the human brain show that we are "wonderfully made"?

blood, or eye cells. All such differentiation is programmed into the cell's "library" of genetic blueprints, the DNA. Interestingly, David was inspired to say to Jehovah: "Your eyes saw even the embryo of me, and in your book all its parts were down in writing."—Psalm 139:16.

¹² Some body parts are immensely complex. Consider, for example, the human brain. Some have called it the most complex object yet discovered in the universe. It contains some 100 billion nerve cells—about as many as the number of stars in our galaxy. Each of those cells branches off into thousands of connections with other cells. Scientists say that a human brain could contain all the information in all the world's libraries and that its storage capacity may, in fact, be unfathomable. Despite decades of studying this "wonderfully made" organ, scientists admit that they may never fully understand how it works.

¹³ Humans, however, are just one example of Jehovah's creative wisdom. Psalm 104:24 says: "How many your works are, O Jehovah! All of them in wisdom you have made. The earth is full of your productions." Jehovah's wisdom is apparent in every creation around us. The ant, for example, is "instinctively wise." (Proverbs 30:24) Indeed, ant colonies are superbly organized. Some ant colonies tend, shelter, and draw nourishment from insects called aphids as if these were livestock. Other ants act as farmers, raising and cultivating "crops" of fungus. Many other creatures have been programmed to do remarkable things by instinct. A common fly performs aerobatic feats that the most advanced of man's aircraft cannot duplicate. Migrating birds navigate by the stars, by the orientation

---

13, 14. (a) How do ants and other creatures show that they are "instinctively wise," and what does that teach us about their Creator? (b) Why might we say that such creations as the spiderweb are made "in wisdom"?

of the earth's magnetic field, or by some form of internal map. Biologists spend years studying the sophisticated behaviors that have been programmed into these creatures. How wise, then, the divine Programmer must be!

[14] Scientists have learned much from Jehovah's creative wisdom. There is even a field of engineering, called biomimetics, that seeks to mimic designs found in nature. For instance, you may have gazed in wonder at the beauty of a spiderweb. But an engineer sees it as a marvel of design. Some frail-looking strands are proportionately stronger than steel, tougher than the fibers in a bulletproof vest. Just how strong? Imagine a spiderweb enlarged in scale until it is the size of a net used on a fishing boat. Such a web could catch a passenger plane in mid-flight! Yes, Jehovah has made all such things "in wisdom."

Wisdom Beyond the Earth

[15] Jehovah's wisdom is evident in his works throughout the universe. The starry heavens, which we discussed at some length in Chapter 5, are not scattered haphazardly throughout space. Thanks to the wisdom of Jehovah's "celestial laws," the heavens are beautifully organized into structured galaxies that, in turn, are grouped into clusters that, in turn, combine to form superclusters. (Job 38:33, *The New Jerusalem Bible*) No wonder that Jehovah refers to the heavenly bodies as an "army"! (Isaiah 40:26) There is another army, though, that even more vividly demonstrates Jehovah's wisdom.

15, 16. (a) The starry heavens give what evidence of Jehovah's wisdom? (b) How does Jehovah's position as Supreme Commander over vast numbers of angels testify to the wisdom of this Administrator?

Who programmed earth's creatures to be "instinctively wise"?

[16] As we noted in Chapter 4, God bears the title "Jehovah of armies" because of his position as Supreme Commander of a vast army of hundreds of millions of spirit creatures. This is proof of Jehovah's power. How, though, is his wisdom involved? Consider: Jehovah and Jesus are never idle. (John 5:17) It stands to reason, then, that the angelic ministers of the Most High are likewise always busy. And remember, they are higher than man, superintelligent and superpowerful. (Hebrews 1:7; 2:7) Yet, Jehovah has kept all those angels busy, happily engaged in fulfilling work—"carrying out his word" and "doing his will"—for billions of years. (Psalm 103:20, 21) How awesome the wisdom of this Administrator must be!

Jehovah Is "Wise Alone"

[17] In view of such evidence, is it any wonder that the Bible shows Jehovah's wisdom to be superlative? For example, it says that Jehovah is "wise alone." (Romans 16:27) Jehovah alone possesses wisdom in the absolute sense. He is the source of all true wisdom. (Proverbs 2:6) That is why Jesus, though the wisest of Jehovah's creatures, did not rely on his own wisdom but spoke as his Father directed him.—John 12:48-50.

[18] Notice how the apostle Paul expressed the uniqueness of Jehovah's wisdom: "O the depth of God's riches and wisdom and knowledge! How unsearchable his judgments are and past tracing out his ways are!" (Romans 11:33) By opening the verse with the exclamation "O," Paul showed strong emotion—in this case, profound awe. The Greek word he chose for "depth" is closely related to the word for "abyss." Hence, his words evoke a vivid mental picture. When we contemplate Jehovah's wisdom, it is as if

17, 18. Why does the Bible say that Jehovah is "wise alone," and why should his wisdom leave us awestruck?

Questions for Meditation

Job 28:11-28 How valuable is divine wisdom, and what good result may come from meditating upon the subject?

Psalm 104:1-25 How is Jehovah's wisdom manifest in creation, and what feelings does that evoke in you?

Proverbs 3:19-26 If we contemplate Jehovah's wisdom and apply it, what may be the effect on our own day-to-day life?

Daniel 2:19-28 Why is Jehovah called a Revealer of secrets, and how should we respond to the prophetic wisdom found in his Word?

---

we were gazing into a limitless, bottomless chasm, a realm so deep, so vast that we could never even grasp its immensity, let alone trace it out or map it in detail. (Psalm 92:5) Is that not a humbling thought?

¹⁹ Jehovah is "wise alone" in another sense: Only he is able to peer into the future. Remember, Jehovah uses the farseeing eagle to symbolize divine wisdom. A golden eagle may weigh a mere ten pounds, but its eyes are larger than those of a full-grown man. The eagle's eyesight is amazingly keen, enabling the bird to spot tiny prey from thousands of feet aloft, perhaps even from miles away! Jehovah himself once said of the eagle: "Far into the distance its eyes keep looking." (Job 39:29) In a similar sense, Jehovah can look "far into the distance" of time—the future!

²⁰ The Bible is full of evidence that this is true. It contains hundreds of prophecies, or history written in advance. The outcome of wars, the rise and fall of world powers, and even the specific battle strategies of military

---

19, 20. (a) Why is the eagle a fitting symbol of divine wisdom? (b) How has Jehovah demonstrated his ability to peer into the future?

commanders were all foretold in the Bible—in some cases, hundreds of years in advance.—Isaiah 44:25–45:4; Daniel 8:2-8, 20-22.

21 Does this mean, though, that God has already fore-seen the choices you will make in life? Some who preach the doctrine of predestination insist that the answer is yes. However, that notion actually undermines Jehovah's wisdom, for it implies that he cannot control his abili-ty to look into the future. To illustrate: If you had a sing-ing voice of unparalleled beauty, would you then have no choice but to sing all the time? The notion is absurd! Like-wise, Jehovah has the ability to foreknow the future, but he does not use it all the time. To do so might infringe upon our own free will, a precious gift that Jehovah will never revoke.—Deuteronomy 30:19, 20.

22 Worse yet, the very notion of predestination suggests that Jehovah's wisdom is cold, devoid of heart, feeling, or compassion. But nothing could be further from the truth! The Bible teaches that Jehovah is "wise *in heart.*" (Job 9:4) Not that he has a literal heart, but the Bible often uses that term in connection with the innermost self, which includes motivations and feelings, such as love. So Jeho-vah's wisdom, like his other qualities, is governed by love. —1 John 4:8.

23 Naturally, Jehovah's wisdom is perfectly trustworthy. It is so far above our own wisdom that God's Word loving-ly urges us: "Trust in Jehovah with all your heart and do not lean upon your own understanding. In all your ways take notice of him, and he himself will make your paths straight." (Proverbs 3:5, 6) Let us now delve into Jehovah's wisdom so that we may draw closer to our all-wise God.

21, 22. (a) Why is there no basis for concluding that Jehovah has foreseen all the choices you will make in life? Illustrate. (b) How do we know that Jehovah's wisdom is not cold or devoid of feeling?
23. The superiority of Jehovah's wisdom should move us to do what?

CHAPTER 18

Wisdom in "the Word of God"

DO YOU recall the last time you received a letter from a loved one who lives far away? Few things bring us as much pleasure as a heartfelt letter from someone we hold dear. We are delighted to hear about his well-being, his experiences, and his plans. Such communication brings loved ones closer, even if they are physically far away.

² What, then, could bring us more pleasure than to receive a written message from the God we love? Jehovah has, in a sense, written us a "letter"—his Word, the Bible. In it he tells us who he is, what he has done, what he purposes to do, and much more. Jehovah has given us his Word because he wants us to be close to him. Our all-wise God chose the best possible way to communicate with us. There is incomparable wisdom in the way the Bible is written and in what it contains.

Why a Written Word?

³ Some may wonder, 'Why did Jehovah not use a more dramatic method—say, a voice from heaven—to communicate with humans?' In fact, Jehovah did at times speak from heaven by means of angelic representatives. He did so, for example, when he gave the Law to Israel. (Galatians 3:19) The voice from heaven was awe-inspiring—so much so that the terrified Israelites asked that Jehovah not speak with them in this manner but that he communicate through Moses. (Exodus 20:18-20) The Law, consisting of some 600 statutes, was thus transmitted to Moses orally, word-for-word.

1, 2. What "letter" has Jehovah written us, and why?
3. In what way did Jehovah transmit the Law to Moses?

⁴ What, though, if that Law had never been put in writing? Would Moses have been able to remember the precise wording of that detailed code and to convey it flawlessly to the rest of the nation? What about later generations? Would they have had to rely solely on word of mouth? That would hardly have been a reliable method of handing down God's laws. Imagine what would happen if you were to transmit a story to a long line of people by telling it to the first person and then having it relayed from one to another down the line. What the person at the end of the line heard would likely differ considerably from the original. The words of God's Law were in no such danger.

⁵ Jehovah wisely chose to have his words put in writing. He instructed Moses: "Write down for yourself these words, because it is in accordance with these words that I do conclude a covenant with you and Israel." (Exodus 34: 27) So began the era of Bible writing, in 1513 B.C.E. Over the next 1,610 years, Jehovah "spoke on many occasions and in many ways" to some 40 human writers who then penned the Bible. (Hebrews 1:1) Along the way, devoted copyists took meticulous care to produce accurate copies so as to preserve the Scriptures.—Ezra 7:6; Psalm 45:1.

⁶ Jehovah has truly blessed us by communicating with us in writing. Have you ever received a letter that was so dear to you—perhaps because it offered needed comfort—that you saved it and read it again and again? So it is with Jehovah's "letter" to us. Because Jehovah put his

---

4. Explain why word-of-mouth transmission would not have been a reliable method of handing down God's laws.
5, 6. What did Jehovah instruct Moses to do with His words, and why is it a blessing for us to have Jehovah's Word in writing?

"All Scripture is inspired of God"

words in written form, we are able to read them regularly and to meditate on what they say. (Psalm 1:2) We can receive "the comfort from the Scriptures" whenever we need it.—Romans 15:4.

Why Human Writers?

7 In his wisdom, Jehovah used humans to pen his Word. Consider this: If Jehovah had used angels to record the Bible, would it have the same appeal? Granted, angels could have portrayed Jehovah from their lofty viewpoint, expressed their own devotion to him, and reported on faithful human servants of God. But would we really have been able to identify with the perspective of perfect spirit creatures, whose knowledge, experience, and strength are far superior to our own?—Hebrews 2:6, 7.

8 Through his use of human writers, Jehovah provided just what we need—a record that is "inspired of God" yet retains the human element. (2 Timothy 3:16) How did he achieve this? In many cases, he evidently allowed the writers to use their own mental faculties in selecting "the delightful words and the writing of correct words of truth." (Ecclesiastes 12:10, 11) This explains the Bible's diversity of style; the writings reflect the background and personality of the individual writers.* Yet, these men "spoke from God as they were borne along by holy spirit." (2 Peter 1: 21) Hence, the end product truly is "the word of God." —1 Thessalonians 2:13.

---

* For example, David, who was a shepherd, uses examples drawn from pastoral life. (Psalm 23) Matthew, who had been a tax collector, makes numerous references to numbers and money values. (Matthew 17:27; 26:15; 27:3) Luke, who was a physician, uses words that reflect his medical background.—Luke 4:38; 14:2; 16:20.

---

7. How is Jehovah's wisdom seen in his use of human penmen?
8. In what way were the Bible writers allowed to use their own mental faculties? (See also footnote.)

⁹ The use of human penmen gives the Bible tremendous warmth and appeal. Its writers were men with feelings like ours. Being imperfect, they faced trials and pressures similar to our own. In some cases, Jehovah's spirit inspired them to write about their own feelings and struggles. (2 Corinthians 12:7-10) So they penned words in the first person, words that no angel could have expressed.

¹⁰ Take, for example, King David of Israel. After he had committed some serious sins, David composed a psalm in which he poured out his heart, begging for God's forgiveness. He wrote: "Cleanse me even from my sin. For my transgressions I myself know, and my sin is in front of me constantly. Look! With error I was brought forth with birth pains, and in sin my mother conceived me. Do not throw me away from before your face; and your holy spirit O do not take away from me. The sacrifices to God are a broken spirit; a heart broken and crushed, O God, you will not despise." (Psalm 51:2, 3, 5, 11, 17) Can you not feel the writer's anguish? Who but an imperfect human could express such heartfelt sentiments?

Why a Book About People?

¹¹ There is something else that contributes to the Bible's appeal. To a large extent, it is a book about people—real people—those serving God and those not serving him. We read about their experiences, hardships, and joys. We see the outcome of their choices in life. Such accounts were included "for our instruction." (Romans 15:4) Through these true-life portrayals, Jehovah teaches in ways that touch our heart. Consider some examples.

9, 10. Why does the use of human writers add to the Bible's warmth and appeal?

11. What kind of true-life portrayals are included in the Bible "for our instruction"?

¹² The Bible tells about unfaithful, even wicked, humans and what befell them. In these accounts, undesirable qualities are seen in action, making them easier for us to comprehend. For instance, what command against disloyalty could be more powerful than the living example of this quality in Judas as he carried out his traitorous plot against Jesus? (Matthew 26:14-16, 46-50; 27:3-10) Accounts such as this reach our heart more effectively, helping us to recognize and reject loathsome traits.

¹³ The Bible also describes many faithful servants of God. We read about their devotion and loyalty. We see living illustrations of the qualities we need to cultivate in order to draw close to God. Take faith, for example. The Bible defines faith and tells us how essential it is if we would please God. (Hebrews 11:1, 6) But the Bible also contains vivid examples of faith in action. Think about the faith Abraham showed when he attempted to offer up Isaac. (Genesis, chapter 22; Hebrews 11:17-19) Through such accounts, the word "faith" takes on added meaning and becomes easier to grasp. How wise that Jehovah not only exhorts us to cultivate desirable qualities but also provides examples of them in action!

¹⁴ The real-life accounts found in the Bible often teach us something about the kind of person Jehovah is. Consider what we read about a woman whom Jesus observed in the temple. While seated near the treasury chests, Jesus was watching as the people dropped in their contributions. Many rich ones came, giving "out of their surplus." But Jesus' gaze became fixed on a lowly widow. Her gift con-

---

12. Bible accounts about unfaithful humans help us in what way?
13. In what way does the Bible help us to grasp desirable qualities?
14, 15. What does the Bible tell us about a certain woman who came to the temple, and what do we learn about Jehovah from this account?

sisted of "two small coins, which have very little value."* It was the last bit of money she had. Jesus, who perfectly reflected Jehovah's mind on matters, noted: "This poor widow dropped in more than all those dropping money into the treasury chests." According to those words, she put in more than all the others combined.—Mark 12:41-44; Luke 21:1-4; John 8:28.

¹⁵ Is it not significant that of all the people who came to the temple that day, this widow was singled out and mentioned in the Bible? Through this example, Jehovah teaches us that he is an appreciative God. He is pleased to accept our whole-souled gifts, no matter how they compare with what others are able to give. Jehovah could hardly have found a better way to teach us this heart-warming truth!

What the Bible Does Not Contain

¹⁶ When you write a letter to a loved one, there is only so much you can include. So you use discretion in choosing what to write. Likewise, Jehovah chose to mention certain individuals and events in his Word. But in these descriptive accounts, the Bible does not always spell out all the details. (John 21:25) For example, when the Bible tells of God's judgment, the information provided may not answer our every question. Jehovah's wisdom is seen even in what he chose to leave out of his Word. How so?

¹⁷ The way in which the Bible is written serves to test what is in our heart. Hebrews 4:12 says: "The word [or,

---

* Each of these coins was a lepton, the smallest Jewish coin in circulation at that time. Two lepta were the equivalent of 1/64 of a day's wage. These two coins were not even enough to buy a single sparrow, the cheapest bird used for food by the poor.

16, 17. How is Jehovah's wisdom seen even in what he chose to leave out of his Word?

message] of God is alive and exerts power and is sharper than any two-edged sword and pierces even to the dividing of soul and spirit . . . and is able to discern thoughts and intentions of the heart." The Bible's message pierces deep, revealing our true thinking and motives. Those who read it with a critical heart are often stumbled by accounts that do not contain enough information to satisfy them. Such ones may even question whether Jehovah really is loving, wise, and just.

18 In contrast, when we make a careful study of the Bible with a sincere heart, we come to see Jehovah in the context in which the Bible as a whole presents him. Hence, we are not disturbed if a particular account raises some questions to which we cannot find immediate answers. To illustrate: When piecing together a large puzzle, perhaps we cannot at first find a particular piece or we cannot see how a certain piece fits in. Yet, we may have assembled enough of the pieces to grasp what the complete picture must look like. Similarly, when we study the Bible, little by little we learn about the kind of God Jehovah is, and a definite picture emerges. Even if we cannot at first understand a certain account or see how it fits in with God's personality, our study of the Bible has already taught us more than enough about Jehovah to enable us to see that he is unfailingly a loving, fair, and just God.

19 To comprehend God's Word, then, we must read and study it with a sincere heart and an open mind. Is this not evidence of Jehovah's great wisdom? Clever humans can write books that only "wise and intellectual ones" can grasp. But to author a book that can be understood only

---

18, 19. (a) Why should we not be disturbed if a particular Bible account raises questions to which we cannot find immediate answers? (b) What is needed in order to comprehend God's Word, and how is this evidence of Jehovah's great wisdom?

by those having the right heart motivation—that takes the wisdom of God!—Matthew 11:25.

A Book of "Practical Wisdom"

[20] In his Word, Jehovah tells us the best way to live. As our Creator, he knows our needs better than we do. And basic human needs—including the desire to find love, to be happy, and to make a success of relationships—have remained the same. The Bible contains a wealth of "practical wisdom" that can help us to live meaningful lives. (Proverbs 2:7) Each section of this study aid contains a chapter showing how we can apply the Bible's wise counsel, but let us here consider just one example.

[21] Have you ever noticed that people who nurse grudges and harbor resentment often end up hurting themselves? Resentment is a heavy burden to carry in life. When we nurture it, it consumes our thoughts, robs us of peace, and stifles our joy. Scientific studies suggest that harboring anger can increase our risk of heart disease and a host of other chronic illnesses. Long before such scientific studies, the Bible wisely said: "Let anger alone and leave rage." (Psalm 37:8) But how can we do that?

[22] God's Word offers this wise counsel: "The insight of a man certainly slows down his anger, and it is beauty on his part to pass over transgression." (Proverbs 19:11) Insight is the ability to see beneath the surface, to look beyond the obvious. Insight nurtures understanding, for it can help us to discern why another person spoke or acted in a certain way. Endeavoring to grasp his genuine motives, feelings, and circumstances may help us to dispel negative thoughts and feelings toward him.

20. Why can Jehovah alone tell us the best way to live, and what does the Bible contain that can help us?
21-23. What wise counsel can help us to avoid harboring anger and resentment?

Questions for Meditation

Proverbs 2:1-6 What effort is needed in order to gain the wisdom found in God's Word?

Proverbs 2:10-22 In what ways will we benefit from living in harmony with the Bible's wise counsel?

Romans 7:15-25 How does this passage illustrate the wisdom of using humans to record God's Word?

1 Corinthians 10:6-12 What can we learn from the Bible's warning examples involving Israel?

---

²³ The Bible contains this further piece of advice: "Continue putting up with one another and forgiving one another freely." (Colossians 3:13) The expression "continue putting up with one another" suggests being patient with others, tolerating the traits we may find irritating. Such forbearance can help us to avoid nursing petty grudges. "Forgiving" conveys the idea of letting go of resentment. Our wise God knows that we need to forgive others when there is sound basis for doing so. This is not only for their benefit but also for our own peace of mind and heart. (Luke 17:3, 4) What wisdom is found in God's Word!

²⁴ Moved by his boundless love, Jehovah wanted to communicate with us. He chose the best possible way—a written "letter" penned by human writers under the guidance of holy spirit. As a result, Jehovah's own wisdom is found in its pages. This wisdom is "very trustworthy." (Psalm 93:5) As we bring our lives into harmony with it and as we share it with others, we are naturally drawn close to our all-wise God. In the next chapter, we will discuss another outstanding example of Jehovah's farsighted wisdom: his ability to foretell the future and to fulfill his purpose.

---

24. What results when we bring our lives into harmony with divine wisdom?

CHAPTER 19

"God's Wisdom in a Sacred Secret"

SECRETS! Because they intrigue, fascinate, and mystify, humans often have difficulty keeping them confidential. However, the Bible says: "The glory of God is the keeping of a matter secret." (Proverbs 25:2) Yes, as Sovereign Ruler and Creator, Jehovah rightfully keeps some things secret from mankind until it is his due time to reveal them.

² However, there is a fascinating, intriguing secret that Jehovah has revealed in his Word. It is called "the sacred secret of [God's] will." (Ephesians 1:9) Learning about it can do more than satisfy your curiosity. Knowledge of this secret can lead to salvation and can provide you with a glimpse into Jehovah's unfathomable wisdom.

Revealed Progressively

³ When Adam and Eve sinned, it may have appeared that Jehovah's purpose to have an earthly paradise inhabited by perfect humans had been thwarted. But God *immediately* addressed the problem. He said: "I shall put enmity between you [the serpent] and the woman and between your seed and her seed. He will bruise you in the head and you will bruise him in the heel."—Genesis 3:15.

⁴ These were puzzling, cryptic words. Who was this woman? Who was the serpent? Who was the "seed" that would bruise the serpent's head? Adam and Eve could only guess. Still, God's words provided hope for any faithful

---

1, 2. What "sacred secret" should interest us, and why?
3, 4. How did the prophecy recorded at Genesis 3:15 provide hope, and what mystery, or "sacred secret," did it encompass?

offspring of that unfaithful pair. Righteousness would triumph. Jehovah's purpose would be realized. But how? Ah, that was a mystery! The Bible calls it "God's wisdom in a sacred secret, the hidden wisdom."—1 Corinthians 2:7.

⁵ As the "Revealer of secrets," Jehovah would eventually unveil pertinent details regarding the outworking of this secret. (Daniel 2:28) But he would do so gradually, progressively. To illustrate, we might think of the way a loving father responds when his little boy asks, "Dad, where did I come from?" A wise father provides only as much information as that little boy can grasp. As the boy gets older, the father tells him more. In a similar way, Jehovah determines when his people are ready for revelations of his will and purpose.—Proverbs 4:18; Daniel 12:4.

⁶ How did Jehovah make such revelations? He used a series of covenants, or contracts, to reveal much. Likely, you have at one time or another entered into some sort of a contract—perhaps to buy a home or to borrow or lend money. Such a contract provided a legal guarantee that the terms agreed upon would be fulfilled. But why would Jehovah need to make formal covenants, or contracts, with humans? Surely, his word is a sufficient guarantee of his promises. That is true, and yet, on a number of occasions, God has kindly backed his word with legal contracts. These ironclad agreements give us imperfect humans an even more solid basis for confidence in the promises of Jehovah.—Hebrews 6:16-18.

5. Illustrate why Jehovah revealed his secret progressively.
6. (a) What purpose does a covenant, or contract, serve? (b) Why is it remarkable that Jehovah would initiate covenants with humans?

"I shall . . . multiply your seed like the stars of the heavens"

The Covenant With Abraham

⁷ Over two thousand years after man's expulsion from Paradise, Jehovah told his faithful servant Abraham: "I shall surely multiply your seed like the stars of the heavens . . . and by means of your seed all nations of the earth will certainly bless themselves due to the fact that you have listened to my voice." (Genesis 22:17, 18) This was more than a promise; Jehovah framed it in the form of a legal covenant and backed it by his unbreakable oath. (Genesis 17: 1, 2; Hebrews 6:13-15) How remarkable that the Sovereign Lord actually *contracted* to bless mankind!

⁸ The Abrahamic covenant revealed that the promised Seed would come as a human, for he would be a descendant of Abraham. But who would he be? In time, Jehovah revealed that of Abraham's sons, Isaac would be a forebear of the Seed. Of Isaac's two sons, Jacob was selected. (Genesis 21:12; 28:13, 14) Later, Jacob uttered these prophetic words over one of his 12 sons: "The scepter will not turn aside from Judah, neither the commander's staff from between his feet, until Shiloh ["He to Whom It Belongs"] comes; and to him the obedience of the peoples will belong." (Genesis 49:10) Now it was known that the Seed would be a king, one who descended from Judah!

The Covenant With Israel

⁹ In 1513 B.C.E., Jehovah made a provision that set the scene for further revelations about the sacred secret. He concluded a covenant with Abraham's descendants, the

---

7, 8. (a) What covenant did Jehovah make with Abraham, shedding what light on the sacred secret? (b) How did Jehovah progressively narrow down the line of descent to the promised Seed?

9, 10. (a) What covenant did Jehovah make with the nation of Israel, and what protection did that covenant provide? (b) How did the Law demonstrate mankind's need for a ransom?

nation of Israel. Although now no longer in force, this Mosaic Law covenant was an essential part of Jehovah's purpose to bring about the promised Seed. How so? Consider three ways. First, the Law was like a protective wall. (Ephesians 2:14) Its righteous statutes acted as a barrier between Jew and Gentile. Thus the Law helped to preserve the line of the Seed of promise. Thanks largely to such protection, the nation still existed when God's due time arrived for the Messiah to be born into the tribe of Judah.

[10] Second, the Law thoroughly demonstrated mankind's need for a ransom. A perfect Law, it exposed the inability of sinful humans to adhere to it fully. It thus served "to make transgressions manifest, until the seed should arrive to whom the promise had been made." (Galatians 3:19) By means of animal sacrifices, the Law offered provisional atonement for sins. But since, as Paul wrote, "it is not possible for the blood of bulls and of goats to take sins away," these sacrifices only foreshadowed Christ's ransom sacrifice. (Hebrews 10:1-4) For faithful Jews, then, that covenant became a "tutor leading to Christ."—Galatians 3:24.

[11] Third, that covenant offered the nation of Israel a glorious prospect. Jehovah told them that if they proved faithful to the covenant, they would become "a kingdom of priests and a holy nation." (Exodus 19:5, 6) Fleshly Israel did eventually provide the first members of a heavenly kingdom of priests. However, as a whole, Israel rebelled against the Law covenant, rejected the Messianic Seed, and lost out on that prospect. Who, then, would complete the kingdom of priests? And how would that blessed nation be related to the promised Seed? Those aspects of the sacred secret would be revealed in God's due time.

---

11. What glorious prospect did the Law covenant offer Israel, but why did that nation as a whole lose out?

The Davidic Kingdom Covenant

¹² In the 11th century B.C.E., Jehovah shed further light on the sacred secret when he made another covenant. He promised faithful King David: "I shall certainly raise up your seed after you, . . . and I shall indeed firmly establish his kingdom. . . . I shall certainly establish the throne of his kingdom firmly to time indefinite." (2 Samuel 7:12, 13; Psalm 89:3) Now the lineage of the promised Seed had been narrowed down to the house of David. But could an ordinary human rule "to time indefinite"? (Psalm 89:20, 29, 34-36) And could such a human king rescue mankind from sin and death?

¹³ Under inspiration, David wrote: "The utterance of Jehovah to my Lord is: 'Sit at my right hand until I place your enemies as a stool for your feet.' Jehovah has sworn (and he will feel no regret): 'You are a priest to time indefinite according to the manner of Melchizedek!'" (Psalm 110: 1, 4) David's words applied directly to the promised Seed, or Messiah. (Acts 2:35, 36) This King would rule, not from Jerusalem, but from heaven at Jehovah's "right hand." That would give him authority not just over the land of Israel but over the whole earth. (Psalm 2:6-8) Something more was here revealed. Note that Jehovah uttered a solemn oath that the Messiah would be "a priest . . . according to the manner of Melchizedek." Like Melchizedek, who served as king-priest in Abraham's day, the coming Seed would have a direct appointment from God to serve as King *and* Priest!—Genesis 14:17-20.

¹⁴ Over the years, Jehovah used his prophets to make further revelations about his sacred secret. Isaiah, for exam-

---

12. What covenant did Jehovah make with David, and what light did it shed on God's sacred secret?
13, 14. (a) According to Psalm 110, what promise does Jehovah make to his anointed King? (b) What further revelations regarding the coming Seed were made through Jehovah's prophets?

ple, revealed that the Seed would die a sacrificial death. (Isaiah 53:3-12) Micah foretold the place of the Messiah's birth. (Micah 5:2) Daniel even prophesied the exact timing of the Seed's appearance and death.—Daniel 9:24-27.

The Sacred Secret Revealed!

15 How these prophecies would be fulfilled remained a mystery until the Seed actually made his appearance. Galatians 4:4 says: "When the full limit of the time arrived, God sent forth his Son, who came to be out of a woman." In the year 2 B.C.E., an angel told a Jewish virgin named Mary: "Look! you will conceive in your womb and give birth to a son, and you are to call his name Jesus. This one will be great and will be called Son of the Most High; and Jehovah God will give him the throne of David his father . . . Holy spirit will come upon you, and power of the Most High will overshadow you. For that reason also what is born will be called holy, God's Son."—Luke 1:31, 32, 35.

16 Later, Jehovah transferred the life of his Son from heaven to Mary's womb, so that he came to be out of a woman. Mary was an imperfect woman. Yet, Jesus did not inherit imperfection from her, for he was "God's Son." At the same time, Jesus' human parents, as descendants of David, provided Him with both the natural and the legal rights of an heir of David. (Acts 13:22, 23) At Jesus' baptism in 29 C.E., Jehovah anointed him with holy spirit and said: "This is my Son, the beloved." (Matthew 3:16, 17) At last, the Seed had arrived! (Galatians 3:16) It was time to reveal more about the sacred secret.—2 Timothy 1:10.

17 During his ministry, Jesus identified the serpent of Genesis 3:15 as Satan and the serpent's seed as Satan's

---

15, 16. (a) How did Jehovah's Son come to be "out of a woman"? (b) What did Jesus inherit from his human parents, and when did he arrive as the Seed of promise?
17. How was light shed on the meaning of Genesis 3:15?

followers. (Matthew 23:33; John 8:44) Later, it was revealed how all of these would be crushed forever. (Revelation 20:1-3, 10, 15) And the woman was identified as "the Jerusalem above," Jehovah's heavenly, wifelike organization of spirit creatures.*—Galatians 4:26; Revelation 12:1-6.

The New Covenant

18 Perhaps the most dramatic revelation of all came on the night before Jesus' death when he told his faithful disciples about "the new covenant." (Luke 22:20) Like its predecessor, the Mosaic Law covenant, this new covenant was to produce "a kingdom of priests." (Exodus 19:6; 1 Peter 2:9) However, this covenant would establish, not a fleshly nation, but a spiritual one, "the Israel of God," made up exclusively of Christ's faithful anointed followers. (Galatians 6:16) These parties to the new covenant would share with Jesus in blessing the human race!

19 But why does the new covenant succeed in producing "a kingdom of priests" to bless mankind? Because instead of condemning Christ's disciples as sinners, it provides for the forgiveness of their sins through his sacrifice. (Jeremiah 31:31-34) Once they receive a clean standing before Jehovah, he adopts them into his heavenly family and anoints them with holy spirit. (Romans 8:15-17; 2 Corinthians 1:21) They thus experience "a new birth to a living hope . . . reserved in the heavens." (1 Peter 1:3, 4) Since

---

* "The sacred secret of . . . godly devotion" was also revealed in Jesus. (1 Timothy 3:16) It had long been a secret, a mystery, as to whether anyone could maintain perfect integrity to Jehovah. Jesus revealed the answer. He kept integrity under every test that Satan put upon him.—Matthew 4:1-11; 27:26-50.

---

18. What is the purpose of "the new covenant"?
19. (a) Why does the new covenant succeed in producing "a kingdom of priests"? (b) Why are anointed Christians called "a new creation," and how many will serve in the heavens with Christ?

such an elevated status is entirely new to humans, spirit-begotten anointed Christians are called "a new creation." (2 Corinthians 5:17) The Bible reveals that 144,000 will eventually share in ruling redeemed mankind from heaven.—Revelation 5:9, 10; 14:1-4.

[20] Along with Jesus, these anointed ones become "Abraham's seed."* (Galatians 3:29) The first ones chosen were fleshly Jews. But in 36 C.E., another aspect of the sacred secret was revealed: Gentiles, or non-Jews, would also share in the heavenly hope. (Romans 9:6-8; 11:25, 26; Ephesians 3:5, 6) Would anointed Christians be the only ones to enjoy the blessings promised to Abraham? No, for Jesus' sacrifice benefits the whole world. (1 John 2:2) In time, Jehovah revealed that an unnumbered "great crowd" would survive the end of Satan's system of things. (Revelation 7:9, 14) Multitudes more would be resurrected with the prospect of living forever in Paradise!—Luke 23:43; John 5:28, 29; Revelation 20:11-15; 21:3, 4.

God's Wisdom and the Sacred Secret

[21] The sacred secret is an astonishing display of "the greatly diversified wisdom of God." (Ephesians 3:8-10) What wisdom Jehovah displayed in formulating this secret, then in revealing it so gradually! He wisely took into consideration the limitations of humans, allowing them to manifest their true heart condition.—Psalm 103:14.

[22] Jehovah also showed matchless wisdom in his choice

---

* Jesus also made "a covenant . . . for a kingdom" with the same group. (Luke 22:29, 30) In effect, Jesus contracted with this "little flock" for them to rule with him in heaven as the *secondary* part of the seed of Abraham.—Luke 12:32.

---

20. (a) What revelation regarding the sacred secret was made in 36 C.E.? (b) Who will enjoy the blessings promised to Abraham?
21, 22. In what ways does Jehovah's sacred secret display his wisdom?

Questions For Meditation

John 16:7-12 How did Jesus imitate his Father's way of revealing truth gradually?

1 Corinthians 2:6-16 Why are many unable to grasp Jehovah's sacred secrets, and how may we understand these secrets?

Ephesians 3:10 What privilege do Christians today have in connection with God's sacred secret?

Hebrews 11:8-10 How did the sacred secret sustain the faith of men of old, even though its details were not understood?

---

of Jesus as King. Jehovah's Son is more trustworthy than any other creature in the universe. In living as a man of blood and flesh, Jesus experienced many kinds of adversity. He fully understands human problems. (Hebrews 5: 7-9) And what about Jesus' corulers? Over the centuries, both men and women—chosen from all races, languages, and backgrounds—have been anointed. There is simply no problem that individuals among them have not faced and overcome. (Ephesians 4:22-24) Living under the rule of these merciful king-priests will be a delight!

²³ The apostle Paul wrote: "The sacred secret that was hidden from the past systems of things and from the past generations . . . has been made manifest to his holy ones." (Colossians 1:26) Yes, Jehovah's anointed holy ones have come to understand much about the sacred secret, and they have shared such knowledge with millions. What a privilege all of us have! Jehovah has "made known to us the sacred secret of his will." (Ephesians 1:9) Let us share this marvelous secret with others, helping them likewise to peer into the unfathomable wisdom of Jehovah God!

---

23. What privilege do Christians have in connection with Jehovah's sacred secret?

CHAPTER 20

"Wise in Heart"—Yet Humble

A FATHER wants to impart a vital lesson to his small child. He is eager to reach the heart. What approach should he take? Should he tower intimidatingly over the child and use harsh language? Or should he bend down to the child's level and speak in a mild, appealing manner? Surely a wise, humble father would choose the mild approach.

2 What kind of Father is Jehovah—haughty or humble, harsh or mild? Jehovah is all-knowing, all-wise. Have you noticed, though, that knowledge and intelligence do not necessarily make people humble? As the Bible says, "knowledge puffs up." (1 Corinthians 3:19; 8:1) But Jehovah, who is "wise in heart," is also humble. (Job 9:4) Not that he is in any way low in position or lacking in grandeur, but he is devoid of haughtiness. Why is that so?

3 Jehovah is holy. So haughtiness, a quality that defiles, is not in him. (Mark 7:20-22) Further, note what the prophet Jeremiah said to Jehovah: "Without fail your soul [Jehovah himself] will remember and bow low over me."* (Lamentations 3:20) Imagine! Jehovah, the Sovereign Lord of the universe, was willing to "bow low," or come down to Jeremiah's level, in order to give that imperfect human favorable attention. (Psalm 113:7) Yes, Jehovah is humble. But what does godly humility involve? How is it related to wisdom? And why is it important to us?

---

* The ancient scribes, or Sopherim, changed this verse to say that Jeremiah, not Jehovah, is the one bowing low. They evidently thought it unfitting to attribute to God such a humble act. As a result, many translations miss the point of this beautiful verse. However, *The New English Bible* accurately has Jeremiah saying to God: "Remember, O remember, and stoop down to me."

1-3. Why can we be certain that Jehovah is humble?

How Jehovah Proves to Be Humble

⁴ Humility is lowliness of mind, absence of arrogance and pride. An inner quality of the heart, humility is manifest in such traits as mildness, patience, and reasonableness. (Galatians 5:22, 23) Never, though, should these godly qualities be mistaken for weakness or timidity. They are not incompatible with Jehovah's righteous anger or his use of destructive power. Rather, by his humility and mildness, Jehovah demonstrates his immense strength, his power to control himself perfectly. (Isaiah 42:14) How is humility related to wisdom? One reference work on the Bible notes: "Humility is finally defined . . . in terms of selflessness and is an essential root of all wisdom." Genuine wisdom, then, cannot exist apart from humility. How does Jehovah's humility benefit us?

4, 5. (a) What is humility, how is it manifest, and why should it never be confused with weakness or timidity? (b) How did Jehovah demonstrate humility in his dealings with David, and how important to us is Jehovah's humility?

A wise father deals humbly and mildly with his children

⁵ King David sang to Jehovah: "You will give me your shield of salvation, and your own right hand will sustain me, and your own humility will make me great." (Psalm 18:35) In effect, Jehovah lowered himself in order to deal with this mere imperfect human, protecting and sustaining him day by day. David realized that if he was to find salvation—and even, eventually, achieve a measure of greatness as a king—it would be only because of Jehovah's willingness to humble Himself in this way. Really, who of us would have any hope of salvation if Jehovah were not humble, willing to lower himself in order to deal with us as a mild and loving Father?

⁶ It is worth noting that there is a distinction between humility and modesty. Modesty is a beautiful quality for faithful humans to cultivate. Like humility, it is associated with wisdom. For example, Proverbs 11:2 says: "Wisdom is with the modest ones." However, the Bible never speaks of Jehovah as being modest. Why not? Modesty, as used in the Scriptures, suggests a proper awareness of one's own limitations. The Almighty has no limitations except for those he imposes upon himself because of his own righteous standards. (Mark 10:27; Titus 1:2) Furthermore, as the Most High, he is subject to no one. So the concept of modesty simply does not apply to Jehovah.

⁷ However, Jehovah is humble and mild. He teaches his servants that mildness is essential to true wisdom. His Word speaks of "mildness that belongs to wisdom."* (James 3:13) Consider Jehovah's example in this regard.

---

* Other versions say "the humility that comes from wisdom" and "that gentleness which is the hallmark of wisdom."

6, 7. (a) Why does the Bible never refer to Jehovah as being modest? (b) What is the relationship between mildness and wisdom, and who sets the ultimate example in this regard?

Jehovah Humbly Delegates and Listens

⁸ There is heartwarming proof of Jehovah's humility in his willingness to delegate responsibility and to listen. That he does so at all is amazing; Jehovah has no need for assistance or counsel. (Isaiah 40:13, 14; Romans 11:34, 35) Nonetheless, the Bible repeatedly shows us that Jehovah condescends in these ways.

⁹ Consider, for example, an outstanding event in the life of Abraham. Abraham had three visitors, one of whom he addressed as "Jehovah." The visitors were actually angels, but one of them came in Jehovah's name and was acting in His name. When that angel spoke and acted, it was, in effect, Jehovah speaking and acting. By this means, Jehovah told Abraham that He had heard a loud "cry of complaint about Sodom and Gomorrah." Jehovah stated: "I am quite determined to go down that I may see whether they act altogether according to the outcry over it that has come to me, and, if not, I can get to know it." (Genesis 18:3, 20, 21) Of course, Jehovah's message did not mean that the Almighty would "go down" in person. Rather, he again sent angels to represent him. (Genesis 19:1) Why? Could the all-seeing Jehovah not "get to know" the true condition of that region on his own? Certainly. But instead, Jehovah humbly gave those angels the assignment to investigate the situation and to visit Lot and his family in Sodom.

¹⁰ Furthermore, Jehovah listens. He once asked his angels to suggest various ways to bring about the downfall of wicked King Ahab. Jehovah did not need such help. Yet, he accepted the suggestion of one angel and commissioned him to follow through on it. (1 Kings 22:19-22) Was that not humble?

8-10. (a) Why is it remarkable that Jehovah shows a willingness to delegate and to listen? (b) How has the Almighty dealt humbly with his angels?

¹¹ Jehovah is even willing to listen to imperfect humans who desire to express their concerns. For instance, when Jehovah first told Abraham of His intention to destroy Sodom and Gomorrah, that faithful man was puzzled. "It is unthinkable of you," Abraham said, adding: "Is the Judge of all the earth not going to do what is right?" He asked whether Jehovah would spare the cities if 50 righteous men could be found there. Jehovah assured him that He would. But Abraham asked again, lowering the number to 45, then 40, and so on. Despite Jehovah's assurances, Abraham persisted until the number was as low as ten. Perhaps Abraham did not yet fully grasp how merciful Jehovah is. At any rate, Jehovah patiently and humbly allowed his friend and servant Abraham to express his concerns in this way.—Genesis 18:23-33.

¹² How many brilliant, learned humans would listen so patiently to a person of vastly inferior intelligence?* Such is the humility of our God. During the same interchange, Abraham also came to see that Jehovah is "slow to anger." (Exodus 34:6) Perhaps realizing that he had no right to question the doings of the Most High, Abraham twice begged: "May Jehovah, please, not grow hot with anger." (Genesis 18:30, 32) Of course, Jehovah did not. He truly does have the "mildness that belongs to wisdom."

Jehovah Is Reasonable

¹³ Jehovah's humility is manifest in yet another beautiful quality—reasonableness. This quality is sadly lacking

---

* Interestingly, the Bible contrasts patience with haughtiness. (Ecclesiastes 7:8) Jehovah's patience provides further evidence of his humility.—2 Peter 3:9.

11, 12. How did Abraham get to see Jehovah's humility?
13. What is the meaning of the word "reasonable" as used in the Bible, and why does this word aptly describe Jehovah?

among imperfect humans. Not only is Jehovah willing to listen to his intelligent creatures but he is also willing to yield when there is no conflict with righteous principles. As used in the Bible, the word "reasonable" literally means "yielding." This quality too is a hallmark of divine wisdom. James 3:17 says: "The wisdom from above is . . . reasonable." In what sense is the all-wise Jehovah reasonable? For one thing, he is adaptable. Remember, his very name teaches us that Jehovah causes himself to become whatever is needed in order to fulfill his purposes. (Exodus 3:14) Does that not indicate a spirit of adaptability and reasonableness?

¹⁴ There is a remarkable Bible passage that helps us begin to grasp Jehovah's adaptability. The prophet Ezekiel was given a vision of Jehovah's heavenly organization of spirit creatures. He saw a chariot of awe-inspiring proportions, Jehovah's own "vehicle" always under His control. Most interesting was the way that it moved. The giant wheels were four-sided and full of eyes so that they could see everywhere and could change direction instantly, without stopping or turning. And this gigantic chariot did not have to lumber along like an unwieldy, man-made vehicle. It could move at the speed of lightning, even making right-angled turns! (Ezekiel 1:1, 14-28) Yes, Jehovah's organization, like the almighty Sovereign in control of it, is supremely adaptable, responsive to the ever-changing situations and needs it must address.

¹⁵ Humans can only try to imitate such perfect adaptability. All too often, though, humans and their organizations are more rigid than adaptable, more unreasonable

---

14, 15. Ezekiel's vision of Jehovah's celestial chariot teaches us what about Jehovah's heavenly organization, and how does it differ from worldly organizations?

than yielding. To illustrate: A supertanker or a freight train might be awesome in terms of size and power. But can either one respond to sudden changes in circumstance? If an obstacle falls across the tracks in front of a freight train, turning is out of the question. Sudden stops are not much easier. A heavy freight train may take over a mile to stop after the brakes are applied! Similarly, a supertanker may coast onward for five miles after the engines are shut off. Even if the engines are thrown into reverse, the tanker may still plow on for two miles! It is similar with human organizations that are prone to rigidity and unreasonableness. Because of pride, men often refuse to adapt to changing needs and circumstances. Such rigidity has bankrupted corporations and even toppled governments. (Proverbs 16:18) How happy we can be that neither Jehovah nor his organization is anything like that!

How Jehovah Displays Reasonableness

¹⁶ Consider again the destruction of Sodom and Gomorrah. Lot and his family received explicit instructions from Jehovah's angel: "Escape to the mountainous region." However, this did not appeal to Lot. "Not that, please, Jehovah!" he begged. Convinced that he would die if he had to flee to the mountains, Lot pleaded that he and his family be allowed to flee to a nearby city named Zoar. Now, Jehovah had intended to destroy that city. Furthermore, Lot's fears had no real basis. Surely Jehovah could preserve Lot alive in the mountains! Nonetheless, Jehovah yielded to Lot's pleas and spared Zoar. "Here I do show you consideration to this extent also," the angel told Lot. (Genesis 19:17-22) Was that not reasonable on Jehovah's part?

---

16. How did Jehovah show reasonableness in dealing with Lot prior to the destruction of Sodom and Gomorrah?

¹⁷ Jehovah also responds to heartfelt repentance, always doing what is merciful and right. Consider what occurred when the prophet Jonah was sent to the wicked, violent city of Nineveh. When Jonah marched through the streets of Nineveh, the inspired message he proclaimed was quite simple: The mighty city would be destroyed in 40 days. However, circumstances changed dramatically. The Ninevites repented!—Jonah, chapter 3.

¹⁸ It is instructive to compare how Jehovah reacted with how Jonah reacted to this turn of events. In this instance, Jehovah adapted, causing himself to become a Forgiver of sins instead of "a manly person of war."* (Exodus 15:3) Jonah, on the other hand, was inflexible and far less merciful. Rather than reflecting Jehovah's reasonableness, he responded more like the freight train or the supertanker mentioned earlier. He had proclaimed doom, so doom it must be! Patiently, though, Jehovah taught his impatient prophet a memorable lesson in reasonableness and mercy.—Jonah, chapter 4.

¹⁹ Finally, Jehovah is reasonable in what he expects of us. King David said: "He himself well knows the formation of us, remembering that we are dust." (Psalm 103:14) Jehovah understands our limitations and our imperfections better than we ourselves do. He never expects of us more than we can do. The Bible contrasts those human masters who are "good and reasonable" with those who are "hard

---

* At Psalm 86:5, Jehovah is said to be "good and ready to forgive." When that psalm was translated into Greek, the expression "ready to forgive" was rendered *e·pi·ei·kes'*, or "reasonable."

17, 18. In dealing with the Ninevites, how did Jehovah show that he is reasonable?
19. (a) Why can we be sure that Jehovah is reasonable in what he expects of us? (b) How does Proverbs 19:17 show that Jehovah is a "good and reasonable" Master and also profoundly humble?

Questions for Meditation

Exodus 32:9-14 How did Jehovah demonstrate humility in responding to Moses' plea in behalf of Israel?

Judges 6:36-40 How did Jehovah show patience and reasonableness in answering Gideon's requests?

Psalm 113:1-9 How does Jehovah prove to be humble in dealing with mankind?

Luke 1:46-55 Mary believed that Jehovah has what view of humble and lowly people? How might his view affect us?

---

to please." (1 Peter 2:18) Which type of Master is Jehovah? Note what Proverbs 19:17 says: "He that is showing favor to the lowly one is lending to Jehovah." Clearly, only a good and reasonable master would take note of every act of kindness performed in behalf of lowly ones. More than that, this scripture suggests that the Creator of the universe, in effect, views himself as indebted to the mere humans who perform such deeds of mercy! Here is humility of the most profound kind.

[20] Jehovah is just as mild and reasonable in his dealings with his servants today. When we pray in faith, he listens. And even though he does not send angelic messengers to speak to us, we should not conclude that our prayers go unanswered by him. Recall that when the apostle Paul asked fellow believers to "carry on prayer" for his release from prison, he added: "That I may be restored to you the sooner." (Hebrews 13:18, 19) So our prayers may actually move Jehovah to do what he might not have done otherwise!—James 5:16.

---

20. What assurance is there that Jehovah hears our prayers and responds to them?

Jehovah is reasonable and understands our limitations

²¹ Of course, none of these manifestations of Jehovah's humility—his mildness, his willingness to listen, his patience, his reasonableness—mean that Jehovah compromises his righteous principles. The clergy of Christendom may think that they are being reasonable when they tickle the ears of their flocks by watering down Jehovah's moral standards. (2 Timothy 4:3) But the human tendency to compromise for the sake of expediency has nothing to do with divine reasonableness. Jehovah is holy; never will he pollute his righteous standards. (Leviticus 11:44) Let us, then, love Jehovah's reasonableness for what it is —a proof of his humility. Do you not thrill to think that Jehovah God, the wisest Being in the universe, is also sublimely humble? What a delight to draw close to this awesome yet mild, patient, reasonable God!

21. What conclusion should we never draw from Jehovah's humility, but rather, what should we appreciate about him?

CHAPTER 21

Jesus Reveals the "Wisdom From God"

THE audience was stunned. The young man Jesus was standing before them in the synagogue and teaching. He was no stranger to them—he had grown up in their city, and for years he had worked among them as a carpenter. Perhaps some of them lived in houses that Jesus had helped to build, or maybe they worked their land with plows and yokes that he had made with his own hands.* But how would they respond to the teaching of this former carpenter?

² Most of those listening were astounded, asking: "Where did this man get this wisdom?" But they also remarked: "This is the carpenter the son of Mary." (Matthew 13:54-58; Mark 6:1-3) Sadly, Jesus' onetime neighbors reasoned, 'This carpenter is just a local man like us.' Despite the wisdom in his words, they rejected him. Little did they know that the wisdom he shared was not his own.

³ Where *did* Jesus get this wisdom? "What I teach is not mine," he said, "but belongs to him that sent me." (John 7:16) The apostle Paul explained that Jesus "has become to us wisdom from God." (1 Corinthians 1:30) Jehovah's own wisdom is revealed through his Son, Jesus. Indeed,

---

* In Bible times, carpenters were employed in building houses, constructing furniture, and making farm implements. Justin Martyr, of the second century C.E., wrote of Jesus: "He was in the habit of working as a carpenter when among men, making ploughs and yokes."

1-3. How did Jesus' former neighbors respond to his teaching, and what did they fail to recognize about him?

this was true to such an extent that Jesus could say: "I and the Father are one." (John 10:30) Let us examine three areas in which Jesus manifested the "wisdom from God."

What He Taught

4 First, consider what Jesus taught. The theme of his message was "the good news of the kingdom." (Luke 4:43) That was highly important because of the role the Kingdom would play in vindicating Jehovah's sovereignty and in bringing lasting blessings to mankind. In his teaching, Jesus also offered wise counsel for everyday living. He proved himself to be the foretold "Wonderful Counselor." (Isaiah 9:6) Indeed, how could his counsel be anything but wonderful? He had a profound knowledge of God's Word and will, a keen understanding of human nature, and a deep love for humankind. Hence, his counsel was always practical and in the best interests of his listeners. Jesus uttered "sayings of everlasting life." Yes, when followed, his counsel leads to salvation.—John 6:68.

5 The Sermon on the Mount is an outstanding example of the unparalleled wisdom found in the teachings of Jesus. This sermon, as recorded at Matthew 5:3–7:27, would likely take only 20 minutes to deliver. Its counsel, however, is timeless—as relevant today as when it was first given. Jesus covered a wide range of subjects, including how to improve relations with others (5:23-26, 38-42; 7:1-5, 12), how to keep morally clean (5:27-32), and how to live a meaningful life (6:19-24; 7:24-27). But Jesus did more than just

---

4. (a) What was the theme of Jesus' message, and why was that highly important? (b) Why was Jesus' counsel always practical and in the best interests of his listeners?
5. What were some of the subjects that Jesus covered in the Sermon on the Mount?

"The crowds were astounded at his way of teaching"

tell his listeners what the course of wisdom is; he *showed* them by explaining, reasoning, and offering proof.

⁶ Consider, for example, Jesus' wise counsel on how to deal with anxiety about material things, as stated in Matthew chapter 6. "Stop being anxious about your souls as to what you will eat or what you will drink, or about your bodies as to what you will wear," Jesus advises us. (Verse 25) Food and clothing are basic necessities, and it is only natural to be concerned about obtaining these. But Jesus tells us to "stop being anxious" about such things.* Why?

⁷ Listen as Jesus reasons convincingly. Since Jehovah has given us life and a body, can he not provide food to sustain that life and raiment to clothe that body? (Verse 25) If God provides birds with food and he clothes flowers with beauty, how much more will he care for his human worshipers! (Verses 26, 28-30) Really, undue anxiety is pointless anyway. It cannot extend our life even by a fraction.# (Verse 27) How can we avoid anxiety? Jesus counsels us: Continue giving worship of God priority in life. Those who do so can be confident that all their daily needs "will be added" to them by their heavenly Father. (Verse 33) Finally, Jesus gives a most practical suggestion—take one day at a time. Why add tomorrow's anxieties to those of today? (Verse 34) Besides, why worry unduly about things that may never happen? Applying such wise counsel can spare us much heartache in this stressful world.

---

* The Greek verb rendered "be anxious" means "to have the mind distracted." As used at Matthew 6:25, it refers to worried fear that distracts or divides the mind, taking the joy out of life.

In fact, scientific research has shown that excessive worry and stress can put us at risk of cardiovascular disease and a host of other ailments that can shorten life.

6-8. (a) What compelling reasons for avoiding anxiety does Jesus give? (b) What shows that Jesus' counsel reflects wisdom from above?

[8] Clearly, the counsel Jesus provided is as practical today as it was when it was given nearly 2,000 years ago. Is that not evidence of wisdom from above? Even the best advice from human counselors tends to become outdated and is soon revised or replaced. The teachings of Jesus, however, have stood the test of time. But that should not surprise us, for this Wonderful Counselor spoke "the sayings of God." —John 3:34.

His Manner of Teaching

[9] A second area in which Jesus reflected God's wisdom was his manner of teaching. On one occasion, some soldiers who had been sent to arrest him returned empty-handed, saying: "Never has another man spoken like this." (John 7: 45, 46) This was no exaggeration. Of all the humans who have ever lived, Jesus, who was "from the realms above," had the greatest reservoir of knowledge and experience from which to draw. (John 8:23) He truly taught as no other human could teach. Consider just two of the methods of this wise Teacher.

[10] *Effective use of illustrations.* "Jesus spoke to the crowds by illustrations," we are told. "Indeed, without an illustration he would not speak to them." (Matthew 13:34) We cannot help but marvel at his matchless ability to teach profound truths through everyday things. Farmers planting seeds, women preparing to bake bread, children playing in the marketplace, fishermen hauling in nets, shepherds searching for lost sheep—these were things his listeners had seen many times. When important truths are tied in with familiar things, such truths are etched quickly

---

9. What did some soldiers say about Jesus' teaching, and why was this no exaggeration?
10, 11. (a) Why can we not help but marvel at Jesus' use of illustrations? (b) What are parables, and what example shows why Jesus' parables are so effective for teaching?

and deeply on the mind and heart.—Matthew 11:16-19; 13:
3-8, 33, 47-50; 18:12-14.

11 Jesus often used parables, short stories from which
moral or spiritual truths are drawn. Since stories are easier to grasp and remember than abstract ideas, the parables
helped to preserve Jesus' teaching. In many parables, Jesus
described his Father with vivid word pictures that could
not easily be forgotten. For example, who cannot comprehend the point of the parable of the prodigal son—that
when one who has gone astray shows genuine repentance,
Jehovah will feel pity and tenderly accept that one back?
—Luke 15:11-32.

12 *Skillful use of questions.* Jesus used questions to get his
listeners to arrive at their own conclusions, examine their
motives, or make decisions. (Matthew 12:24-30; 17:24-27;
22:41-46) When the religious leaders questioned whether
he had God-given authority, Jesus replied: "Was the baptism by John from heaven or from men?" Stunned by
the question, they reasoned among themselves: "If we say,
'From heaven,' he will say to us, 'Why, then, did you not
believe him?' If, though, we say, 'From men,' we have the
crowd to fear, for they all hold John as a prophet." Finally,
they answered: "We do not know." (Mark 11:27-33; Matthew 21:23-27) With a simple question, Jesus left them
speechless and revealed the treachery in their hearts.

13 Jesus sometimes combined methods by weaving
thought-provoking questions into his illustrations. When
a Jewish lawyer asked Jesus what was required to gain everlasting life, Jesus referred him to the Mosaic Law, which
commands love of God and neighbor. Wanting to prove

----

12. (a) In what way did Jesus use questions in his teaching? (b) How
did Jesus silence those who questioned his authority?
13-15. How does the parable of the neighborly Samaritan reflect the
wisdom of Jesus?

himself righteous, the man asked: "Who really is my neighbor?" Jesus answered by telling a story. A certain Jewish man was traveling alone when he was assaulted by robbers, who left him half dead. Along came two Jews, first a priest and then a Levite. Both ignored him. But then a certain Samaritan came upon the scene. Moved with pity, he gently dressed the victim's wounds and lovingly carried the man to the safety of an inn where he could recover. Concluding the story, Jesus asked his inquirer: "Who of these three seems to you to have made himself neighbor to the man that fell among the robbers?" The man was compelled to answer: "The one that acted mercifully toward him."—Luke 10:25-37.

¹⁴ How does the parable reflect the wisdom of Jesus? In Jesus' day, the Jews applied the term "neighbor" only to those who kept their traditions—certainly not to Samaritans. (John 4:9) Had Jesus told the story with a Samaritan victim and a Jewish helper, would that have overturned the prejudice? Jesus wisely framed the story so that a Samaritan tenderly cared for a Jew. Notice, too, the question Jesus asked at the end of the story. He shifted the focus of the term "neighbor." The lawyer had, in effect, asked: 'Who should be the object of my neighborly love?' But Jesus asked: "Who of these three seems to you to have made himself neighbor?" Jesus focused, not on the one who *received* the kindness, the victim, but on the one who *showed* the kindness, the Samaritan. A true neighbor takes the initiative to show love to others regardless of their ethnic background. Jesus could hardly have made his point more effectively.

¹⁵ Is it any wonder that people were astounded at Jesus' "way of teaching" and were drawn to him? (Matthew 7:28, 29) On one occasion "a big crowd" remained near him for three days, even going without food!—Mark 8:1, 2.

His Way of Life

¹⁶ A third area in which Jesus reflected Jehovah's wisdom was his manner of life. Wisdom is practical; it works. "Who among you is wise?" asked the disciple James. Then he answered his own question, saying: "Let his right conduct give practical proof of it." (James 3:13, *The New English Bible*) The way Jesus conducted himself gave "practical proof" that he was governed by divine wisdom. Let us consider how he demonstrated sound judgment, both in his way of life and in his dealings with others.

¹⁷ Have you noticed that people who lack good judgment often go to extremes? Yes, it takes wisdom to be balanced. Reflecting godly wisdom, Jesus had perfect balance. Above all else, he gave spiritual things first place in his life. He was intensely occupied with the work of declaring the good news. "It is for this purpose I have gone out," he said. (Mark 1:38) Naturally, material things were not of primary importance to him; it seems that he had very little materially. (Matthew 8:20) However, he was not an ascetic. Like his Father, "the happy God," Jesus was a joyful person, and he added to the joy of others. (1 Timothy 1:11; 6:15) When he attended a wedding feast—typically an event marked by music, singing, and rejoicing—he was not there to cast a pall over the occasion. When the wine ran out, he turned water into fine wine, a beverage that "makes the heart of mortal man rejoice." (Psalm 104:15; John 2:1-11) Jesus accepted many invitations to meals, and he often used such occasions to teach. —Luke 10:38-42; 14:1-6.

---

16. In what way did Jesus give "practical proof" that he was governed by divine wisdom?
17. What indications are there that Jesus had perfect balance in his life?

Questions for Meditation

Proverbs 8:22-31 How does the description of wisdom personified match what the Bible says about Jehovah's firstborn Son?

Matthew 13:10-15 How were Jesus' illustrations effective in revealing the heart attitude of his listeners?

John 1:9-18 Why was Jesus able to reveal the wisdom of God?

John 13:2-5, 12-17 How did Jesus employ an object lesson, and what did he thereby teach his apostles?

---

¹⁸ Jesus manifested flawless judgment in his dealings with others. His insight into human nature gave him a clear-sighted view of his disciples. He well knew that they were not perfect. Yet, he discerned their good qualities. He saw the potential in these men whom Jehovah had drawn. (John 6:44) Despite their shortcomings, Jesus showed a willingness to trust them. Demonstrating that trust, he delegated a heavy responsibility to his disciples. He commissioned them to preach the good news, and he had confidence in their ability to fulfill that commission. (Matthew 28:19, 20) The book of Acts testifies that they faithfully followed through on the work he had commanded them to do. (Acts 2:41, 42; 4:33; 5:27-32) Clearly, then, Jesus had been wise to trust them.

¹⁹ As we noted in Chapter 20, the Bible associates humility and mildness with wisdom. Jehovah, of course, sets the best example in this regard. But what about Jesus? It is heartwarming to see the humility Jesus showed in dealing with his disciples. As a perfect man, he was superior to

---

18. How did Jesus manifest flawless judgment in his dealings with his disciples?
19. How did Jesus demonstrate that he was "mild-tempered and lowly in heart"?

them. Yet, he did not look down on his disciples. Never did he seek to make them feel inferior or incompetent. On the contrary, he was considerate of their limitations and patient with their shortcomings. (Mark 14:34-38; John 16:12) Is it not significant that even children felt at ease with Jesus? Surely they felt drawn to him because they sensed that he was "mild-tempered and lowly in heart."—Matthew 11:29; Mark 10:13-16.

20 Jesus showed godly humility in yet another important way. He was reasonable, or yielding, when mercy made this proper. Recall, for example, the time when a Gentile woman begged him to cure her badly demonized daughter. In three different ways, Jesus initially indicated that he was not going to help her—first, by refraining from answering her; second, by stating directly that he had been sent forth, not to the Gentiles, but to the Jews; and third, by giving an illustration that kindly made the same point. However, the woman persisted, giving evidence of extraordinary faith. In the light of this exceptional circumstance, how did Jesus respond? He did exactly what he had indicated he would not do. He cured the woman's daughter. (Matthew 15:21-28) Remarkable humility, is it not? And remember, humility is at the root of genuine wisdom.

21 How thankful we can be that the Gospels reveal to us the words and actions of the wisest man who ever lived! Let us remember that Jesus was a perfect reflection of his Father. By imitating the personality, speech, and ways of Jesus, we will be cultivating the wisdom from above. In the next chapter, we will see how we can put godly wisdom to work in our life.

---

20. How did Jesus display reasonableness in dealing with the Gentile woman whose daughter was demonized?
21. Why should we endeavor to imitate the personality, speech, and ways of Jesus?

CHAPTER 22

Is "the Wisdom From Above" at Work in Your Life?

IT WAS a difficult case—two women arguing over a baby. The women shared a home, and each had given birth to a son, just days apart. One of the babies had died, and now each woman claimed to be the mother of the living baby.* There were no other witnesses to what had happened. The case had likely been heard in a lower court but not resolved. Finally, the dispute was taken to Solomon, the king of Israel. Would he be able to uncover the truth?

2 After listening for a while as the women argued, Solomon called for a sword. Then, with seeming conviction, he ordered that the child be cut in two, with half given to each woman. At once, the real mother pleaded with the king to give the baby—her precious child—to the other woman. But the other woman kept insisting that the child be cut in two. Solomon now knew the truth. He had knowledge of a mother's tender compassion for the child of her womb, and he used that knowledge to settle this dispute. Imagine the mother's relief when Solomon awarded her the baby and said: "She is his mother." —1 Kings 3:16-27.

3 Extraordinary wisdom, was it not? When the people

---

* According to 1 Kings 3:16, the two women were prostitutes. *Insight on the Scriptures* states: "These women may have been prostitutes, not in a commercial sense, but women who had committed fornication, either Jewish women or, quite possibly, women of foreign descent."—Published by Jehovah's Witnesses.

1-3. (a) How did Solomon display extraordinary wisdom in the way he handled a maternity dispute? (b) What does Jehovah promise to give us, and what questions arise?

heard how Solomon had resolved the case, they were in awe, "for they saw that the wisdom of God was within him." Yes, Solomon's wisdom was a divine gift. Jehovah had given him "a wise and understanding heart." (1 Kings 3:12, 28) But what about us? May we too receive godly wisdom? Yes, for under inspiration, Solomon wrote: "Jehovah himself gives wisdom." (Proverbs 2:6) Jehovah promises to give wisdom—the ability to put knowledge, understanding, and discernment to good use—to those who sincerely seek it. How may we acquire wisdom from above? And how can we put it to work in our life?

"Acquire Wisdom"—How?

⁴ Must we have great intelligence or be highly educated in order to receive godly wisdom? No. Jehovah is willing to share his wisdom with us regardless of our background and education. (1 Corinthians 1:26-29) But we must take the initiative, for the Bible urges us to "acquire wisdom." (Proverbs 4:7) How can we do so?

⁵ First, we need to fear God. "The fear of Jehovah is the start of wisdom ["the first step to wisdom," *The New English Bible*]," says Proverbs 9:10. Fear of God is the foundation of true wisdom. Why? Recall that wisdom involves the ability to use knowledge successfully. To fear God is, not to cower before him in terror, but to bow before him in awe, respect, and trust. Such fear is wholesome and powerfully motivating. It moves us to bring our life into harmony with our knowledge of God's will and ways. There is no wiser course that we could take, for Jehovah's standards always promote the highest good for those who follow them.

⁶ Second, we must be humble and modest. Godly wis-

4-7. What are four requirements for acquiring wisdom?

dom cannot exist without humility and modesty. (Proverbs 11:2) Why is that? If we are humble and modest, we are willing to admit that we do not have all the answers, that our opinions are not always right, and that we need to know Jehovah's mind on matters. Jehovah "opposes the haughty ones," but he is pleased to grant wisdom to those who are humble at heart.—James 4:6.

⁷ A third essential is the study of God's written Word. Jehovah's wisdom is revealed in his Word. To acquire that wisdom, we must put forth the effort to dig for it. (Proverbs 2:1-5) A fourth requirement is prayer. If we sincerely ask God for wisdom, he will be generous in giving it. (James 1:5) Our prayers for the help of his spirit will not go unanswered. And his spirit can enable us to find the treasures in his Word that can help us to solve problems, ward off danger, and make wise decisions.—Luke 11:13.

⁸ As we noted in Chapter 17, Jehovah's wisdom is practical. Hence, if we have truly acquired godly wisdom, it will be evident in the way we conduct ourselves. The disciple James described the fruits of divine wisdom when he wrote: "The wisdom from above is first of all chaste, then peaceable, reasonable, ready to obey, full of mercy and good fruits, not making partial distinctions, not hypocritical." (James 3:17) As we discuss each of these aspects of divine wisdom, we might ask ourselves, 'Is the wisdom from above at work in my life?'

"Chaste, Then Peaceable"

⁹ *"First of all chaste."* To be chaste means to be pure and undefiled not just outwardly but inwardly. The Bible associates wisdom with the heart, but heavenly wisdom

---

8. If we have truly acquired godly wisdom, how will it be evident?
9. What does it mean to be chaste, and why is it fitting that chasteness is the first quality of wisdom listed?

cannot enter into a heart that is defiled by wicked thoughts, desires, and motives. (Proverbs 2:10; Matthew 15:19, 20) However, if our heart is chaste—that is, as far as is possible for imperfect humans—we will "turn away from what is bad and do what is good." (Psalm 37:27; Proverbs 3:7) Is it not fitting that chasteness is the first quality of wisdom listed? After all, if we are not morally and spiritually clean, how can we truly reflect the other qualities of the wisdom from above?

10 *"Then peaceable."* Heavenly wisdom moves us to pursue peace, which is a fruit of God's spirit. (Galatians 5:22) We strive to avoid disrupting the "bond of peace" that unites Jehovah's people. (Ephesians 4:3) We also do our best to restore peace when it is disturbed. Why is this important? The Bible says: "Continue . . . to live peaceably; and the God of love and of peace will be with you." (2 Corinthians 13:11) So as long as we continue to live peaceably, the God of peace will be with us. The way we treat fellow worshipers has a direct bearing on our relationship with Jehovah. How can we prove ourselves to be peacemakers? Consider an example.

11 What should you do if you sense that you have offended a fellow worshiper? Jesus said: "If, then, you are bringing your gift to the altar and you there remember that your brother has something against you, leave your gift there in front of the altar, and go away; first make your peace with your brother, and then, when you have come back, offer up your gift." (Matthew 5:23, 24) You can apply that counsel by taking the initiative to go to your brother. With what objective? To "make your peace" with

___

10, 11. (a) Why is it important that we be peaceable? (b) If you sense that you have offended a fellow worshiper, how can you prove yourself to be a peacemaker? (See also footnote.)

*To acquire godly wisdom, we must
put forth effort to dig for it*

him.* To that end, you may need to acknowledge, not
deny, his hurt feelings. If you approach him with the goal
of restoring peace and maintain that attitude, likely any
misunderstanding can be cleared up, appropriate apolo-
gies made, and forgiveness extended. When you go out of
your way to make peace, you show that you are guided by
godly wisdom.

"Reasonable, Ready to Obey"

12 *"Reasonable."* What does it mean to be reasonable?
According to scholars, the original Greek word rendered

---

* The Greek expression rendered "make your peace" comes from a
verb that means " 'to effect an alteration, to exchange,' and hence, 'to
reconcile.' " So your goal is to effect a change, to remove, if possible,
ill will from the offended one's heart.—Romans 12:18.

12, 13. (a) What is the meaning of the word rendered "reasonable"
at James 3:17? (b) How can we demonstrate that we are reasonable?

"reasonable" at James 3:17 is difficult to translate. Translators have used such words as "gentle," "forbearing," and "considerate." A footnote in the *New World Translation* indicates that the literal meaning is "yielding." How can we demonstrate that this aspect of the wisdom from above is at work in us?

¹³ "Let your reasonableness become known to all men," says Philippians 4:5. Another translation reads: "Have a reputation for being reasonable." (*The New Testament in Modern English,* by J. B. Phillips) Notice that it is not so much a question of how we see ourselves; it is a question of how others see us, of how we are known. A reasonable person does not always insist on the letter of the law or on having his own way. Instead, he is willing to listen to others and, when appropriate, to yield to their wishes. He is also gentle, not rough or harsh, in his dealings with others. While this is essential for all Christians, it is especially important for those serving as elders. Gentleness attracts, making elders approachable. (1 Thessalonians 2:7, 8) We all do well to ask ourselves, 'Do I have a reputation for being considerate, yielding, and gentle?'

¹⁴ *"Ready to obey."* The Greek word rendered "ready to obey" is not found elsewhere in the Christian Greek Scriptures. According to one scholar, this word "is often used of military discipline." It conveys the idea of "easy to be persuaded" and "submissive." One who is governed by the wisdom from above readily submits to what the Scriptures say. He is not known as one who makes up his mind and then refuses to be influenced by any facts that contradict him. Rather, he is quick to change when he is presented with clear Scriptural evidence that he has taken a wrong stand or has drawn erroneous conclusions. Is that how you are known by others?

---

14. How can we demonstrate that we are "ready to obey"?

"Full of Mercy and Good Fruits"

15 *"Full of mercy and good fruits."** Mercy is an important part of the wisdom from above, for such wisdom is said to be *"full* of mercy." Notice that "mercy" and "good fruits" are mentioned together. This is fitting, for in the Bible, mercy most often refers to an active concern for others, a compassion that produces a rich crop of kindly deeds. One reference work defines mercy as "a feeling of sorrow over someone's bad situation and trying to do something about it." Hence, godly wisdom is not dry, heartless, or merely intellectual. Instead, it is warm, heartfelt, and sensitive. How can we show that we are full of mercy?

16 Surely an important way is by sharing the good news of God's Kingdom with others. What motivates us to do this work? Primarily, it is love for God. But we are also motivated by mercy, or compassion for others. (Matthew 22: 37-39) Many today are "skinned and thrown about like sheep without a shepherd." (Matthew 9:36) They have been neglected and blinded spiritually by false religious shepherds. As a result, they do not know of the wise guidance found in God's Word or of the blessings that the Kingdom will soon bring to this earth. When we thus ponder the spiritual needs of those around us, our heartfelt compassion moves us to do all we can to tell them of Jehovah's loving purpose.

17 In what other ways can we show that we are full

---

* Another translation renders these words "full of compassion and good deeds."—*A Translation in the Language of the People,* by Charles B. Williams.

---

15. What is mercy, and why is it fitting that "mercy" and "good fruits" are mentioned together at James 3:17?
16, 17. (a) In addition to love for God, what motivates us to share in the preaching work, and why? (b) In what ways can we show that we are full of mercy?

of mercy? Recall Jesus' illustration of the Samaritan who found a traveler lying by the roadside, robbed and beaten. Moved with compassion, the Samaritan "acted mercifully," binding the victim's wounds and caring for him. (Luke 10:29-37) Does this not illustrate that mercy involves offering practical help to those in need? The Bible tells us to "work what is good toward all, but especially toward those related to us in the faith." (Galatians 6:10) Consider some possibilities. An older fellow believer may need transportation to and from Christian meetings. A widow in the congregation may need help with repairs on her home. (James 1:27) A discouraged one may need a "good word" to cheer him up. (Proverbs 12:25) When we show mercy in such ways, we give proof that the wisdom from above is at work in us.

"Not Making Partial Distinctions, Not Hypocritical"

[18] *"Not making partial distinctions."* Godly wisdom rises above racial prejudice and national pride. If we are guided by such wisdom, we endeavor to root out of our hearts any tendency to show favoritism. (James 2:9) We do not give preferential treatment to others on the basis of their educational background, financial standing, or congregational responsibility; nor do we look down on any of our fellow worshipers, regardless of how lowly they may seem to be. If Jehovah has made such ones recipients of *his* love, we should certainly deem them worthy of *our* love.

[19] *"Not hypocritical."* The Greek word for "hypocrite" can

---

18. If we are guided by the wisdom from above, what must we endeavor to root out of our hearts, and why?

19, 20. (a) What is the background of the Greek word for "hypocrite"? (b) How do we demonstrate "unhypocritical brotherly affection," and why is this important?

When we show mercy, or compassion, to others, we reflect "the wisdom from above"

refer to "an actor who played a role." In ancient times, Greek and Roman actors wore large masks when performing. Hence, the Greek word for "hypocrite" came to apply to one putting on a pretense, or one playing false. This aspect of godly wisdom should influence not just how we treat fellow worshipers but also how we feel about them.

²⁰ The apostle Peter noted that our "obedience to the truth" should result in "unhypocritical brotherly affection." (1 Peter 1:22) Yes, our affection for our brothers must not be put on for show. We do not wear masks or play roles in order to deceive others. Our affection must be genuine, heartfelt. If it is, we will earn the trust of our fellow believers, for they will know that we are what we appear to be. Such sincerity paves the way for open and honest relationships between Christians and helps to create a trusting atmosphere in the congregation.

Questions for Meditation

Deuteronomy 4:4-6 How do we prove ourselves wise?

Psalm 119:97-105 How will we benefit if we diligently study and apply God's Word?

Proverbs 4:10-13, 20-27 Why do we need Jehovah's wisdom?

James 3:1-16 How can those entrusted with oversight in the congregation show that they are wise and understanding?

"Safeguard Practical Wisdom"

²¹ Godly wisdom is a gift from Jehovah, one that we should safeguard. Solomon said: "My son, . . . safeguard practical wisdom and thinking ability." (Proverbs 3:21) Sadly, Solomon himself failed to do that. He remained wise as long as he kept an obedient heart. But in the end, his many foreign wives turned his heart away from the pure worship of Jehovah. (1 Kings 11:1-8) Solomon's outcome illustrates that knowledge is of little value if we do not put it to good use.

²² How can we safeguard practical wisdom? Not only must we regularly read the Bible and the Bible-based publications provided by "the faithful and discreet slave" but we must also endeavor to apply what we learn. (Matthew 24:45) We have every reason to apply divine wisdom. It means a better way of life now. It enables us to "get a firm hold on the real life"—life in God's new world. (1 Timothy 6:19) And most important, cultivating the wisdom from above draws us closer to the source of all wisdom, Jehovah God.

21, 22. (a) How did Solomon fail to safeguard wisdom? (b) How can we safeguard wisdom, and how will we benefit from doing so?

"GOD IS LOVE"

Of all the qualities that Jehovah possesses, love is the dominant one. It is also the most appealing. As we examine some of the beautiful facets of this gemlike quality, we will come to see why the Bible says that "God is love."
—*1 John 4:8.*

CHAPTER 23

"He First Loved Us"

ON A spring day nearly 2,000 years ago, an innocent man was tried, convicted of crimes he had never committed, and then tortured to death. It was not the first cruel and unjust execution in history; nor, sadly, was it the last. Yet, that death was unlike any other.

2 As that man suffered through his final, agonizing hours, heaven itself marked the significance of the event. Though it was the middle of the day, darkness suddenly descended on the land. As one historian put it, "the sunlight failed." (Luke 23:44, 45) Then, just before the man breathed his last, he said these unforgettable words: "It has been accomplished!" Indeed, by laying down his life, he accomplished something wonderful. His sacrifice was the greatest act of love ever performed by any human. —John 15:13; 19:30.

3 That man, of course, was Jesus Christ. His suffering and death on that dark day, Nisan 14, 33 C.E., are well-known. However, an important fact has often been ignored. Though Jesus suffered intensely, someone else suffered even more. In fact, someone else made an even greater sacrifice that day—the greatest act of love ever performed by anyone in the universe. What act was that? The answer provides a fitting introduction to the most important of subjects: Jehovah's love.

1-3. What are some factors that made Jesus' death unlike any other in history?

"God . . . gave his only-begotten Son"

The Greatest Act of Love

⁴ The Roman centurion who supervised the execution of Jesus was astonished both by the darkness that preceded Jesus' death and by the violent earthquake that followed it. "Certainly this was God's Son," he said. (Matthew 27: 54) Clearly, Jesus was no ordinary man. That soldier had helped to execute the only-begotten Son of the Most High God! Just how dear was this Son to his Father?

⁵ The Bible calls Jesus "the firstborn of all creation." (Colossians 1:15) Just think—Jehovah's Son was in existence before the physical universe. How long, then, were Father and Son together? Some scientists estimate that the universe is 13 billion years old. Can you even imagine that much time? To help people grasp the age of the universe as estimated by scientists, one planetarium features a time line 360 feet long. As visitors walk along that time line, each step they take represents about 75 million years in the life of the universe. At the end of the time line, all human history is represented by a single mark the thickness of one human hair! Yet, even if this estimate is correct, that *entire* time line would not be long enough to represent the life span of Jehovah's Son! How was he occupied during all those ages?

⁶ The Son happily served as his Father's "master worker." (Proverbs 8:30) The Bible says: "Apart from [the Son] not even one thing came into existence." (John 1:3) So Jehovah and his Son worked together to bring all other things into being. What thrilling, happy times they had! Now, many will agree that the love between parent and

---

4. How did a Roman soldier come to see that Jesus was no ordinary man, and what did that soldier conclude?
5. How might the vast amount of time that Jehovah and his Son spent together in heaven be illustrated?
6. (a) How was Jehovah's Son occupied during his prehuman existence? (b) What kind of bond exists between Jehovah and his Son?

child is amazingly strong. And love "is a perfect bond of union." (Colossians 3:14) Who of us, then, can begin to fathom the power of a bond that has existed over such an immense span of time? Clearly, Jehovah God and his Son are united by the strongest bond of love ever forged.

[7] Nevertheless, the Father dispatched his Son to the earth to be born as a human baby. Doing so meant that for some decades, Jehovah had to forgo intimate association with his beloved Son in heaven. With intense interest, He watched from heaven as Jesus grew up to be a perfect man. At about 30 years of age, Jesus got baptized. We do not have to guess how Jehovah felt about him. The Father spoke personally from heaven: "This is my Son, the beloved, whom I have approved." (Matthew 3:17) Seeing that Jesus faithfully did all that had been prophesied, all that was asked of him, his Father must have been so pleased!—John 5:36; 17:4.

[8] How, though, did Jehovah feel on Nisan 14, 33 C.E.? How did he feel as Jesus was betrayed and then arrested by a mob in the night? As Jesus was deserted by his friends and subjected to an illegal trial? As he was ridiculed, spat upon, and struck with fists? As he was scourged, his back torn to ribbons? As he was nailed, hands and feet, to a wooden pole and left to hang there while people reviled him? How did the Father feel as his beloved Son cried out to him in the throes of agony? How did Jehovah feel as Jesus breathed his last, and for the first time since the dawn of all creation, His dear Son was not in existence?—Matthew 26:14-16, 46, 47, 56, 59, 67; 27:38-44, 46; John 19:1.

[9] Words fail us. Since Jehovah has feelings, the pain he

---

7. When Jesus got baptized, how did Jehovah express his feelings about his Son?

8, 9. (a) What was Jesus put through on Nisan 14, 33 C.E., and how was his heavenly Father affected? (b) Why did Jehovah allow his Son to suffer and die?

suffered over the death of his Son is beyond the power of our words to express. What *can* be expressed is Jehovah's motive for having allowed it to happen. Why
did the Father subject himself to such feelings? Jehovah
reveals something wonderful to us at John 3:16—a Bible
verse so important that it has been called the Gospel in
miniature. It says: "God loved the world so much that he
gave his only-begotten Son, in order that everyone exercising faith in him might not be destroyed but have everlasting life." So Jehovah's motive amounted to this: love.
Jehovah's gift—his sending his Son to suffer and die for
us—was the greatest act of love ever.

Divine Love Defined

[10] What does this word "love" mean? Love has been described as the greatest need humans have. From the cradle
to the grave, people strive after love, thrive in its warmth,
even pine away and die for lack of it. Nonetheless, it is sur-
prisingly difficult to define. Of course, people talk a lot
about love. There is an endless stream of books, songs,
and poems about it. The results do not always clarify the
meaning of love. If anything, the word is so overused that
its true meaning seems ever more elusive.

[11] The Bible, however, teaches with clarity about love.
Vine's *Expository Dictionary of New Testament Words*
notes: "Love can be known only from the actions it
prompts." The Bible record of Jehovah's actions teaches
us a great deal about his love—the benevolent affection
he has for his creatures. For example, what could reveal

---

10. Humans have what need, and what has happened to the meaning of the word "love"?
11, 12. (a) Where can we learn a great deal about love, and why
there? (b) What types of love were specified in the ancient Greek language, and what word for "love" was used most often in the Christian
Greek Scriptures? (See also footnote.) (c) What is *a·ga'pe?*

more about this quality than Jehovah's own supreme act of love described earlier? In the chapters to follow, we will see many other examples of Jehovah's love in action. Additionally, we can gain some insight from the original words for "love" used in the Bible. In the ancient Greek tongue, there were four words for "love."* Of these, the one used most often in the Christian Greek Scriptures is *a·ga'pe*. One Bible dictionary calls this "the most powerful word imaginable for love." Why?

¹² *A·ga'pe* refers to love that is guided by principle. So it is more than just an emotional response to another person. It is broader in scope, more thoughtful and deliberate in its basis. Above all, *a·ga'pe* is utterly unselfish. For example, look again at John 3:16. What is "the world" that God loved so much that he gave his only-begotten Son? It is the world of redeemable mankind. That includes many people who are pursuing a sinful course in life. Does Jehovah love each one as a personal friend, the way he loved faithful Abraham? (James 2:23) No, but Jehovah lovingly extends goodness toward all, even at great cost to himself. He wants all to repent and change their ways. (2 Peter 3:9) Many do. These he happily receives as his friends.

¹³ Some, though, have the wrong idea about *a·ga'pe*. They think that it means a cold, intellectual type of love. The fact is that *a·ga'pe* often includes warm personal affection. For example, when John wrote, "The Father loves the Son," he used a form of the word *a·ga'pe*. Is that

---

* The verb *phi·le'o*, meaning "to have affection for, to be fond of, or to like (as one might feel about a close friend or a brother)," is used often in the Christian Greek Scriptures. A form of the word *stor·ge'*, or close familial love, is used at 2 Timothy 3:3 to show that such love would be sorely lacking during the last days. *E'ros*, or romantic love between the sexes, is not used in the Christian Greek Scriptures, although that type of love is discussed in the Bible.—Proverbs 5:15-20.

13, 14. What shows that *a·ga'pe* often includes warm affection?

love devoid of warm affection? Note that Jesus said, "The Father has affection for the Son," using a form of the word *phi·le'o.* (John 3:35; 5:20) Jehovah's love often includes tender affection. However, his love is never swayed by mere sentiment. It is always guided by his wise and just principles.

¹⁴ As we have seen, all of Jehovah's qualities are sterling, perfect, and appealing. But love is the most appealing of all. Nothing draws us so powerfully to Jehovah. Happily, love is also his dominant quality. How do we know that?

"God Is Love"

¹⁵ The Bible says something about love that it never says about Jehovah's other cardinal attributes. The Scriptures do not say that God is power or that God is justice or even that God is wisdom. He *possesses* those qualities, is the ultimate source of them, and is beyond comparison in regard to all three. About the fourth attribute, though, something more profound is said: "God is love."* (1 John 4:8) What does that mean?

¹⁶ "God is love" is not a simple equation, as if to say, "God equals love." We cannot rightly reverse the statement and say that "love is God." Jehovah is much more than an abstract quality. He is a person with a wide array

---

* Other Scriptural statements have a comparable structure. For example, "God is light" and "God is . . . a consuming fire." (1 John 1:5; Hebrews 12:29) But these must be understood as metaphors, for they liken Jehovah to physical things. Jehovah is *like* light, for he is holy and upright. There is no "darkness," or uncleanness, in him. And he may be likened to fire for his use of destructive power.

---

15. What statement does the Bible make about Jehovah's attribute of love, and in what way is this statement unique? (See also footnote.) 16-18. (a) Why does the Bible say that "God is love"? (b) Of all the creatures on earth, why is man a fitting symbol of Jehovah's attribute of love?

of feelings and characteristics in addition to love. Yet, love runs very deep in Jehovah. One reference work thus says regarding this verse: "God's essence or nature is love." Generally, we might think of it this way: Jehovah's power *enables* him to act. His justice and his wisdom *guide* the way he acts. But Jehovah's love *motivates* him to act. And his love is always present in the way he uses his other attributes.

¹⁷ It is often said that Jehovah is the very personification of love. Hence, if we want to learn about principled love, we must learn about Jehovah. Of course, we may see this beautiful quality in humans as well. But why is it there? At the time of creation, Jehovah spoke these words, evidently to his Son: "Let us make man in our image, according to our likeness." (Genesis 1:26) Of all the creatures on this earth, only men and women can choose to love and thus imitate their heavenly Father. Recall that Jehovah used various creatures to symbolize his cardinal attributes. Yet, Jehovah chose his highest earthly creation, man, as the symbol of His dominant quality, love.—Ezekiel 1:10.

¹⁸ When we love in an unselfish, principled way, we are reflecting Jehovah's dominant quality. It is just as the apostle John wrote: "As for us, we love, because he first loved us." (1 John 4:19) But in what ways has Jehovah loved us first?

Jehovah Took the Initiative

¹⁹ Love is not new. After all, what moved Jehovah to begin creating? It was not that he was lonely and needed companionship. Jehovah is complete and self-contained, lacking nothing that someone else might supply. But his love, an active quality, naturally moved him to want to

---

19. Why might it be said that love played a key role in Jehovah's creative work?

share the joys of life with intelligent creatures who could appreciate such a gift. "The beginning of the creation by God" was his only-begotten Son. (Revelation 3:14) Then Jehovah used this Master Worker to bring all other things into existence, starting with the angels. (Job 38:4, 7; Colossians 1:16) Blessed with freedom, intelligence, and feelings, these mighty spirits had the opportunity to form loving attachments of their own—with one another and, above all, with Jehovah God. (2 Corinthians 3:17) Thus, they loved because they were loved first.

20 So it was with mankind as well. From the start, Adam and Eve were virtually bathed in love. Everywhere they looked in their Paradise home in Eden, they could see evidence of the Father's love for them. Note what the Bible says: "Jehovah God planted a garden in Eden, toward the east, and there he put the man whom he had formed." (Genesis 2:8) Have you ever been in a truly beautiful garden or park? What pleased you most? The light filtering through the leaves in a shady alcove? The stunning array of colors in a bed of flowers? The background music of a gurgling brook, singing birds, and humming insects? What about the scents of trees, fruits, and blossoms? In any case, no park today could compare with the one in Eden. Why?

21 That garden was planted by Jehovah himself! It must have been indescribably lovely. Every tree delightful for beauty or for delicious fruit was there. The garden was well watered, spacious, and alive with a fascinating variety of animals. Adam and Eve had everything to make their lives happy and full, including rewarding work and perfect companionship. Jehovah first loved them, and they had every reason to respond in kind. Yet, they failed to do

20, 21. Adam and Eve were exposed to what evidence that Jehovah loved them, yet how did they respond?

Questions for Meditation

Psalm 63:1-11 What value should we place on Jehovah's love, and what confidence can that love build in us?

Hosea 11:1-4; 14:4-8 In what ways did Jehovah show fatherly love toward Israel (or, Ephraim), despite what record of disobedience?

Matthew 5:43-48 How does Jehovah show fatherly love toward mankind in general?

John 17:15-26 How does Jesus' prayer in behalf of his followers assure us of Jehovah's love for us?

so. Instead of lovingly obeying their heavenly Father, they selfishly rebelled against him.—Genesis, chapter 2.

²² How painful that must have been for Jehovah! But did this rebellion embitter his loving heart? No! "His loving-kindness [or, "loyal love," footnote] is to time indefinite." (Psalm 136:1) Thus, he immediately purposed to make loving provisions to redeem any rightly disposed offspring of Adam and Eve. As we have seen, those provisions included the ransom sacrifice of his beloved Son, which cost the Father so dearly.—1 John 4:10.

²³ Yes, from the beginning Jehovah has taken the initiative in showing love to mankind. In countless ways, "he first loved us." Love promotes harmony and joy, so it is no wonder that Jehovah is described as "the happy God." (1 Timothy 1:11) However, an important question arises. Does Jehovah really love us as individuals? The next chapter will address that matter.

---

22. How did Jehovah's response to the rebellion in Eden prove that his love is loyal?
23. What is one of the reasons that Jehovah is "the happy God," and what vital question will be addressed in the next chapter?

CHAPTER 24

Nothing Can "Separate Us From God's Love"

DOES Jehovah God love you personally? Some agree that God loves mankind in general, as John 3:16 says. But they feel, in effect: 'God could never love *me* as an individual.' Even true Christians may occasionally have doubts in that respect. Discouraged, one man said: "I find it very difficult to believe that God cares anything about me." Do similar doubts afflict you at times?

² Satan is eager for us to believe that Jehovah God neither loves us nor values us. True, Satan often seduces people by appealing to their vanity and pride. (2 Corinthians 11:3) But he also delights in crushing the self-respect of vulnerable ones. (John 7:47-49; 8:13, 44) This is particularly so in these critical "last days." Many today grow up in families where there is "no natural affection." Others are constantly exposed to those who are fierce, selfish, and headstrong. (2 Timothy 3:1-5) Years of being subjected to ill-treatment, racism, or hatred may have convinced such ones that they are worthless or unlovable.

³ If you sense such negative feelings in yourself, do not despair. Many of us are unreasonably hard on ourselves from time to time. But remember, God's Word is designed for "setting things straight" and for "overturning strongly entrenched things." (2 Timothy 3:16; 2 Corinthians 10:4) The Bible says: "We shall assure our hearts before him as regards whatever our hearts may condemn

---

1. What negative feeling afflicts many people, including some true Christians?
2, 3. Who wants us to believe that we are worthless or unlovable in Jehovah's eyes, and how can we combat that notion?

us in, because God is greater than our hearts and knows all things." (1 John 3:19, 20) Let us consider four ways in which the Scriptures help us to "assure our hearts" of Jehovah's love.

Jehovah Values You

4 First, the Bible directly teaches that God sees worth in each of his servants. For example, Jesus said: "Do not two sparrows sell for a coin of small value? Yet not one of them will fall to the ground without your Father's knowledge. But the very hairs of your head are all numbered. Therefore have no fear: you are worth more than many sparrows." (Matthew 10:29-31) Consider what those words meant to Jesus' first-century listeners.

5 We may wonder why anyone would buy a sparrow. Well, in Jesus' day the sparrow was the cheapest of the birds sold as food. Notice that for one coin of small value, a purchaser got two sparrows. But Jesus later stated that if a person was prepared to spend two coins, he got, not four sparrows, but *five*. The extra bird was added as though it had no value at all. Perhaps such creatures were worthless in the eyes of men, but how did the Creator view them? Said Jesus: "Not one of them [not even the one added in] goes forgotten before God." (Luke 12:6, 7) Now we may begin to see Jesus' point. If Jehovah places such value on a single sparrow, of how much greater worth is a human! As Jesus explained, Jehovah knows every detail about us. Why, the very hairs of our head are numbered!

6 Our hairs numbered? Some might assume that Jesus

4, 5. How does Jesus' illustration of the sparrows show that we have value in Jehovah's eyes?
6. Why are we certain that Jesus was being realistic when he spoke of the hairs of our head being numbered?

was being unrealistic here. Just think, though, about the hope of the resurrection. How intimately Jehovah must know us in order to recreate us! He values us so much that he remembers every detail, including our genetic code and all our years of memories and experiences.* Numbering our hairs—of which the average head grows about 100,000—would be a simple feat by comparison.

What Does Jehovah See in Us?

7 Second, the Bible teaches us what Jehovah values in his servants. Simply put, he delights in our good qualities and in the efforts we put forth. King David told his son Solomon: "All hearts Jehovah is searching, and every inclination of the thoughts he is discerning." (1 Chronicles 28:9) As God searches through billions of human hearts in this violent, hate-filled world, how delighted he must be when he comes upon a heart that loves peace, truth, and righteousness! What happens when God finds a heart that swells with love for him, that seeks to learn about him and to share such knowledge with others? Jehovah tells us that he takes note of those who tell others about him. He even has "a book of remembrance" for all "those in fear of Jehovah and for those thinking upon his name." (Malachi 3:16) Such qualities are precious to him.

8 What are some good works that Jehovah values? Cer-

---

* The Bible repeatedly connects the resurrection hope with Jehovah's memory. The faithful man Job said to Jehovah: "O . . . that you would set a time limit for me and *remember* me!" (Job 14:13) Jesus referred to the resurrection of "all those in the *memorial* tombs." This was appropriate because Jehovah perfectly remembers the dead whom he intends to resurrect.—John 5:28, 29.

7, 8. (a) What are some qualities that Jehovah is delighted to find as he searches through human hearts? (b) What are some of the works we do that Jehovah values?

"You are worth more than many sparrows"

tainly our efforts to imitate his Son, Jesus Christ. (1 Peter 2:21) One vital work that God values is the spreading of the good news of his Kingdom. At Romans 10:15, we read: "How comely are the feet of those who declare good news of good things!" We may not normally think of our lowly feet as being "comely," or beautiful. But here they represent the efforts Jehovah's servants make in preaching the good news. All such efforts are beautiful and precious in his eyes.—Matthew 24:14; 28:19, 20.

⁹ Jehovah also values our endurance. (Matthew 24:13) Remember, Satan wants you to turn your back on Jehovah. Each day that you remain loyal to Jehovah is another day that you have helped to furnish a reply to Satan's taunts. (Proverbs 27:11) Sometimes endurance is no easy matter. Health problems, financial woes, emotional distress, and other obstacles can make each passing day

9, 10. (a) Why may we be assured that Jehovah values our endurance in the face of various hardships? (b) Jehovah never takes what negative views of his faithful servants?

a trial. Postponed expectations can prove discouraging too. (Proverbs 13:12) Endurance in the face of such challenges is all the more precious to Jehovah. That is why King David asked Jehovah to store up his tears in a "skin bottle," adding confidently: "Are they not in your book?" (Psalm 56:8) Yes, Jehovah treasures up and remembers all the tears and suffering we endure while maintaining our loyalty to him. They too are precious in his eyes.

[10] Now, the self-condemning heart may resist such evidence of our value in the eyes of God. It may insistently whisper: 'But there are so many others who are more exemplary than I am. How disappointed Jehovah must be when he compares me with them!' Jehovah does not compare; nor is he rigid or harsh in his thinking. (Galatians 6:4) It is with great subtlety that he reads our hearts, and he values the good—even small measures of it.

Jehovah Sifts the Good From the Bad

[11] Third, as Jehovah searches through us, he carefully sifts, looking for the good. For instance, when Jehovah decreed that the entire apostate dynasty of King Jeroboam was to be executed, He ordered that one of the king's sons, Abijah, be given a decent burial. Why? "Something good toward Jehovah the God of Israel has been found in him." (1 Kings 14:1, 10-13) Jehovah, in effect, sifted through the heart of that young man and found "something good" there. However small or insignificant that bit of good may have been, Jehovah found it worth noting in his Word. He even rewarded it, showing an appropriate degree of mercy to that one member of an apostate household.

---

11. What may we learn about Jehovah from the way he handled the case of Abijah?

¹² An even more positive example may be found in good King Jehoshaphat. When the king committed a foolish act, Jehovah's prophet told him: "For this there is indignation against you from the person of Jehovah." What a sobering thought! But Jehovah's message did not end there. It went on: "Nevertheless, there are good things that have been found with you." (2 Chronicles 19:1-3) So Jehovah's righteous anger did not blind him to the good in Jehoshaphat. How unlike imperfect humans! When upset with others, we may tend to become blind to the good in them. And when we sin, the disappointment, shame, and guilt that we feel may blind us to the good in ourselves. Remember, though, that if we repent of our sins and strive hard not to repeat them, Jehovah forgives us.

¹³ As Jehovah sifts through you, he discards such sins, much the way a prospector

12, 13. (a) How does the case of King Jehoshaphat show that Jehovah looks for the good in us even when we sin? (b) When it comes to our good works and qualities, how does Jehovah act as a fond Parent?

Jehovah values our endurance in the face of trials

panning for gold discards worthless gravel. What about your good qualities and works? Ah, these are the "nuggets" he keeps! Have you ever noticed the way fond parents treasure their children's drawings or school projects, sometimes for decades after the children have forgotten them? Jehovah is the fondest Parent. As long as we remain faithful to him, he *never* forgets our good works and qualities. In fact, he would view it as unrighteous to forget these, and he is never unrighteous. (Hebrews 6:10) He also sifts us in another way.

¹⁴ Jehovah looks beyond our imperfections and sees our potential. To illustrate: People who love works of art will go to great lengths to restore badly damaged paintings or other works. When, for example, in the National Gallery in London, England, someone with a shotgun damaged a Leonardo da Vinci drawing worth some $30 million, no one suggested that since the drawing was now damaged, it should be discarded. Work to restore the nearly 500-year-old masterpiece began immediately. Why? Because it was precious in the eyes of art lovers. Are you not worth more than a chalk and charcoal drawing? In God's eyes you certainly are—however damaged you may be by inherited imperfection. (Psalm 72:12-14) Jehovah God, the skilled Creator of the human family, will do what is necessary to restore to perfection all of those who respond to his loving care.—Acts 3:21; Romans 8:20-22.

¹⁵ Yes, Jehovah sees the good in us that we may not see in ourselves. And as we serve him, he will make the good grow until we are eventually perfect. No matter how Satan's world has treated us, Jehovah values his faithful servants as desirable, or precious.—Haggai 2:7; footnote.

14, 15. (a) Why do our imperfections never blind Jehovah to the good in us? Illustrate. (b) What will Jehovah do with the good things he finds in us, and how does he view his faithful people?

Jehovah Actively Demonstrates His Love

¹⁶ Fourth, Jehovah does much to prove his love for us. Surely, Christ's ransom sacrifice is the most potent answer to the satanic lie that we are worthless or unlovable. Never should we forget that the agonizing death that Jesus suffered on the torture stake and the even greater agony that Jehovah endured in watching his beloved Son die are proof of their love for us. Sadly, many people find it hard to believe that this gift could be meant for them personally. They feel unworthy. Remember, though, that the apostle Paul had been a persecutor of Christ's followers. Yet, he wrote: "The Son of God . . . loved *me* and handed himself over for *me*."—Galatians 1:13; 2:20.

¹⁷ Jehovah proves his love for us by helping us individually to take advantage of the benefits of Christ's sacrifice. Jesus said: "No man can come to me unless the Father, who sent me, draws him." (John 6:44) Yes, Jehovah personally draws us toward his Son and the hope of eternal life. How? By means of the preaching work, which reaches us individually, and by means of his holy spirit, which Jehovah uses to help us grasp and apply spiritual truths despite our limitations and imperfections. Jehovah can therefore say of us as he said of Israel: "With a love to time indefinite I have loved you. That is why I have drawn you with loving-kindness."—Jeremiah 31:3.

¹⁸ Perhaps it is through the privilege of prayer that we experience Jehovah's love in the most intimate way. The Bible invites each of us to "pray incessantly" to God.

---

16. What is the greatest proof of Jehovah's love for us, and how do we know that this gift is meant for us personally?
17. By what means does Jehovah draw us to himself and to his Son?
18, 19. (a) What is the most intimate way in which Jehovah demonstrates his love for us, and what shows that he cares for this personally? (b) How does God's Word assure us that Jehovah is an empathetic listener?

(1 Thessalonians 5:17) He listens. He is even called the "Hearer of prayer." (Psalm 65:2) He has not delegated this office to anyone else, not even to his own Son. Just think: The Creator of the universe urges us to approach him in prayer, with freeness of speech. And what kind of listener is he? Cold, impassive, uncaring? Not at all.

[19] Jehovah is empathetic. What is empathy? One faithful elderly Christian said: "Empathy is *your* pain in *my* heart." Is Jehovah really affected by our pain? We read regarding the sufferings of his people Israel: "During all their distress it was distressing to him." (Isaiah 63:9) Not only did Jehovah see their troubles; he felt for the people. Just how intensely he feels is illustrated by Jehovah's own words to his servants: "He that is touching you is touching my eyeball."* (Zechariah 2:8) How painful that would be! Yes, Jehovah feels for us. When we hurt, he hurts.

[20] No balanced Christian would use such evidence of God's love and esteem as an excuse for pride or egotism. The apostle Paul wrote: "Through the undeserved kindness given to me I tell everyone there among you not to think more of himself than it is necessary to think; but to think so as to have a sound mind, each one as God has distributed to him a measure of faith." (Romans 12:3) Another translation says here: "I would say to every one of you not to estimate himself above his real value, but to make a sober rating of himself." (*A Translation in the*

---

* Some translations here imply that the one touching God's people is touching his *own* eye or Israel's eye, not God's eye. This error was introduced by some scribes who viewed this passage as irreverent and therefore emended it. Their misguided effort obscured the intensity of Jehovah's personal empathy.

---

20. What unbalanced thinking must we avoid if we are to obey the counsel found at Romans 12:3?

Questions for Meditation

Psalm 139:1-24 How do King David's inspired words show that Jehovah is keenly interested in us as individuals?

Isaiah 43:3, 4, 10-13 How does Jehovah feel about those who serve as his Witnesses, and how are his feelings expressed in actions?

Romans 5:6-8 Why can we be sure that our sinful state does not prevent Jehovah's love from reaching and benefiting us?

Jude 17-25 How can we keep ourselves in God's love, and what influences work against our doing so?

Language of the People, by Charles B. Williams) So while we bask in the warmth of our heavenly Father's love, let us be sound in mind and remember that we neither earn nor deserve God's love.—Luke 17:10.

²¹ Let each of us do everything in our power to reject all of Satan's lies, including the lie that we are worthless or unlovable. If your experiences in life have taught you to see yourself as an obstacle too daunting even for God's immense love to surmount, or your good works as too insignificant even for his all-seeing eyes to notice, or your sins as too vast even for the death of his precious Son to cover, you have been taught a lie. Reject such lies with all your heart! Let us continue to assure our hearts with the truth expressed in Paul's inspired words: "I am convinced that neither death nor life nor angels nor governments nor things now here nor things to come nor powers nor height nor depth nor any other creation will be able to separate us from God's love that is in Christ Jesus our Lord."—Romans 8:38, 39.

---

21. What satanic lies must we continually resist, and with what divine truth may we continue to assure our hearts?

CHAPTER 25

"The Tender Compassion of Our God"

IN THE middle of the night, a baby cries. Immediately, the mother wakes up. She does not sleep as soundly as she used to—not since her baby was born. She has learned to distinguish her infant's different types of crying. Hence, she can often tell whether her newborn needs to be fed, cuddled, or otherwise tended to. But regardless of the reason for the baby's crying, the mother responds. Her heart cannot let her ignore the needs of her child.

[2] The compassion that a mother feels for the child of her womb is among the most tender feelings known to humans. There is, however, a feeling that is infinitely stronger—the tender compassion of our God, Jehovah. A consideration of this endearing quality can help us draw closer to Jehovah. Let us, then, discuss what compassion is and how our God manifests it.

What Is Compassion?

[3] In the Bible, there is a close relationship between compassion and mercy. A number of Hebrew and Greek words convey the sense of tender compassion. Consider, for example, the Hebrew verb *ra·cham'*, which is often rendered "show mercy" or "have pity." One reference work explains that the verb *ra·cham'* "expresses a deep and tender feeling of compassion, such as is aroused by the sight of weakness or suffering in those that are dear to us or

---

1, 2. (a) How does a mother naturally respond to the crying of her baby? (b) What feeling is even stronger than a mother's compassion?
3. What is the meaning of the Hebrew verb rendered "show mercy" or "have pity"?

need our help." This Hebrew term, which Jehovah applies to himself, is related to the word for "womb" and can be described as "motherly compassion."*—Exodus 33:19; Jeremiah 33:26.

4 The Bible uses the feelings that a mother has for her baby to teach us about the meaning of Jehovah's compassion. At Isaiah 49:15, we read: "Can a woman forget her nursing child, that she should not have compassion [*racham*'] on the son of her womb? Yes, they may forget, yet I will not forget you." (*The Amplified Bible*) That touching description underscores the depth of Jehovah's compassion for his people. How so?

5 It is difficult to imagine that a mother would forget to nourish and care for her nursing child. After all, an infant is helpless; night and day a baby needs its mother's attention and affection. Sad to say, however, maternal neglect is not unheard of, especially in these "critical times" characterized by a lack of "natural affection." (2 Timothy 3: 1, 3) "Yet," Jehovah declares, "I will not forget you." The tender compassion that Jehovah has for his servants is unfailing. It is immeasurably stronger than the most tender natural feeling that we can imagine—the compassion that a mother normally feels for her infant child. Little wonder that one commentator said of Isaiah 49:15: "This is one of the strongest, if not the strongest expression of God's love in the Old Testament."

6 Is tender compassion a sign of weakness? Many imperfect humans have held that view. For instance, the Roman

---

* Interestingly, though, at Psalm 103:13, the Hebrew verb *ra·cham*' connotes the mercy, or compassion, that a father shows to his children.

4, 5. How does the Bible use the feelings that a mother has for her baby to teach us about Jehovah's compassion?
6. Many imperfect humans have viewed tender compassion in what way, but of what does Jehovah assure us?

philosopher Seneca, who was a contemporary of Jesus and a leading intellectual figure in Rome, taught that "pity is a weakness of the mind." Seneca was an advocate of Stoicism, a philosophy stressing calmness that is devoid of feeling. A wise person may help those in distress, said Seneca, but he must not allow himself to feel pity, for such a feeling would deprive him of serenity. That self-centered view of life allowed no room for heartfelt compassion. But that is not at all what Jehovah is like! In his Word, Jehovah assures us that he "is very tender in affection and compassionate."(James 5:11, footnote) As we will see, compassion is not a weakness but a strong, vital quality. Let us examine how Jehovah, like a loving parent, manifests it.

When Jehovah Showed Compassion to a Nation

⁷ The compassion of Jehovah is clearly seen in the way he dealt with the nation of Israel. By the end of the 16th century B.C.E., millions of Israelites were enslaved in ancient Egypt, where they were severely oppressed. The Egyptians "kept making their life bitter with hard slavery at clay mortar and bricks." (Exodus 1:11, 14) In their distress, the Israelites cried out to Jehovah for help. How did the God of tender compassion respond?

⁸ Jehovah's heart was touched. He said: "Unquestionably I have seen the affliction of my people who are in Egypt, and I have heard their outcry as a result of those who drive them to work; because I well know the pains they suffer." (Exodus 3:7) Jehovah could not see the sufferings of his people or hear their outcries without feeling

---

7, 8. In what way did the Israelites suffer in ancient Egypt, and how did Jehovah respond to their suffering?

"Can a woman forget . . . the son of her womb?"

for them. As we saw in Chapter 24 of this book, Jehovah is a God of empathy. And empathy—the ability to identify with the pain of others—is akin to compassion. But Jehovah did not just *feel* for his people; he was moved to act in their behalf. Isaiah 63:9 says: "In his love and in his compassion he himself repurchased them." With "a strong hand," Jehovah rescued the Israelites out of Egypt. (Deuteronomy 4:34) Thereafter, he provided them with miraculous food and delivered them into a fruitful land of their own.

⁹ Jehovah's compassion did not stop there. When settled in the Promised Land, Israel repeatedly lapsed into unfaithfulness and suffered as a result. But then the people would come to their senses and call out to Jehovah. Again and again he delivered them. Why? "Because he felt compassion for his people."—2 Chronicles 36:15; Judges 2: 11-16.

¹⁰ Consider what happened in the days of Jephthah. Since the Israelites had turned to serving false gods, Jehovah allowed them to be oppressed by the Ammonites for 18 years. Finally, the Israelites repented. The Bible tells us: "They began to remove the foreign gods from their midst and to serve Jehovah, so that his soul became impatient because of the trouble of Israel."* (Judges 10:6-16) Once his people manifested genuine repentance, Jehovah could no longer bear to see them suffer. So the God of tender

---

* The expression "his soul became impatient" literally means "his soul was shortened; his patience was exhausted." *The New English Bible* reads: "He could endure no longer to see the plight of Israel." *Tanakh —A New Translation of the Holy Scriptures* renders it: "He could not bear the miseries of Israel."

9, 10. (a) Why did Jehovah repeatedly deliver the Israelites after they were settled in the Promised Land? (b) In the days of Jephthah, Jehovah delivered the Israelites from what oppression, and what moved him to do so?

compassion empowered Jephthah to deliver the Israelites out of the hands of their enemies.—Judges 11:30-33.

[11] What do Jehovah's dealings with the nation of Israel teach us about tender compassion? For one thing, we see that it is more than just a sympathetic awareness of the adversities that people experience. Recall the example of a mother whose compassion moves her to respond to the crying of her baby. Similarly, Jehovah is not deaf to the outcries of his people. His tender compassion moves him to relieve their suffering. In addition, the way Jehovah dealt with the Israelites teaches us that compassion is by no means a weakness, for this tender quality moved him to take strong, decisive action in behalf of his people. But does Jehovah show compassion only to his servants as a group?

Jehovah's Compassion for Individuals

[12] The Law that God gave to the nation of Israel showed his compassion for individuals. Take, for example, his concern for the poor. Jehovah knew that unforeseen circumstances might arise that could plunge an Israelite into poverty. How were poor ones to be treated? Jehovah strictly commanded the Israelites: "You must not harden your heart or be closefisted toward your poor brother. You should by all means give to him, and your heart should not be stingy in your giving to him, because on this account Jehovah your God will bless you in every deed of yours." (Deuteronomy 15:7, 10) Jehovah further commanded that the Israelites not harvest the edges of their fields completely or pick up any leftovers. Such gleanings were for disadvantaged ones. (Leviticus 23:22; Ruth 2:2-7) When the nation observed this considerate legislation in

---

11. From Jehovah's dealings with the Israelites, what do we learn about compassion?
12. How did the Law reflect Jehovah's compassion for individuals?

behalf of the poor in their midst, needy individuals in Israel did not have to beg for food. Was that not a reflection of Jehovah's tender compassion?

¹³ Today, too, our loving God is deeply concerned about us as individuals. We can be sure that he is keenly aware of any suffering we may undergo. The psalmist David wrote: "The eyes of Jehovah are toward the righteous ones, and his ears are toward their cry for help. Jehovah is near to those that are broken at heart; and those who are crushed in spirit he saves." (Psalm 34:15, 18) Regarding those described by these words, one Bible commentator notes: "They are of a broken heart and a contrite spirit, that is, humbled for sin, and emptied of self; they are low in their own eyes, and have no confidence in their own merit." Such ones may feel that Jehovah is far away and that they are too insignificant for him to care about them. But that is not the case. David's words assure us that Jehovah does not abandon those who are "low in their own eyes." Our compassionate God knows that at such times, we need him more than ever, and he is near.

¹⁴ Consider an experience. A mother in the United States rushed her two-year-old son to the hospital because he was suffering from a bad case of croup. After examining the boy, the doctors informed the mother that they would have to keep him in the hospital overnight. Where did the mother spend that night? In a chair in the hospital room, right next to her son's bed! Her little boy was sick, and she just had to be near him. Surely we can expect even more from our loving heavenly Father! After all, we are made in his image. (Genesis 1:26) The touching words

---

13, 14. (a) How do David's words assure us that Jehovah is deeply concerned about us as individuals? (b) How could it be illustrated that Jehovah is near to those who are "broken at heart" or "crushed in spirit"?

of Psalm 34:18 tell us that when we are "broken at heart" or "crushed in spirit," Jehovah, like a loving parent, "is near"—ever compassionate and ready to help.

¹⁵ How, then, does Jehovah help us as individuals? He does not necessarily remove the cause of our suffering. But Jehovah has made abundant provisions for those who cry out to him for help. His Word, the Bible, offers practical counsel that can make a difference. In the congregation, Jehovah provides spiritually qualified overseers, who endeavor to reflect his compassion in helping fellow worshipers. (James 5:14, 15) As the "Hearer of prayer," he gives "holy spirit to those asking him." (Psalm 65:2; Luke 11:13) That spirit can infuse us with "power beyond what is normal" in order to endure until God's Kingdom removes all stressful problems. (2 Corinthians 4:7) Are we not grateful for all these provisions? Let us not forget that they are expressions of Jehovah's tender compassion.

¹⁶ Of course, the greatest example of Jehovah's compassion is his giving the One dearest to him as a ransom for us. It was a loving sacrifice on Jehovah's part, and it opened the way for our salvation. Remember, that ransom provision applies to us personally. With good reason, Zechariah, the father of John the Baptizer, foretold that this provision magnified "the tender compassion of our God."—Luke 1:78.

When Jehovah Withholds Compassion

¹⁷ Are we to imagine that Jehovah's tender compassion is

15. In what ways does Jehovah help us as individuals?
16. What is the greatest example of Jehovah's compassion, and how does it affect us as individuals?
17-19. (a) How does the Bible show that Jehovah's compassion is not without limits? (b) What caused Jehovah's compassion for his people to reach its limit?

without limits? On the contrary, the Bible clearly shows that in the case of individuals who set themselves against his righteous ways, Jehovah rightly withholds compassion. (Hebrews 10:28) To see why he does so, recall the example of the nation of Israel.

[18] Although Jehovah repeatedly delivered the Israelites from their enemies, his compassion eventually reached its limit. This stubborn people practiced idolatry, even bringing their disgusting idols right into Jehovah's temple! (Ezekiel 5:11; 8:17, 18) Further, we are told: "They were continually making jest at the messengers of the true God and despising his words and mocking at his prophets, until the rage of Jehovah came up against his people, until there was no healing." (2 Chronicles 36:16) The Israelites reached a point where there was no longer any proper basis for compassion, and they provoked Jehovah to righteous anger. With what result?

[19] Jehovah could no longer feel compassion for his people. He proclaimed: "I shall show no compassion, nor feel any sorrow, and I shall not have the mercy to keep from bringing them to ruin." (Jeremiah 13:14) Thus, Jerusalem and its temple were destroyed, and the Israelites were taken captive to Babylon. How tragic it is when sinful humans get so rebellious that they exhaust the limits of divine compassion!—Lamentations 2:21.

[20] What about today? Jehovah has not changed. Out of compassion, he has commissioned his Witnesses to preach the "good news of the kingdom" in all the inhabited earth. (Matthew 24:14) When righthearted peo-

---

20, 21. (a) What will happen when divine compassion reaches its limit in our day? (b) What compassionate provision of Jehovah will be discussed in the next chapter?

Questions for Meditation

Jeremiah 31:20 What tender feelings does Jehovah have for his people, and how does this make you feel toward him?

Joel 2:12-14, 17-19 What did Jehovah's people need to do in order to be shown compassion, and what do we learn from this?

Jonah 4:1-11 How did Jehovah teach Jonah a lesson about the importance of compassion?

Hebrews 10:26-31 Why can we not presume on Jehovah's mercy, or compassion?

ple respond, Jehovah helps them to grasp the Kingdom message. (Acts 16:14) But this work will not go on forever. It would hardly be compassionate for Jehovah to allow this wicked world, with all its misery and suffering, to continue indefinitely. When divine compassion has reached its limit, Jehovah will come to execute judgment on this system of things. Even then, he will be acting out of compassion—compassion for his "holy name" and for his devoted servants. (Ezekiel 36:20-23) Jehovah will clear away wickedness and usher in a righteous new world. Regarding the wicked, Jehovah declares: "My eye will not feel sorry, neither shall I show compassion. Their way I shall certainly bring upon their own head." —Ezekiel 9:10.

²¹ Until then, Jehovah feels compassion for people, even those who face destruction. Sinful humans who are sincerely repentant can benefit from one of Jehovah's most compassionate provisions—forgiveness. In the next chapter, we will discuss some of the beautiful word pictures in the Bible that convey the completeness of Jehovah's forgiveness.

CHAPTER 26

A God Who Is "Ready to Forgive"

"MY OWN errors have passed over my head," wrote the psalmist David. "Like a heavy load they are too heavy for me. I have grown numb and become crushed to an extreme degree." (Psalm 38:4, 8) David knew how heavy the burden of a guilty conscience could be. But he found comfort for his troubled heart. He understood that while Jehovah hates sin, He does not hate the sinner if that one is truly repentant and rejects his sinful course. With full faith in Jehovah's willingness to extend mercy to repentant ones, David said: "You, O Jehovah, are . . . ready to forgive."—Psalm 86:5.

² When we sin, we too may carry the crushing burden of a pained conscience. This feeling of remorse is healthy. It can move us to take positive steps to correct our mistakes. There is, however, a danger of becoming overwhelmed by guilt. Our self-condemning heart might insist that Jehovah will not forgive us, no matter how repentant we are. If we become "swallowed up" by guilt, Satan may try to get us to give up, to feel that Jehovah views us as worthless, unfit to serve him.—2 Corinthians 2:5-11.

³ Is that how Jehovah views matters? Not at all! Forgiveness is a facet of Jehovah's great love. In his Word, he assures us that when we manifest genuine, heartfelt repentance, he is willing to forgive. (Proverbs 28:13) Lest Jehovah's forgiveness ever seem unattainable to us, let us examine why and how he forgives.

1-3. (a) What heavy burden did the psalmist David carry, and how did he find comfort for his troubled heart? (b) When we sin, what burden may we carry as a result, but of what does Jehovah assure us?

Why Jehovah Is "Ready to Forgive"

⁴ Jehovah is aware of our limitations. "He himself well knows the formation of us, remembering that we are dust," says Psalm 103:14. He does not forget that we are creatures of dust, having frailties, or weaknesses, as a result of imperfection. The expression that he knows "the formation of us" reminds us that the Bible likens Jehovah to a potter and us to the clay vessels he forms.* (Jeremiah 18:2-6) The Great Potter tempers his dealings with us according to the frailty of our sinful nature and the way we respond or fail to respond to his guidance.

⁵ Jehovah understands how powerful sin is. His Word describes sin as a potent force that has man in its deadly grip. Just how strong is sin's hold? In the book of Romans, the apostle Paul explains: We are "under sin," as soldiers are under their commander (Romans 3:9); sin has "ruled" over mankind like a king (Romans 5:21); it "resides," or is "dwelling," within us (Romans 7:17, 20); its "law" is continually at work in us, in effect trying to control our course. (Romans 7:23, 25) What a powerful hold sin has on our fallen flesh!—Romans 7:21, 24.

⁶ Hence, Jehovah knows that perfect obedience is not possible for us, no matter how earnestly we may yearn to give it to him. He lovingly assures us that when we seek his mercy with a contrite heart, he will extend forgiveness. Psalm 51:17 says: "The sacrifices to God are a broken spirit; a heart broken and crushed, O God, you

---

* The Hebrew word rendered "the formation of us" is also used concerning the clay vessels formed by a potter.—Isaiah 29:16.

---

4. What does Jehovah remember about our nature, and how does this affect the way he treats us?
5. How does the book of Romans describe sin's powerful grip?
6, 7. (a) How does Jehovah view those who seek his mercy with a contrite heart? (b) Why should we not presume on God's mercy?

will not despise." Jehovah will never reject, or turn away, a heart that is "broken and crushed" by the burden of guilt.

7 Does this mean, though, that we can presume on God's mercy, using our sinful nature as an excuse to sin? Certainly not! Jehovah is not guided by mere sentiment. His mercy has limits. He will by no means forgive those who hardheartedly practice willful sin, not showing any repentance. (Hebrews 10:26) On the other hand, when he sees a contrite heart, he is ready to forgive. Let us now consider some of the expressive language used in the Bible to describe this marvelous facet of Jehovah's love.

How Completely Does Jehovah Forgive?

8 A repentant David said: "My sin I finally confessed to you, and my error I did not cover. . . . And you yourself *pardoned* the error of my sins." (Psalm 32:5) The term "pardoned" translates a Hebrew word that basically means "lift up" or "carry." Its use here signifies to take away "guilt, iniquity, transgression." So Jehovah, in effect, lifted up David's sins and carried them away. This no doubt eased the feelings of guilt that David had been carrying. (Psalm 32:3) We too can have full confidence in the God who carries away the sins of those who seek his forgiveness on the basis of their faith in Jesus' ransom sacrifice.—Matthew 20:28.

9 David used another vivid expression to describe Jehovah's forgiveness: "As far as *the east is from the west,* so far has He removed our transgressions from us." (Psalm 103:12, *The Amplified Bible*) How far is east from west? In a sense, east is always at the utmost distance imaginable from west; the two points can never meet. One schol-

8. What does Jehovah, in effect, do when he pardons our sins, and what confidence does this give us?
9. How far away from us does Jehovah put our sins?

ar notes that this expression means "as far as possible; as far as we can imagine." David's inspired words tell us that when Jehovah forgives, he puts our sins as far away from us as we can imagine.

¹⁰ Have you ever tried to remove a stain from a light-colored garment? Perhaps despite your best efforts, the stain remained visible. Notice how Jehovah describes his capacity for forgiveness: "Though the sins of you people should prove to be as scarlet, they will be made *white just like snow;* though they should be red like crimson cloth, they will become even like wool." (Isaiah 1:18) The word "scarlet" denotes a bright red color.* "Crimson" was one of the deep colors of dyed material. (Nahum 2:3) We can

---

* One scholar says that scarlet "was a *fast,* or *fixed* colour. Neither dew, nor rain, nor washing, nor long usage, would remove it."

---

10. When Jehovah forgives our sins, why should we not feel that we bear the stain of such sins for the rest of our life?

"The sins of you people . . . will be made white just like snow"

never through our own efforts remove the stain of sin. But Jehovah can take sins that are like scarlet and crimson and make them white like snow or undyed wool. When Jehovah forgives our sins, we need not feel that we bear the stain of such sins for the rest of our life.

¹¹ In a moving song of gratitude that Hezekiah composed after he was spared from a deadly sickness, he said to Jehovah: "You have *thrown behind your back* all my sins." (Isaiah 38:17) Jehovah is here portrayed as taking the sins of a repentant wrongdoer and throwing them behind Him where He neither sees them nor takes notice of them anymore. According to one source, the idea conveyed may be expressed: "You have made [my sins] as if they had not happened." Is that not reassuring?

¹² In a promise of restoration, the prophet Micah expressed his conviction that Jehovah would forgive his repentant people: "Who is a God like you, . . . passing over transgression of the remnant of his inheritance? . . . And you will throw *into the depths of the sea* all their sins." (Micah 7:18, 19) Imagine what those words meant to those living in Bible times. Was there any chance of retrieving something that had been hurled "into the depths of the sea"? Micah's words thus indicate that when Jehovah forgives, he removes our sins permanently.

¹³ Jesus drew on the relationship between creditors and debtors to illustrate Jehovah's forgiveness. Jesus urged us to pray: "Forgive us our *debts.*" (Matthew 6:12) Jesus thus likened sins to debts. (Luke 11:4) When we sin, we become "debtors" to Jehovah. Regarding the meaning of the Greek verb translated "forgive," one reference work

11. In what sense does Jehovah throw our sins behind his back?
12. How does the prophet Micah indicate that when Jehovah forgives, He removes our sins permanently?
13. What is the meaning of Jesus' words "Forgive us our debts"?

says: "To let go, give up, a debt, by not demanding it." In a sense, when Jehovah forgives, he cancels the debt that would otherwise be charged against our account. Repentant sinners can thus take comfort. Jehovah will never demand payment for a debt he has canceled!—Psalm 32:1, 2.

14 Jehovah's forgiveness is further described at Acts 3:19: "Repent, therefore, and turn around so as to get your sins *blotted out.*" That last phrase translates a Greek verb that can mean "to wipe out, . . . cancel or destroy." According to some scholars, the image expressed is that of erasing handwriting. How was this possible? The ink commonly used in ancient times was made of a mixture that included carbon, gum, and water. Soon after working with such ink, a person could take a wet sponge and wipe the writing away. Therein is a beautiful picture of Jehovah's mercy. When he forgives our sins, it is as though he takes a sponge and wipes them away.

15 When we reflect on these varied word pictures, is it not clear that Jehovah wants us to know that he is truly ready to forgive our sins as long as he finds us sincerely repentant? We need not fear that he will hold such sins against us in the future. This is shown by something else that the Bible reveals about Jehovah's great mercy: When he forgives, he forgets.

"Their Sin I Shall Remember No More"

16 Jehovah promised regarding those in the new covenant: "I shall forgive their error, and their sin I shall remember no more." (Jeremiah 31:34) Does this mean that when Jehovah forgives he is unable to recall sins

---

14. The phrase "get your sins blotted out" evokes what mental image?
15. What does Jehovah want us to know about him?
16, 17. When the Bible says that Jehovah forgets our sins, what does it mean, and why do you so answer?

Jehovah wants us to know that he is "ready to forgive"

anymore? That could hardly be the case. The Bible tells us of the sins of many individuals whom Jehovah forgave, including David. (2 Samuel 11:1-17; 12:13) Jehovah is obviously still aware of the errors they committed. The record of their sins, as well as that of their repentance and forgiveness by God, has been preserved for our benefit. (Romans 15:4) What, then, does the Bible mean when it says that Jehovah does not "remember" the sins of those whom he forgives?

¹⁷ The Hebrew verb rendered "I shall remember" implies more than simply to recall the past. The *Theological Wordbook of the Old Testament* notes that it includes "the additional implication of taking appropriate action."

So in this sense, to "remember" sin involves taking action against sinners. (Hosea 9:9) But when God says "their sin I shall remember no more," he is assuring us that once he forgives repentant sinners, he will not at some future time act against them because of those sins. (Ezekiel 18:21, 22) Jehovah thus forgets in the sense that he does not bring our sins up again and again in order to accuse or punish us over and over. Is it not comforting to know that our God forgives *and forgets?*

What About the Consequences?

¹⁸ Does Jehovah's readiness to forgive mean that a repentant sinner is exempted from all consequences of his wrong course? Not at all. We cannot sin with impunity. Paul wrote: "Whatever a man is sowing, this he will also reap." (Galatians 6:7) We may face certain consequences of our actions. This does not mean that after extending forgiveness Jehovah causes adversity to befall us. When troubles arise, a Christian should not feel, 'Perhaps Jehovah is punishing me for past sins.' (James 1:13) On the other hand, Jehovah does not shield us from all the effects of our wrong actions. Divorce, unwanted pregnancy, sexually transmitted disease, loss of trust or respect—all of these may be the sad, unavoidable consequences of sin. Recall that even after forgiving David for his sins in connection with Bath-sheba and Uriah, Jehovah did not protect David from the disastrous consequences that followed.—2 Samuel 12:9-12.

¹⁹ Our sins may have additional consequences, especially if others have been hurt by our actions.

---

18. Why does forgiveness not mean that a repentant sinner is exempted from all consequences of his wrong course?
19-21. (a) How did the law recorded at Leviticus 6:1-7 benefit both the victim and the offender? (b) If others have been hurt by our sins, Jehovah is pleased when we take what action?

Consider, for example, the account in Leviticus chapter 6. The Mosaic Law here addresses the situation wherein a person commits a serious wrong by seizing a fellow Israelite's goods through robbery, extortion, or fraud. The sinner then denies that he is guilty, even being so daring as to swear falsely. It is one person's word against another's. Later, however, the offender becomes stricken in conscience and confesses his sin. To gain God's forgiveness, he has to do three more things: restore what he had taken, pay the victim a fine totaling 20 percent of the value of the stolen items, and provide a ram as a guilt offering. Then, the law says: "The priest must make an atonement for him before Jehovah, and so it must be forgiven him."—Leviticus 6:1-7.

[20] This law was a merciful provision from God. It benefited the victim, whose property was returned and who no doubt felt much relief when the offender finally acknowledged his sin. At the same time, the law benefited the one whose conscience at last moved him to admit his guilt and correct his wrong. Indeed, if he refused to do so, there would be no forgiveness for him from God.

[21] Although we are not under the Mosaic Law, that Law gives us insight into Jehovah's mind, including his thinking on forgiveness. (Colossians 2:13, 14) If others have been hurt by our sins, God is pleased when we do what we can to right the wrong. (Matthew 5:23, 24) This may involve acknowledging our sin, admitting our guilt, and even apologizing to the victim. Then we can appeal to Jehovah on the basis of Jesus' sacrifice and experience the assurance that we have been forgiven by God.—Hebrews 10:21, 22.

[22] Like any loving parent, Jehovah may offer forgiveness

22. What may accompany Jehovah's forgiveness?

Questions for Meditation

2 Chronicles 33:1-13 Why did Jehovah forgive Manasseh, and what does this teach us about His mercy?

Matthew 6:12, 14, 15 Why should we forgive others when there is a sound basis for doing so?

Luke 15:11-32 What does this parable teach us about Jehovah's willingness to forgive, and how does that make you feel?

2 Corinthians 7:8-11 What must we do in order to receive divine forgiveness?

---

along with a measure of discipline. (Proverbs 3:11, 12) A repentant Christian may have to relinquish his privilege of serving as an elder, a ministerial servant, or a full-time evangelizer. It may be painful for him to lose for a period of time privileges that were precious to him. Such discipline, however, does not mean that Jehovah has withheld forgiveness. We must remember that discipline from Jehovah is proof of his love for us. Accepting and applying it is in our best interests.—Hebrews 12:5-11.

23 How refreshing to know that our God is "ready to forgive"! Despite the mistakes we may have made, we should never conclude that we are beyond the reach of Jehovah's mercy. If we truly repent, take steps to right the wrong, and earnestly pray for forgiveness on the basis of Jesus' shed blood, we can have full confidence that Jehovah will forgive us. (1 John 1:9) Let us imitate his forgiveness in our dealings with one another. After all, if Jehovah, who does not sin, can so lovingly forgive us, should not we sinful humans do our best to forgive one another?

---

23. Why should we never conclude that we are beyond the reach of Jehovah's mercy, and why should we imitate his forgiveness?

CHAPTER 27

"O How Great
His Goodness Is!"

BATHED in the warm light of sunset, a few longtime friends enjoy an outdoor meal together, laughing and talking as they admire the view. Far away, a farmer looks out at his fields and smiles in satisfaction because dark clouds have gathered and the first drops of rain are falling on thirsty crops. Elsewhere, a husband and wife are delighted to see their child take his first wobbly steps.

² Whether they know it or not, such people are all benefiting from the same thing—the goodness of Jehovah God. Religious people often repeat the phrase "God is good." The Bible is far more emphatic. It says: "O how great his goodness is!" (Zechariah 9:17) But it seems that few today really know what those words mean. What does the goodness of Jehovah God actually involve, and how does this quality of God affect each one of us?

An Outstanding Facet of Divine Love

³ In many modern languages, "goodness" is a somewhat bland word. As revealed in the Bible, though, goodness is far from bland. Primarily, it refers to virtue and moral excellence. In a sense, then, we might say that goodness permeates Jehovah. All his attributes—including his power, his justice, and his wisdom—are good through and through. Still, goodness might best be described as an expression of Jehovah's love. Why?

1, 2. How far-reaching is the goodness of God, and what emphasis does the Bible place on this quality?

3, 4. What is goodness, and why might Jehovah's goodness best be described as an expression of divine love?

⁴ Goodness is an active, outgoing quality. The apostle Paul indicated that in humans it is even more appealing than righteousness. (Romans 5:7) The righteous man can be counted on to adhere faithfully to the requirements of the law, but a good man does more. He takes the initiative, actively seeking ways to benefit others. As we shall see, Jehovah is certainly good in that sense. Clearly, such goodness springs from Jehovah's boundless love.

⁵ Jehovah is also unique in his goodness. Not long before Jesus died, a man approached him to ask a question, addressing him with the words "Good Teacher." Jesus replied: "Why do you call me good? Nobody is good, except one, God." (Mark 10:17, 18) Now, that response may strike you as puzzling. Why would Jesus correct the man? Was not Jesus, in fact, a "Good Teacher"?

⁶ Evidently, the man was using the words "Good Teacher" as a flattering title. Jesus modestly directed such glory to his heavenly Father, who is good in the supreme sense. (Proverbs 11:2) But Jesus was also affirming a profound truth. Jehovah alone is the standard for what is good. Only he has the sovereign right to determine what is good and what is bad. Adam and Eve, by rebelliously partaking of the tree of the knowledge of good and bad, sought to assume that right themselves. Unlike them, Jesus humbly leaves the setting of standards to his Father.

⁷ Moreover, Jesus knew that Jehovah is the source of all that is truly good. He is the Giver of "every good gift and every perfect present." (James 1:17) Let us examine how Jehovah's goodness is evident in his generosity.

5-7. Why did Jesus refuse to be called "Good Teacher," and what profound truth did he thereby affirm?

Jehovah is "giving you rains from heaven and fruitful seasons"

Evidence of Jehovah's Abundant Goodness

⁸ Everyone who has ever lived has benefited from Jehovah's goodness. Psalm 145:9 says: "Jehovah is good to *all.*" What are some examples of his all-embracing goodness? The Bible says: "He did not leave himself without witness in that he did good, giving you rains from heaven and fruitful seasons, filling your hearts to the full with food and good cheer." (Acts 14:17) Have you ever felt your spirits lift when enjoying a delightful meal? Were it not for Jehovah's goodness in designing this earth with its ever-recycling fresh water supply and "fruitful seasons" to produce an abundance of food, there would be no meals. Jehovah has directed such goodness not just to those who love him but to *everyone.* Jesus said: "He

────

8. How has Jehovah shown goodness toward all mankind?

makes his sun rise upon wicked people and good and makes it rain upon righteous people and unrighteous." —Matthew 5:45.

9 Many take for granted the sheer generosity that is heaped upon mankind because of the continued action of the sun, the rain, and the fruitful seasons. For example, consider the apple. Throughout the temperate regions of the earth, it is a common fruit. Yet, it is beautiful, delicious to eat, and full of refreshing water and vital nutrients. Did you know that worldwide there are some 7,500 different varieties of apples, ranging in color from

9. How does the apple illustrate Jehovah's goodness?

From this tiny seed grows a tree that can feed and delight people for decades

red to gold to yellow to green and in size from slightly larger than a cherry to the size of a grapefruit? If you hold a tiny apple seed in your hand, it looks insignificant. But from it grows one of the loveliest of trees. (Song of Solomon 2:3) Every spring the apple tree is crowned with a glorious halo of blossoms; every autumn it produces fruit. Each year—for up to 75 years—the average apple tree will yield enough fruit to fill 20 cartons to a weight of 42 pounds each!

10 In his infinite goodness, Jehovah has given us a body that is "wonderfully made," with senses designed to help us perceive his works and delight in them. (Psalm 139: 14) Think again of those scenes described at the outset of this chapter. What *sights* bring joy to such moments? The flushed cheeks of a delighted child. The curtains of rain descending on the fields. The reds, golds, and violets of a sunset. The human eye is designed to detect over 300,000 different colors! And our sense of *hearing* catches the nuances of tone in a well-loved voice, the whisper of the wind through the trees, the toddler's ecstatic laugh. Why are we able to enjoy such sights and sounds? The Bible says: "The hearing ear and the seeing eye—Jehovah himself has made even both of them." (Proverbs 20:12) But those are only two of the senses.

11 The sense of *smell* is another evidence of Jehovah's goodness. The human nose can distinguish some 10,000 different odors. Think of just a few: your favorite food cooking, flowers, fallen leaves, the hint of smoke from a cozy fire. And your sense of *touch* enables you to feel the caress of the breeze on your face, the reassuring embrace of a loved one, the satisfying smoothness of a piece of fruit in your hand. When you take a bite, your sense

10, 11. How do the senses demonstrate God's goodness?

of *taste* comes into play. A symphony of flavor greets you as your taste buds detect subtleties created by the fruit's complex chemical makeup. Yes, we have every reason to exclaim regarding Jehovah: "How abundant your goodness is, which you have treasured up for those fearing you!" (Psalm 31:19) How, though, has Jehovah "treasured up" goodness for those who have godly fear?

Goodness With Everlasting Benefits

[12] Jesus said: "It is written, 'Man must live, not on bread alone, but on every utterance coming forth through Jehovah's mouth.'" (Matthew 4:4) Indeed, Jehovah's spiritual provisions can do us even more good than can the physical kind, for they lead to everlasting life. In Chapter 8 of this book, we noted that Jehovah has used his restorative power during these last days to bring into being a spiritual paradise. A key feature of that paradise is the abundance of spiritual food.

[13] In one of the Bible's great restoration prophecies, the prophet Ezekiel was given a vision of a restored and glorified temple. From that temple flowed a stream of water, widening and deepening as it went until it became a "double-size torrent." Wherever it flowed, that river brought blessings. On its banks flourished a crop of trees that provided food and healing. And the river even brought life and productivity to the salty, lifeless Dead Sea! (Ezekiel 47:1-12) But what did all of that mean?

[14] The vision meant that Jehovah would restore his arrangement for pure worship, as pictured by the temple

---

12. What provisions from Jehovah are the most important, and why?
13, 14. (a) What did the prophet Ezekiel see in vision, with what meaning for us today? (b) What life-giving spiritual provisions does Jehovah make for his faithful servants?

Ezekiel saw. Like that visionary river, God's provisions for life would flow out to his people in ever-greater abundance. Since the restoration of pure worship in 1919, Jehovah has blessed his people with life-giving provisions. How? Well, Bibles, Bible literature, meetings, and conventions have all served to bring vital truths to millions. By such means Jehovah has taught people about the most important of his provisions for life—Christ's ransom sacrifice, which brings a clean standing before Jehovah and the hope of everlasting life to all those who truly love and fear God.* Hence, throughout these last days, while the world has suffered a spiritual famine, Jehovah's people have enjoyed a spiritual feast.—Isaiah 65:13.

¹⁵ But Ezekiel's visionary river does not stop flowing when this old system of things meets its end. On the contrary, it will flow even more abundantly during Christ's Millennial Reign. Then, by means of the Messianic Kingdom, Jehovah will apply the full value of Jesus' sacrifice, gradually lifting faithful mankind to perfection. How we will then exult over Jehovah's goodness!

Additional Facets of Jehovah's Goodness

¹⁶ Jehovah's goodness involves more than generosity. God told Moses: "I myself shall cause all my goodness to pass before your face, and I will declare the name of Jehovah before you." Later the account says: "Jehovah went passing by before his face and declaring: 'Jehovah, Jeho-

---

* There can be no greater example of Jehovah's goodness than the ransom. Of all the millions of spirit creatures to choose from, Jehovah selected his beloved, only-begotten Son to die in our behalf.

15. In what sense will Jehovah's goodness flow to faithful mankind during Christ's Millennial Reign?
16. How does the Bible show that Jehovah's goodness embraces other qualities, and what are some of these?

vah, a God merciful and gracious, slow to anger and abundant in loving-kindness and truth.'" (Exodus 33:19; 34:6) So Jehovah's goodness embraces a number of fine qualities. Let us consider just two of these.

17 *"Gracious."* This quality tells us much about Jehovah's manner of dealing with his creatures. Instead of being brusque, cold, or tyrannical, as is often true of the powerful, Jehovah is gentle and kind. For example, Jehovah said to Abram: "Raise your eyes, please, and look from the place where you are, northward and southward and eastward and westward." (Genesis 13:14) Many translations omit the word "please." But Bible scholars note that the wording in the original Hebrew includes a word particle that changes the statement from a command to a polite request. There are other, similar instances. (Genesis 31:12; Ezekiel 8:5) Imagine, the Sovereign of the universe says "please" to mere humans! In a world where harshness, pushiness, and rudeness are so common, is it not refreshing to contemplate the graciousness of our God, Jehovah?

18 *"Abundant in . . . truth."* Dishonesty has become the way of the world today. But the Bible reminds us: "God is not a man that he should tell lies." (Numbers 23:19) In fact, Titus 1:2 says that "God . . . *cannot* lie." He is far too good for that. Thus, Jehovah's promises are completely reliable; his words, always sure of fulfillment. Jehovah is even called "the God of truth." (Psalm 31:5) Not only does he refrain from telling falsehoods but he dispenses an abundance of truth. He is not closed, guarded, or secretive; rather, he generously enlightens his faithful servants

---

17. What is graciousness, and how has Jehovah displayed it to mere imperfect humans?
18. In what sense is Jehovah "abundant . . . in truth," and why are those words reassuring?

from his boundless store of wisdom.* He even teaches them how to live by the truths he dispenses so that they may "go on walking in the truth." (3 John 3) In general, how should Jehovah's goodness affect us individually?

"Become Radiant Over the Goodness of Jehovah"

¹⁹ When Satan tempted Eve in the garden of Eden, he began by subtly undermining her trust in Jehovah's goodness. Jehovah had told Adam: "From every tree of the garden you may eat to satisfaction." Of the thousands of trees that must have graced that garden, only one was placed off-limits by Jehovah. Yet, notice how Satan worded his first question to Eve: "Is it really so that God said you must not eat from every tree of the garden?" (Genesis 2:9, 16; 3:1) Satan twisted Jehovah's words to make Eve think that Jehovah was holding back something good. Sadly, the tactic worked. Eve, like so many men and women after her, began to doubt the goodness of God, who had given her everything she had.

²⁰ We know the depth of sorrow and misery brought on by such doubts. So let us take to heart the words of Jeremiah 31:12: "They will certainly . . . become radiant over the goodness of Jehovah." Jehovah's goodness should indeed make us radiant with joy. We need never doubt the motives of our God, who is so full of goodness. We may trust in him completely, for he wants nothing but good for those who love him.

---

* For good reason, the Bible associates truth with light. "Send out your light and your truth," sang the psalmist. (Psalm 43:3) Jehovah sheds an abundance of spiritual light upon those willing to be taught, or enlightened, by him.—2 Corinthians 4:6; 1 John 1:5.

19, 20. (a) How did Satan seek to undermine Eve's confidence in Jehovah's goodness, and with what result? (b) Jehovah's goodness should rightly have what effect on us, and why?

Questions for Meditation

1 Kings 8:54-61, 66 How did Solomon express appreciation for Jehovah's goodness, and with what effect on the Israelites?

Psalm 119:66, 68 How might our prayers reflect a desire to imitate Jehovah's goodness?

Luke 6:32-38 What can help to motivate us to imitate Jehovah's spirit of generosity?

Romans 12:2, 9, 17-21 How can we demonstrate goodness in our day-to-day life?

---

²¹ Further, when we get an opportunity to talk to others about God's goodness, we are delighted. Regarding Jehovah's people, Psalm 145:7 says: "With the mention of the abundance of your goodness they will bubble over." Every day that we live, we benefit in some way from Jehovah's goodness. Why not make it a practice each day to thank Jehovah for his goodness, being as specific as possible? Thinking about that quality, thanking Jehovah for it daily, and telling others about it will help us to imitate our good God. And as we seek ways to do good, as Jehovah does, we will draw ever closer to him. The aged apostle John wrote: "Beloved one, be an imitator, not of what is bad, but of what is good. He that does good originates with God."—3 John 11.

²² Jehovah's goodness is also associated with other qualities. For example, God is "abundant in loving-kindness," or loyal love. (Exodus 34:6) This quality is more specific in its focus than is goodness, for Jehovah expresses it particularly toward his faithful servants. In the next chapter, we will learn how he does so.

21, 22. (a) What are some ways in which you would like to respond to Jehovah's goodness? (b) What quality will we discuss in the next chapter, and how does it differ from goodness?

CHAPTER 28

"You Alone Are Loyal"

KING DAVID was no stranger to disloyalty. At one point his tumultuous reign was beset by intrigue, with members of his own nation plotting against him. Furthermore, David was betrayed by some of those whom we would expect to have been his closest companions. Consider Michal, David's first wife. Initially, she "was in love with David," no doubt supporting him in his kingly endeavors. Later, however, she "began to despise him in her heart," even considering David to be "just as one of the empty-headed men."—1 Samuel 18:20; 2 Samuel 6: 16, 20.

² Then there was David's personal adviser, Ahithophel. His counsel was esteemed as if it were the direct word of Jehovah. (2 Samuel 16:23) But, in time, this trusted confidant turned traitor and joined in an organized rebellion against David. And who was the instigator of the conspiracy? Absalom, David's own son! That scheming opportunist "kept stealing the hearts of the men of Israel," setting himself up as a rival king. Absalom's revolt gained so much momentum that King David was forced to flee for his life.—2 Samuel 15:1-6, 12-17.

³ Was there no one who remained loyal to David? Throughout all his adversity, David knew that indeed there was. Who? None other than Jehovah God. "With someone loyal you will act in loyalty," David said of Jehovah. (2 Samuel 22:26) What is loyalty, and how does Jehovah provide the loftiest example of this quality?

1, 2. Why can it be said that King David was no stranger to disloyalty?

3. What confidence did David have?

*The moon is called a faithful witness,
but only intelligent living creatures
can truly reflect Jehovah's loyalty*

What Is Loyalty?

⁴ "Loyalty" as used in the Hebrew Scriptures is kindness that lovingly attaches itself to an object and does not let go until its purpose in connection with that object is realized. More is involved than faithfulness. After all, a person might be faithful merely out of a sense of duty. In contrast, loyalty is rooted in love.* Then, too, the word "faithful" can be applied to inanimate things. For example, the psalmist called the moon "a faithful witness in the skies" because of its regular nightly appearance. (Psalm 89:37) But the moon cannot be described as being loyal. Why? Because loyalty is an expression of love—something that inanimate things cannot display.

⁵ In its Scriptural sense, loyalty is warm. Its very manifestation indicates that a relationship exists between the person who displays the quality and the one toward whom it is shown. Such loyalty is not fickle. It is not like waves of the sea blown about by changing winds. On the contrary,

---

* Interestingly, the word rendered "loyalty" at 2 Samuel 22:26 is elsewhere translated "loving-kindness" or "loyal love."

4, 5. (a) What is "loyalty"? (b) How does loyalty differ from faithfulness?

loyalty, or loyal love, has the stability and strength to overcome the most daunting of obstacles.

⁶ Granted, such loyalty is rare today. All too often, close companions are "disposed to break one another to pieces." Increasingly, we hear of spouses who abandon their mates. (Proverbs 18:24; Malachi 2:14-16) Treacherous acts are so common that we might find ourselves echoing the words of the prophet Micah: "The loyal one has perished from the earth." (Micah 7:2) Although humans often fail to show loving-kindness, loyalty outstandingly characterizes Jehovah. In fact, the best way to learn just what loyalty entails is to examine how Jehovah displays this grand facet of his love.

Jehovah's Matchless Loyalty

⁷ The Bible says of Jehovah: "You alone are loyal." (Revelation 15:4) How can that be? Have not both humans and angels at times displayed remarkable loyalty? (Job 1:1; Revelation 4:8) And what of Jesus Christ? Is he not God's chief "loyal one"? (Psalm 16:10) How, then, can it be said that Jehovah *alone* is loyal?

⁸ First of all, remember that loyalty is a facet of love. Since "God *is* love"—he being the very personification of this quality—who could display loyalty more completely than Jehovah? (1 John 4:8) Really, angels and humans may reflect God's attributes, but only Jehovah is loyal to the superlative degree. As "the Ancient of Days," he has been displaying loving-kindness longer than any creature, earthly or heavenly. (Daniel 7:9) Hence, Jehovah is the very epitome of loyalty. He displays this quality in a manner that no creature can match. Consider some examples.

---

6. (a) How rare is loyalty among humans, and how is this indicated in the Bible? (b) What is the best way to learn what loyalty entails, and why?

7, 8. How can it be said that Jehovah alone is loyal?

⁹ Jehovah is "loyal in all his works." (Psalm 145:17) In what way? Psalm 136 provides an answer. There a number of Jehovah's saving acts are cited, including the dramatic deliverance of the Israelites through the Red Sea. Significantly, each verse of this psalm is punctuated with the phrase: "For his loving-kindness [or, loyalty] is to time indefinite." This psalm is included in the Questions for Meditation on page 289. As you read those verses, you cannot help but be struck by the many ways in which Jehovah demonstrated loving-kindness toward his people. Yes, Jehovah displays loyalty to his faithful servants by hearing their cries for help and by taking action at the appointed time. (Psalm 34:6) Jehovah's loyal love for his servants does not waver as long as they remain loyal to him.

¹⁰ In addition, Jehovah demonstrates loyalty to his servants by remaining true to his standards. Unlike some erratic humans, who are guided by mere whim and sentiment, Jehovah does not vacillate in his view of what is right and what is wrong. Throughout the millenniums, his view of such things as spiritism, idolatry, and murder has remained unchanged. "Even to one's old age I am the same One," he stated through his prophet Isaiah. (Isaiah 46:4) Hence, we can have confidence that we will benefit by following the clear moral direction found in God's Word.—Isaiah 48:17-19.

¹¹ Jehovah also shows loyalty by remaining faithful to his word of promise. When he foretells something, it comes to pass. Jehovah thus stated: "My word that goes forth from my mouth . . . will not return to me without results, but it will certainly do that in which I have delighted, and it

---

9. How is Jehovah "loyal in all his works"?
10. How does Jehovah demonstrate loyalty regarding his standards?
11. Give examples to show that Jehovah is faithful to his word of promise.

will have certain success in that for which I have sent it."
(Isaiah 55:11) By remaining faithful to his word, Jehovah
shows loyalty to his people. He does not keep them anx-
iously awaiting something that he does not intend to bring
about. Jehovah's reputation is so impeccable in this regard
that his servant Joshua was able to say: "Not a promise
failed out of all the good promise that Jehovah had made
to the house of Israel; it all came true." (Joshua 21:45) We
can be confident, then, that we will never be led to disappointment because of some failure on Jehovah's part to
live up to his promises.—Isaiah 49:23; Romans 5:5.

¹² As noted earlier, the Bible tells us that Jehovah's loving-
kindness "is to time indefinite." (Psalm 136:1) How is this
so? For one thing, Jehovah's forgiveness of sins is permanent. As discussed in Chapter 26, Jehovah does not bring
up errors of the past for which a person has been pardoned. Since "all have sinned and fall short of the glory of
God," each of us should be grateful that Jehovah's loving-
kindness is to time indefinite.—Romans 3:23.

¹³ But Jehovah's loving-kindness is to time indefinite in
another sense as well. His Word says that the righteous
one "will certainly become like a tree planted by streams
of water, that gives its own fruit in its season and the fo-
liage of which does not wither, and everything he does will
succeed." (Psalm 1:3) Imagine a luxuriant tree whose fo-
liage never withers! So, too, if we take genuine delight in
God's Word, our lives will be long, peaceful, and fruitful.
The blessings that Jehovah loyally extends to his faithful
servants are everlasting. Truly, in the righteous new world
that Jehovah will bring, obedient mankind will experience
his loving-kindness to time indefinite.—Revelation 21:3, 4.

12, 13. In what ways is Jehovah's loving-kindness "to time indefinite"?

Jehovah "Will Not Leave His Loyal Ones"

14 Jehovah has time and again demonstrated his loyalty. Since Jehovah is perfectly consistent, the loyalty he shows toward his faithful servants never wanes. The psalmist wrote: "A young man I used to be, I have also grown old, and yet I have not seen anyone righteous left entirely, nor his offspring looking for bread. For Jehovah is a lover of justice, and he will not leave his loyal ones." (Psalm 37: 25, 28) True, as the Creator, Jehovah deserves our worship. (Revelation 4:11) Still, because he is loyal, Jehovah treasures our faithful acts.—Malachi 3:16, 17.

15 In his loving-kindness, Jehovah repeatedly comes to the aid of his people when they are in distress. The psalmist tells us: "He is guarding the souls of his loyal ones; out of the hand of the wicked ones he delivers them." (Psalm 97:10) Consider his dealings with the nation of Israel. After their miraculous deliverance through the Red Sea, the Israelites proclaimed in song to Jehovah: "You in your loving-kindness [or, "loyal love," footnote] have led the people whom you have recovered." (Exodus 15:13) The deliverance at the Red Sea certainly was an act of loyal love on Jehovah's part. Moses therefore told the Israelites: "It was not because of your being the most populous of all the peoples that Jehovah showed affection for you so that he chose you, for you were the least of all the peoples. But it was because of Jehovah's loving you, and because of his keeping the sworn statement that he had sworn to your forefathers, that Jehovah brought you out with a strong hand, that he might redeem you from the house of slaves, from the hand of Pharaoh the king of Egypt."—Deuteronomy 7:7, 8.

---

14. How does Jehovah show appreciation for the loyalty of his servants?
15. Explain how Jehovah's dealings with Israel highlight His loyalty.

¹⁶ Of course, as a nation the Israelites failed to demonstrate appreciation for Jehovah's loving-kindness, for after their deliverance "they kept sinning still more against [Jehovah] by rebelling against the Most High." (Psalm 78:17) Over the centuries, they rebelled again and again, leaving Jehovah and turning to false gods and pagan practices that brought nothing but defilement. Still, Jehovah did not break his covenant. Instead, through the prophet Jeremiah, Jehovah implored his people: "Do return, O renegade Israel . . . I shall not have my face drop angrily upon you people, for I am loyal." (Jeremiah 3:12) As noted in Chapter 25, however, most of the Israelites were not moved. Indeed, "they were continually making jest at the messengers of the true God and despising his words and mocking at his prophets." With what result? Finally, "the rage of Jehovah came up against his people, until there was no healing."—2 Chronicles 36:15, 16.

¹⁷ What do we learn from this? That Jehovah's loyalty is neither blind nor gullible. True, Jehovah is "abundant in loving-kindness," and he delights to show mercy when there is a basis for it. But what happens when a wrongdoer proves to be incorrigibly wicked? In such a case, Jehovah adheres to his own righteous standards and renders adverse judgment. As Moses was told, "by no means will [Jehovah] give exemption from punishment."—Exodus 34:6, 7.

¹⁸ God's punishment of the wicked is in itself an act of loyalty. How? One indication is found in the book of Rev-

---

16, 17. (a) What shocking lack of appreciation did the Israelites display, yet how did Jehovah show compassion toward them? (b) How did most Israelites show that "there was no healing" for them, and what warning example does this provide for us?

18, 19. (a) How is Jehovah's punishment of the wicked in itself an act of loyalty? (b) In what way will Jehovah demonstrate his loyalty to those of his servants who have been persecuted to the point of death?

Jehovah will loyally remember and resurrect those who have proved loyal even to death

Bernard Luimes (above) and Wolfgang Kusserow (center) were executed by the Nazis

Moses Nyamussua was speared to death by a political group

elation in the commands that Jehovah issues to seven angels: "Go and pour out the seven bowls of the anger of God into the earth." When the third angel pours his bowl "into the rivers and the fountains of the waters," they become blood. Then the angel says to Jehovah: "You, the One who is and who was, *the loyal One,* are righteous, because you have rendered these decisions, because they poured out the blood of holy ones and of prophets, and you have given them blood to drink. They deserve it."—Revelation 16:1-6.

¹⁹ Note that in the midst of delivering that message of judgment, the angel refers to Jehovah as "the loyal One." Why? Because by destroying the wicked, Jehovah is displaying loyalty to his servants, many of whom have been persecuted to the point of death. Loyally, Jehovah keeps such ones very much alive in his memory. He yearns to see these departed faithful ones again, and the Bible confirms that his purpose is to reward them with a resurrection. (Job 14:14, 15) Jehovah does not forget his loyal servants simply because they are no longer alive. On the contrary, "they are all living to him." (Luke 20:37, 38) Jehovah's purpose

to bring back to life those who are in his memory is powerful evidence of his loyalty.

Jehovah's Loyal Love Opens Up the Way of Salvation

²⁰ Throughout history, Jehovah has shown remarkable loyalty toward faithful humans. In fact, for thousands of years, Jehovah has "tolerated with much long-suffering vessels of wrath made fit for destruction." Why? "In order that he might make known the riches of his glory upon vessels of mercy, which he prepared beforehand for glory." (Romans 9:22, 23) These "vessels of mercy" are rightly disposed ones who are anointed by holy spirit to be joint heirs with Christ in his Kingdom. (Matthew 19:28)

20. Who are the "vessels of mercy," and how does Jehovah show loyalty to them?

Because of Jehovah's loyalty, all his faithful servants have a reliable hope for the future

---

Questions for Meditation

1 Samuel 24:1-22 In his treatment of King Saul, how did David display the kind of loyalty that Jehovah values?

Esther 3:7-9; 4:6-14 How did Esther demonstrate godly loyalty toward her people, even at the risk of her life?

Psalm 136:1-26 What does this psalm teach us about Jehovah's loving-kindness, or loyal love?

Obadiah 1-4, 10-16 How did Jehovah's loyalty to his people move him to punish the Edomites for their disloyal conduct?

By opening up the way of salvation for these vessels of mercy, Jehovah remained loyal to Abraham, to whom he had made this covenant promise: "By means of your seed all nations of the earth will certainly bless themselves due to the fact that you have listened to my voice."—Genesis 22:18.

²¹ Jehovah shows similar loyalty to "a great crowd" who have the prospect of coming out of "the great tribulation" and of living forever on a paradise earth. (Revelation 7:9, 10, 14) Although his servants are imperfect, Jehovah loyally extends to them the opportunity to live forever on a paradise earth. How does he do so? By means of the ransom —the greatest demonstration of Jehovah's loyalty. (John 3:16; Romans 5:8) Jehovah's loyalty attracts those who, in their hearts, hunger for righteousness. (Jeremiah 31:3) Do you not feel closer to Jehovah for the deep loyalty he has shown and will yet show? Since it is our desire to draw close to God, may we respond to his love by strengthening our resolve to serve him with loyalty.

---

21. (a) How does Jehovah show loyalty to "a great crowd" who have the prospect of coming out of "the great tribulation"? (b) What does Jehovah's loyalty move you to do?

CHAPTER 29

"To Know the Love of the Christ"

HAVE you ever seen a little boy trying to be like his father? The son may imitate the way his father walks, talks, or acts. In time, the boy may even absorb his father's moral and spiritual values. Yes, the love and admiration that a son feels for a loving father moves the boy to want to be like his dad.

² What about the relationship between Jesus and his heavenly Father? "I love the Father," Jesus said on one occasion. (John 14:31) No one can possibly love Jehovah more than this Son, who was with the Father long before any other creatures came into existence. That love moved this devoted Son to want to be like his Father.—John 14:9.

³ In earlier chapters of this book, we discussed how Jesus perfectly imitated Jehovah's power, justice, and wisdom. How, though, did Jesus reflect his Father's love? Let us examine three facets of Jesus' love—his self-sacrificing spirit, his tender compassion, and his willingness to forgive.

"No One Has Love Greater Than This"

⁴ Jesus set an outstanding example of self-sacrificing love. Self-sacrifice involves unselfishly putting the needs and concerns of others ahead of our own. How did Jesus demonstrate such love? He himself explained: "No one has love greater than this, that someone should surrender his soul in behalf of his friends." (John 15:13) Jesus willingly

1-3. (a) What moved Jesus to want to be like his Father? (b) What facets of Jesus' love will we examine?
4. How did Jesus set the greatest human example of self-sacrificing love?

gave his perfect life for us. It was the greatest expression of love ever made by any human. But Jesus showed self-sacrificing love in other ways as well.

5 In his prehuman existence, the only-begotten Son of God had a privileged and exalted position in the heavens. He had intimate association with Jehovah and with multitudes of spirit creatures. Despite these personal advantages, this dear Son "emptied himself and took a slave's form and came to be in the likeness of men." (Philippians 2:7) He willingly came to live among sinful humans in a world "lying in the power of the wicked one." (1 John 5:19) Was that not a loving sacrifice on the part of God's Son?

6 Throughout his earthly ministry, Jesus showed self-sacrificing love in various ways. He was totally unselfish. He was so absorbed in his ministry that he sacrificed normal comforts to which humans are accustomed. "Foxes have dens and birds of heaven have roosts," he said, "but the Son of man has nowhere to lay down his head." (Matthew 8:20) Being a skilled carpenter, Jesus could have taken some time off to build a comfortable home for himself or to make beautiful furniture to sell so that he would have had some extra money. But he did not use his skills to gain material things.

7 A truly touching example of Jesus' self-sacrificing love is recorded at John 19:25-27. Imagine the many things that must have occupied the mind and heart of Jesus on the afternoon of his death. As he suffered on the stake, he was concerned about his disciples, the preaching work, and

---

5. Why was leaving the heavens a loving sacrifice on the part of God's only-begotten Son?

6, 7. (a) In what ways did Jesus show self-sacrificing love during his earthly ministry? (b) What touching example of unselfish love is recorded at John 19:25-27?

especially his integrity and how it would reflect on his Father's name. Really, the entire future of mankind rested on his shoulders! Yet, just moments before he died, Jesus also showed concern for his mother, Mary, who was apparently a widow by then. Jesus asked the apostle John to look after Mary as if she were John's own mother, and the apostle thereafter took Mary to his home. Jesus thus arranged for the physical and spiritual care of his mother. What a tender expression of unselfish love!

"He Was Moved With Pity"

8 Like his Father, Jesus was compassionate. The Scriptures describe Jesus as one who reached out to those in distress because he was deeply moved. To describe the compassion of Jesus, the Bible uses a Greek word that is rendered "moved with pity." Says one scholar: "It describes . . . an emotion which moves a man to the very depths of his being. It is the strongest word in Greek for the feeling of compassion." Consider some situations in which Jesus was moved by a deep compassion that compelled him to act.

9 *Moved to respond to spiritual needs.* The account at Mark 6:30-34 shows what principally moved Jesus to express his pity. Picture the scene. The apostles were excited, for they had just completed an extensive preaching tour. They returned to Jesus and eagerly reported all that they had seen and heard. But a large crowd gathered, leaving Jesus and his apostles no time even to eat. Ever observant, Jesus noticed that the apostles were tired. "Come, you yourselves,

8. What is the meaning of the Greek word that the Bible uses to describe the compassion of Jesus?
9, 10. (a) What circumstances caused Jesus and his apostles to seek out a quiet place? (b) When his privacy was disturbed by a crowd, how did Jesus react, and why?

privately into a lonely place and rest up a bit," he told them. Boarding a boat, they sailed across the northern tip of the Sea of Galilee to a quiet place. But the crowd saw them leave. Others also heard about it. All of these ran along the northern shoreline and arrived on the other side ahead of the boat!

[10] Was Jesus upset that his privacy was disturbed? Not at all! His heart was touched by the sight of this crowd, numbering in the thousands, who awaited him. Mark wrote: "He saw a great crowd, but he was moved with pity for them, because they were as sheep without a shepherd. And he started to teach them many things." Jesus saw these people as individuals having spiritual needs. They were like sheep straying helplessly, having no shepherd to guide or protect them. Jesus knew that the common people were neglected by the coldhearted religious leaders, who were supposed to be caring shepherds. (John 7: 47-49) His heart went out to the people, so he began teaching them "about the kingdom of God." (Luke 9: 11) Notice that Jesus was moved with pity for the people even before seeing their reaction to what he would teach. In other words, tender compassion was, not the *result* of his teaching the crowd, but rather the *motive* for his doing so.

[11] *Moved to relieve suffering.* People with various ailments sensed that Jesus had compassion, so they were drawn to him. This was especially evident when Jesus, with crowds following him, was approached by a man "full of leprosy." (Luke 5:12) In Bible times, lepers were quarantined so as to protect others from contamination. (Numbers 5:1-4)

───

11, 12. (a) How were lepers regarded in Bible times, but how did Jesus respond when he was approached by a man "full of leprosy"? (b) How might Jesus' touch have affected the leper, and how does the experience of one doctor illustrate this?

In time, however, rabbinic leaders fostered a heartless view of leprosy and imposed their own oppressive rules.* Notice, though, how Jesus responded to the leper: "There also came to him a leper, entreating him even on bended knee, saying to him: 'If you just want to, you can make me clean.' At that he was moved with pity, and he stretched out his hand and touched him, and said to him: 'I want to. Be made clean.' And immediately the leprosy vanished from him." (Mark 1:40-42) Jesus knew that it was unlawful for the leper even to be there. Yet, instead of turning him away, Jesus was so deeply moved that he did something unthinkable. Jesus touched him!

¹² Can you imagine what that touch meant to the leper? To illustrate, consider an experience. Dr. Paul Brand, a leprosy specialist, tells of a leper he treated in India. During the examination, the doctor laid his hand on the leper's shoulder and explained, through an interpreter, the treatment that the man would have to undergo. Suddenly, the leper began to weep. "Have I said something wrong?" the doctor asked. The interpreter questioned the young man in his language and replied: "No, doctor. He says he is crying because you put your hand around his shoulder. Until he came here no one had touched him for many years." For the leper who approached Jesus, being touched had even greater meaning. Following that one touch, the disease that had made him an outcast was gone!

---

* Rabbinic rules stated that no one should come within four cubits (about six feet) of a leper. But if a wind was blowing, the leper had to be kept at least 100 cubits (about 150 feet) away. The *Midrash Rabbah* tells of one rabbi who hid from lepers and of another who threw stones at lepers to keep them away. Lepers thus knew the pain of rejection and the feeling of being despised and unwanted.

"He stretched out his hand and touched him"

¹³ *Moved to dispel grief.* Jesus was deeply moved by the grief of others. Consider, for example, the account at Luke 7:11-15. It took place when, about halfway through his ministry, Jesus approached the outskirts of the Galilean city of Nain. As Jesus got near the gate of the city, he met a funeral procession. The circumstances were especially tragic. A young man who had been an only son had died, and the mother was a widow. Once before, she had likely been in such a procession—that of her husband. This time it was her son, who perhaps had been her only support. The crowd accompanying her may have included additional mourners chanting lamentations and musicians playing mournful tunes. (Jeremiah 9:17, 18; Matthew 9:23) Jesus' gaze, however, became fixed on the grief-stricken mother, no doubt walking near the bier that carried the body of her son.

¹⁴ Jesus "was moved with pity" for the bereaved mother. In a reassuring tone, he said to her: "Stop weeping." Unbidden, he approached and touched the bier. The bearers —and perhaps the rest of the crowd—came to a halt. With the voice of authority, Jesus spoke to the lifeless body: "Young man, I say to you, Get up!" What happened next? "The dead man sat up and started to speak" as if awakened from a deep sleep! Then follows a most touching statement: "And [Jesus] gave him to his mother."

¹⁵ What do we learn from these accounts? In each case, notice the connection between compassion and action. Jesus could not see the plight of others without being moved with pity, and he could not feel such compassion without

---

13, 14. (a) What procession did Jesus meet when approaching the city of Nain, and what made this an especially sad situation? (b) Jesus' compassion moved him to take what action in behalf of the widow of Nain?
15. (a) The Bible accounts about Jesus' being moved with pity show what connection between compassion and action? (b) How can we imitate Jesus in this regard?

acting on it. How can we follow his example? As Christians, we have an obligation to preach the good news and to make disciples. Primarily, we are motivated by love for God. Let us remember, though, that this is also a work of compassion. When we feel for people as Jesus did, our heart will move us to do all we can to share the good news with them. (Matthew 22:37-39) What about showing compassion to fellow believers who are suffering or grieving? We cannot miraculously cure physical suffering or raise the dead. However, we can put compassion into action by taking the initiative to express our concern or provide appropriate practical help.—Ephesians 4:32.

"Father, Forgive Them"

16 Jesus perfectly reflected his Father's love in another important way—he was "ready to forgive." (Psalm 86:5) This willingness was evident even when he was on the torture stake. Subjected to a shameful death, with nails piercing his hands and feet, what did Jesus speak about? Did he call out to Jehovah to punish his executioners? On the contrary, among Jesus' last words were: "Father, forgive them, for they do not know what they are doing."—Luke 23:34.*

17 Perhaps an even more touching example of Jesus'

---

* The first part of Luke 23:34 is omitted from certain ancient manuscripts. However, because these words are found in many other authoritative manuscripts, they are included in the *New World Translation* and numerous other translations. Jesus was evidently speaking about the Roman soldiers who impaled him. They did not know what they were doing, being ignorant of who Jesus really was. Of course, the religious leaders who instigated that execution were far more reprehensible, for they acted knowingly and maliciously. For many of them, no forgiveness was possible.—John 11:45-53.

---

16. How was Jesus' willingness to forgive evident even when he was on the torture stake?
17-19. In what ways did Jesus demonstrate that he forgave the apostle Peter for denying Him three times?

forgiveness can be seen in the way he dealt with the apostle Peter. There is no question that Peter dearly loved Jesus. On Nisan 14, the final night of Jesus' life, Peter told him: "Lord, I am ready to go with you both into prison and into death." Yet, just a few hours later, Peter three times denied even knowing Jesus! The Bible tells us what happened as Peter uttered his third denial: "The Lord turned and looked upon Peter." Crushed by the weight of his sin, Peter "went outside and wept bitterly." When Jesus died later that day, the apostle may well have wondered, 'Did my Lord forgive me?'—Luke 22:33, 61, 62.

[18] Peter did not have to wait long for an answer. Jesus was resurrected on the morning of Nisan 16, and evidently on that same day, he made a personal visit to Peter. (Luke 24: 34; 1 Corinthians 15:4-8) Why did Jesus give such special attention to the apostle who had so vigorously denied Him? Jesus may have wanted to assure the repentant Peter that he was still loved and valued by his Lord. But Jesus did even more to reassure Peter.

[19] Some time later, Jesus appeared to the disciples at the Sea of Galilee. On this occasion, Jesus three times questioned Peter (who had three times denied his Lord) as to Peter's love for him. After the third time, Peter replied: "Lord, you know all things; you are aware that I have affection for you." Indeed, Jesus, who could read hearts, was fully aware of Peter's love and affection for him. Yet, Jesus gave Peter an opportunity to affirm his love. More than that, Jesus commissioned Peter to "feed" and "shepherd" His "little sheep." (John 21:15-17) Earlier, Peter had received an assignment to preach. (Luke 5:10) But now, in a remarkable demonstration of trust, Jesus gave him a further weighty responsibility—to care for those who would become Christ's followers. Shortly afterward, Jesus gave Peter a prominent role in the activity of the disciples. (Acts

---

Questions for Meditation

Matthew 9:35-38 In what significant way did Jesus show pity, or compassion, and what effect should this have on us?

John 13:34, 35 Why is it important for us to reflect the love of the Christ?

Romans 15:1-6 How can we imitate the unselfish mental attitude of Christ?

2 Corinthians 5:14, 15 Appreciation for the ransom should have what effect on our outlook, goals, and life-style?

2:1-41) How relieved Peter must have been to know that Jesus had forgiven him and still trusted him!

Do You "Know the Love of the Christ"?

²⁰ Truly, Jehovah's Word beautifully describes the love of the Christ. How, though, should we respond to Jesus' love? The Bible urges us "to know the love of the Christ which surpasses knowledge." (Ephesians 3:19) As we have seen, the Gospel accounts of Jesus' life and ministry teach us much about Christ's love. However, fully coming "to know the love of the Christ" involves more than learning what the Bible says about him.

²¹ The Greek term rendered "to know" means to know "practically, through experience." When we show love the way Jesus did—unselfishly giving of ourselves in behalf of others, compassionately responding to their needs, forgiving them from our hearts—then we can genuinely appreciate his feelings. In this way, by experience we come "to know the love of the Christ which surpasses knowledge." And let us never forget that the more we become like Christ, the closer we will draw to the one whom Jesus perfectly imitated, our loving God, Jehovah.

20, 21. How can we fully come "to know the love of the Christ"?

CHAPTER 30

"Go On Walking in Love"

"THERE is more happiness in giving than there is in receiving." (Acts 20:35) Those words of Jesus underscore this important truth: Unselfish love brings its own reward. Although there is much happiness in *receiving* love, there is even greater happiness in *giving,* or *showing,* love to others.

² No one knows this better than our heavenly Father does. As we saw in the preceding chapters of this section, Jehovah is the ultimate example of love. No one has shown love in greater ways or over a longer period of time than he has. Is it any wonder, then, that Jehovah is called "the happy God"?—1 Timothy 1:11.

³ Our loving God wants us to try to be like him, especially when it comes to showing love. Ephesians 5:1, 2 tells us: "Become imitators of God, as beloved children, and go on walking in love." When we imitate Jehovah's example of showing love, we experience the greater happiness that comes from giving. We also have the satisfaction of knowing that we are pleasing to Jehovah, for his Word urges us "to love one another." (Romans 13:8) But there are yet other reasons why we should "go on walking in love."

Why Love Is Essential

⁴ Why is it important that we show love to fellow believers? Put simply, love is the essence of true Christianity. Without love we cannot have a close bond with fellow Christians, and more important, we amount to nothing

---

1-3. What results when we imitate Jehovah's example of showing love?
4, 5. Why is it important that we show self-sacrificing love to fellow believers?

in Jehovah's sight. Consider how God's Word highlights these truths.

5 On the final night of his earthly life, Jesus told his followers: "I am giving you a new commandment, that you love one another; just as I have loved you, that you also love one another. By this all will know that you are my disciples, if you have love among yourselves." (John 13: 34, 35) "Just as I have loved you"—yes, we are commanded to show the kind of love that Jesus displayed. In Chapter 29, we noted that Jesus set a superb example in showing self-sacrificing love, putting the needs and interests of others ahead of self. We too are to display unselfish love, and we are to do it so plainly that our love is evident even to those outside the Christian congregation. Indeed, self-sacrificing brotherly love is the mark by which we are identified as true followers of Christ.

6 What if love is lacking in us? "If I . . . do not have love," said the apostle Paul, "I have become a sounding piece of brass or a clashing cymbal." (1 Corinthians 13:1) A clashing cymbal produces a harsh noise. What about a sounding piece of brass? Other versions say "a noisy gong" or "a resounding gong." What apt illustrations! A loveless person is like a musical instrument making a loud, jarring noise that repels rather than attracts. How could such a person enjoy a close relationship with others? Paul also said: "If I have all the faith so as to transplant mountains, but do not have love, I am nothing." (1 Corinthians 13:2) Just imagine, a person without love is "a useless nobody," despite any works that he might perform! (*The Amplified Bible*) Is it not clear that Jehovah's Word places a high value on showing love?

6, 7. (a) How do we know that Jehovah's Word places a high value on showing love? (b) Paul's words recorded at 1 Corinthians 13:4-8 focus on what aspect of love?

Love moves us to express confidence in our brothers

⁷ How, though, can we display this quality in our dealings with others? To answer that, let us examine Paul's words found at 1 Corinthians 13:4-8. The emphasis in these verses is neither on God's love for us nor on our love for God. Rather, Paul focused on how we should show love to one another. He described certain things that love is and certain things that it is not.

What Love Is

⁸ *"Love is long-suffering."* Being long-suffering means patiently putting up with others. (Colossians 3:13) Do we not need such patience? Because we are imperfect creatures serving shoulder to shoulder, it is only realistic to expect that from time to time, our Christian brothers may irritate us and we may do the same to them. But pa-

---

8. How can long-suffering help us in our dealings with others?

tience and forbearance can help us to cope with the minor scrapes and scratches we sustain in our dealings with others—without disrupting the peace of the congregation.

⁹ *"Love is . . . kind."* Kindness is shown by helpful acts and considerate words. Love moves us to look for ways to show kindness, especially toward those most in need. For instance, an older fellow believer may be lonely and in need of an encouraging visit. A single mother or a sister living in a religiously divided home may need some assistance. One who is ill or facing some adversity may need to hear kind words from a loyal friend. (Proverbs 12:25; 17: 17) When we take the initiative to show kindness in such ways, we demonstrate the genuineness of our love.—2 Corinthians 8:8.

¹⁰ *"Love . . . rejoices with the truth."* Another version says: "Love . . . joyfully sides with the truth." Love moves us to uphold truth and to "speak truthfully with one another." (Zechariah 8:16) If, for example, a loved one has been involved in serious sin, love for Jehovah—and for the erring one—will help us hold to God's standards rather than trying to conceal, rationalize, or even lie about the wrongdoing. Granted, the truth of the situation may be hard to accept. But having the best interests of our loved one at heart, we would want him to receive and respond to an expression of God's loving discipline. (Proverbs 3:11, 12) As loving Christians, we also wish to "conduct ourselves honestly in all things."—Hebrews 13:18.

¹¹ *"Love . . . bears all things."* That expression literally means "all things it is covering." (*Kingdom Interlinear*) First Peter 4:8 states: "Love covers a multitude of

---

9. In what ways can we show kindness to others?
10. How does love help us uphold and speak the truth, even when it is not easy to do so?
11. Because love "bears all things," what should we endeavor to do with respect to the shortcomings of fellow believers?

sins." Yes, a Christian who is governed by love is not eager to drag into the light of day all the imperfections and shortcomings of his Christian brothers. In many cases, the mistakes and faults of fellow believers are minor in nature and can be covered by the cloak of love.—Proverbs 10:12; 17:9.

¹² *"Love . . . believes all things."* Moffatt's translation says that love is "always eager to believe the best." We are not unduly suspicious of fellow believers, questioning their every motive. Love helps us "to believe the best" about our brothers and to trust them.* Note an example in Paul's letter to Philemon. Paul was writing in order to encourage Philemon to welcome kindly the return of the runaway slave Onesimus, who had become a Christian. Instead of trying to coerce Philemon, Paul made an appeal based on love. He expressed confidence that Philemon would do the right thing, saying: "Trusting in your compliance, I am writing you, knowing you will even do more than the things I say." (Verse 21) When love moves us to express such confidence in our brothers, we bring out the best in them.

¹³ *"Love . . . hopes all things."* Even as love is trustful, it is also hopeful. Motivated by love, we hope the best for our brothers. For example, if a brother takes a "false step before he is aware of it," we hope that he will respond to loving efforts to readjust him. (Galatians 6:1) We also hold out hope that those who are weak in faith will recover. We are patient with such ones, doing what we can to help

---

* Of course, Christian love is by no means gullible. The Bible exhorts us: "Keep your eye on those who cause divisions and occasions for stumbling . . . , and avoid them."—Romans 16:17.

---

12. How did the apostle Paul show that he believed the best about Philemon, and what can we learn from Paul's example?
13. How can we show that we hope the best for our brothers?

them become strong in faith. (Romans 15:1; 1 Thessalonians 5:14) Even if a loved one goes astray, we do not give up hope that someday he will come to his senses and return to Jehovah, like the prodigal son in Jesus' illustration. —Luke 15:17, 18.

14 *"Love . . . endures all things."* Endurance enables us to stand firm in the face of disappointments or hardships. Tests of endurance do not come only from outside the congregation. At times, we may be tested from within. Because of imperfection, our brothers may on occasion disappoint us. A thoughtless remark may hurt our feelings. (Proverbs 12:18) Perhaps a congregation matter is not handled as we think it should be. The conduct of a respected brother may be upsetting, causing us to wonder, 'How can a Christian act like that?' When faced with such situations, will we withdraw from the congregation and stop serving Jehovah? Not if we have love! Yes, love prevents us from becoming so blinded by the failings of a brother that we can no longer see any good in him or in the congregation as a whole. Love enables us to remain faithful to God and supportive of the congregation regardless of what another imperfect human may say or do.—Psalm 119:165.

What Love Is Not

15 *"Love is not jealous."* Improper jealousy can cause us to become envious of what others have—their belongings, blessings, or abilities. Such jealousy is a selfish, destructive emotion that, left unchecked, can disrupt the peace of the congregation. What will help us to resist the "tendency to envy"? (James 4:5) In a word, love. This precious quality can enable us to rejoice with those who seem to have

---

14. In what ways may our endurance be tested within the congregation, and how will love help us to respond?
15. What is improper jealousy, and how does love help us to avoid this destructive emotion?

certain advantages in life that we ourselves do not have. (Romans 12:15) Love helps us not to view it as a personal affront when someone receives praise for some exceptional ability or outstanding achievement.

16 *"Love . . . does not brag, does not get puffed up."* Love restrains us from flaunting our talents or accomplishments. If we truly love our brothers, how could we constantly brag about our success in the ministry or our privileges in the congregation? Such boasting can tear others down, causing them to feel inferior in comparison. Love does not allow us to brag about what God lets us do in his service. (1 Corinthians 3:5-9) After all, love "does not get puffed up," or as *The New Testament in Modern English* says, it does not "cherish inflated ideas of its own importance." Love prevents us from having an elevated view of ourselves.—Romans 12:3.

17 *"Love . . . does not behave indecently."* A person who behaves indecently acts in an unseemly or offensive manner. Such a course is unloving, for it shows an utter disregard for the feelings and welfare of others. In contrast, there is a graciousness in love that moves us to show consideration for others. Love promotes good manners, godly conduct, and respect for our fellow believers. Thus, love will not permit us to engage in "shameful conduct"—really, any behavior that would shock or offend our Christian brothers.—Ephesians 5:3, 4.

18 *"Love . . . does not look for its own interests."* The *Revised Standard Version* says here: "Love does not insist on its own way." A loving person does not demand that every-

---

16. If we truly love our brothers, why would we avoid boasting about what we are doing in Jehovah's service?
17. Love moves us to show what consideration for others, and what kind of conduct will we thus avoid?
18. Why does a loving person not demand that everything be done his way?

thing be done his way, as if his opinions were always correct. He does not manipulate others, using his powers of persuasion to wear down those who have a different view. Such stubbornness would reveal a measure of pride, and the Bible says: "Pride is before a crash." (Proverbs 16:18) If we really love our brothers, we will respect their views, and where possible, we will show a willingness to yield. A yielding spirit is in harmony with Paul's words: "Let each one keep seeking, not his own advantage, but that of the other person."—1 Corinthians 10:24.

[19] *"Love . . . does not become provoked . . . , does not keep account of the injury."* Love is not easily provoked by what others say or do. True, it is only natural to become upset when others offend us. But even if we get justifiably angry, love does not let us *remain* provoked. (Ephesians 4:26, 27) We would not keep a record of hurtful words or deeds, as if writing them in a ledger so that they will not be forgotten. Instead, love moves us to imitate our loving God. As we saw in Chapter 26, Jehovah forgives when there is sound reason for doing so. When he forgives us, he forgets, that is, he does not hold those sins against us at some future time. Are we not thankful that Jehovah does not keep account of the injury?

[20] *"Love . . . does not rejoice over unrighteousness." The New English Bible* here reads: "Love . . . does not gloat over other men's sins." Moffatt's translation says: "Love is never glad when others go wrong." Love finds no pleasure in unrighteousness, so we do not wink at immorality of any kind. How do we react if a fellow believer is ensnared by sin and fares badly as a result? Love will not let us rejoice, as if to say 'Good! He deserved it!' (Proverbs 17:5) We

19. How does love help us to respond when others offend us?
20. How should we react if a fellow believer is ensnared by wrongdoing and fares badly as a result?

Jehovah's people are identified by their love for one another

do rejoice, however, when a brother who has erred takes positive steps to recover from his spiritual fall.

"A Surpassing Way"

21 *"Love never fails."* What did Paul mean by those words? As seen in the context, he was discussing the gifts of the spirit that were present among early Christians. Those gifts served as signs that God's favor was on the newly formed congregation. But not all Christians could heal, prophesy, or speak in tongues. However, that did not matter; the miraculous gifts would eventually cease anyway. Yet, something else would remain, something every

---

21-23. (a) What did Paul mean when he said that "love never fails"? (b) What will be considered in the final chapter?

Questions for Meditation

2 Corinthians 6:11-13 What does it mean to "widen out" in our affections, and how can we apply this counsel?

1 Peter 1:22 How do these words show that our love for fellow believers must be sincere, genuine, and warm?

1 John 3:16-18 How can we demonstrate that "the love of God" remains in us?

1 John 4:7-11 What is the strongest motivation for showing love to our fellow believers?

Christian could cultivate. It was more outstanding, more enduring, than any miraculous gift. In fact, Paul called it "a surpassing way." (1 Corinthians 12:31) What was this "surpassing way"? It was the way of love.

²² Indeed, the Christian love that Paul described "never fails," that is, it will never come to an end. To this day, self-sacrificing brotherly love identifies Jesus' true followers. Do we not see evidence of such love in the congregations of Jehovah's worshipers earth wide? That love will last forever, for Jehovah promises everlasting life to his faithful servants. (Psalm 37:9-11, 29) May we continue to do our best to "go on walking in love." By doing so, we can experience the greater happiness that comes from giving. More than that, we can keep on living—yes, keep on loving—for all eternity, in imitation of our loving God, Jehovah.

²³ In this chapter concluding the section on love, we have discussed how we can show love for one another. But in view of the many ways in which we benefit from Jehovah's love—as well as from his power, justice, and wisdom—we do well to ask, 'How can I show Jehovah that I truly love him?' That question will be considered in our final chapter.

CHAPTER 31

"Draw Close to God, and He Will Draw Close to You"

PARENTS love to see their newborn baby smile. They often put their faces close to that of the infant, cooing and smiling expressively. They are eager to see a response. And before long, it comes—the baby's cheeks dimple, the lips curl, and a delightful smile appears. In its own small way, that smile seems to express affection, the dawning love of the baby in response to the love of the parents.

² The baby's smile reminds us of something important about human nature. Our natural response to love is love. That is simply the way we are made. (Psalm 22:9) As we grow, we mature in our ability to respond to love. Perhaps you can recall from your own childhood how your parents, relatives, or friends expressed love for you. In your heart a warm feeling took root, grew, and blossomed into action. You showed your love in return. Is a similar process unfolding in your relationship with Jehovah God?

³ The Bible says: "As for us, we love, because he first loved us." (1 John 4:19) In Sections 1 through 3 of this book, you were reminded that Jehovah God has exercised his power, his justice, and his wisdom in loving ways to your benefit. And in Section 4, you saw that he has directly expressed his love for mankind—and for you personally—in remarkable ways. Now comes a question. In a way, it is the most important question you can ask yourself: 'How will I respond to Jehovah's love?'

1-3. (a) What may we learn about human nature by observing the interaction between parents and their baby? (b) What process naturally unfolds when someone shows us love, and what important question can we ask ourselves?

What It Means to Love God

4 Jehovah, the Originator of love, well knows that love has immense power to bring out the best in others. So despite the persistent rebelliousness of unfaithful mankind, he has remained confident that some humans would respond to his love. And, indeed, millions have. Sadly, though, the religions of this corrupt world have left people confused about what it means to love God. Countless people say that they love God, but they seem to think that such love is merely a feeling to be expressed in words. Love for God may begin that way, just as a baby's love for his parents may first show itself in a smile. In mature people, however, love involves more.

5 Jehovah defines what it means to love him. His Word says: "This is what the love of God means, that we observe his commandments." Love of God, then, needs to be expressed in action. Granted, many do not find the thought of obedience appealing. But the same verse kindly adds: "And yet [God's] commandments are not burdensome." (1 John 5:3) Jehovah's laws and principles are designed to benefit us, not to oppress us. (Isaiah 48:17, 18) God's Word is full of principles that help us draw closer to him. How so? Let us review three aspects of our relationship with God. These involve communication, worship, and imitation.

Communicating With Jehovah

6 Chapter 1 opened with the question, "Can you imagine having a conversation with God?" We saw that this

---

4. In what way are people confused about what it means to love God?
5. How does the Bible define love of God, and why should that definition appeal to us?
6-8. (a) By what means can we listen to Jehovah? (b) How can we make the Scriptures *live* when we read them?

was not a fanciful concept. Moses, in effect, had such a conversation. What about us? Now is not Jehovah's time to send his angels to converse with humans. But Jehovah has excellent means of communicating with us today. How can we listen to Jehovah?

⁷ Because "all Scripture is inspired of God," we listen to Jehovah by reading his Word, the Bible. (2 Timothy 3:16) The psalmist thus urged servants of Jehovah to do such reading "day and night." (Psalm 1:1, 2) Doing so requires considerable effort on our part. But all efforts of that kind are well spent. As we saw in Chapter 18, the Bible is like a precious letter to us from our heavenly Father. So reading it should not be a chore. We must make the Scriptures *live* when we read them. How can we do that?

⁸ Visualize the Bible accounts as you read. Try to see the Bible characters as real people. Seek to grasp their background, circumstances, and motives. Then, think deeply about what you read, asking yourself such questions as: 'What does this account teach me about Jehovah? Which of his qualities do I see? What principle does Jehovah want me to learn, and how can I put it to work in my life?' Read, meditate, and apply—as you do, God's Word will come alive for you.—Psalm 77:12; James 1:23-25.

⁹ Jehovah also speaks to us by means of "the faithful and discreet slave." As Jesus foretold, a class of anointed Christians has been appointed to provide spiritual "food at the proper time" during these troublesome last days. (Matthew 24:45-47) When we read literature prepared to help us acquire accurate knowledge of the Bible and when we attend Christian meetings and conventions, we are being fed spiritually by that slave class. Because it is Christ's slave, we wisely apply Jesus' words: "Pay attention to *how*

9. Who is "the faithful and discreet slave," and why is it important that we listen attentively to that "slave"?

you listen." (Luke 8:18) We listen attentively because we recognize the slave class as one of Jehovah's means of communicating with us.

¹⁰ But what about communicating with God? Can we speak to Jehovah? It is an awe-inspiring thought. If you were to try to approach the most powerful ruler in your land in order to talk about some personal concern of yours, what would be your chances of success? In some cases, the very attempt might prove dangerous! In the days of Esther and Mordecai, a person could be put to death for approaching the Persian monarch without a royal invitation to do so. (Esther 4:10, 11) Now imagine coming before the Sovereign Lord of the universe, compared to whom even the most powerful of humans "are as grasshoppers." (Isaiah 40:22) Should we feel too intimidated to approach him? By no means!

¹¹ Jehovah has provided an open, yet simple, means of approach to him—prayer. Even a very young child can pray to Jehovah in faith, doing so in the name of Jesus. (John 14:6; Hebrews 11:6) Yet, prayer also enables us to transmit our most complex, intimate thoughts and feelings—even the painful ones that we find difficult to put into words. (Romans 8:26) It does no good to try to impress Jehovah with eloquent, flowery speech or with lengthy, wordy prayers. (Matthew 6:7, 8) On the other hand, Jehovah puts no limits on how long we may speak to him or how often. His Word even invites us to "pray incessantly."—1 Thessalonians 5:17.

¹² Remember that Jehovah alone is called the "Hearer of prayer," and he listens with genuine empathy. (Psalm 65:2) Does he merely tolerate the prayers of his

---

10-12. (a) Why is prayer a wonderful gift from Jehovah? (b) How can we pray in a manner pleasing to Jehovah, and why may we be confident that he values our prayers?

faithful servants? No, he actually finds pleasure in them. His Word compares such prayers to incense, the burning of which sends sweet-smelling, restful smoke upward. (Psalm 141:2; Revelation 5:8; 8:4) Is it not comforting to think that our sincere prayers likewise ascend and please the Sovereign Lord? So if you want to draw close to Jehovah, humbly pray to him often, every day. Pour out your heart to him; hold nothing back. (Psalm 62:8) Share your concerns, your joys, your thanks, and your praise with your heavenly Father. As a result, the bond between you and him will grow ever stronger.

Worshiping Jehovah

¹³ When we communicate with Jehovah God, we are not simply listening and speaking as we might with a friend or relative. We are actually worshiping Jehovah, according him the reverent honor that he so richly deserves. True worship is our whole life. It is how we express to Jehovah our whole-souled love and devotion, and it unites all of Jehovah's faithful creatures, whether in heaven or on earth. In a vision, the apostle John heard an angel proclaiming this commandment: "Worship the One who made the heaven and the earth and sea and fountains of waters."—Revelation 14:7.

¹⁴ Why should we worship Jehovah? Think of the qualities we have discussed, such as holiness, power, self-restraint, justice, courage, mercy, wisdom, humility, love, compassion, loyalty, and goodness. We have seen that Jehovah represents the very pinnacle, the loftiest standard possible, of every precious attribute. When we try to grasp the sum of his qualities, we perceive that he is far more than a great, admirable Personage. He is overwhelmingly

---

13, 14. What does it mean to worship Jehovah, and why is it fitting that we do so?

Christian meetings are delightful occasions to worship Jehovah

glorious, immeasurably higher than we are. (Isaiah 55:9) Without question, Jehovah is our rightful Sovereign, and he certainly deserves our worship. How, though, should we worship Jehovah?

¹⁵ Jesus said: "God is a Spirit, and those worshiping him must worship with spirit and truth." (John 4:24) That means to worship Jehovah with a heart full of faith and love, guided by his spirit. It also means to worship in harmony with the truth, the accurate knowledge found in God's Word. We have a precious opportunity to worship Jehovah "with spirit and truth" whenever we gather with fellow worshipers. (Hebrews 10:24, 25) When we sing praises to Jehovah, unite in prayer to him, and listen to

15. How may we worship Jehovah "with spirit and truth," and what opportunity do Christian meetings afford us?

and take part in discussions of his Word, we express love for him in pure worship.

16 We also worship Jehovah when we speak about him to others, publicly praising him. (Hebrews 13:15) Indeed, to preach the good news of Jehovah's Kingdom is one of the greatest commandments laid upon true Christians. (Matthew 24:14) We obey eagerly because we love Jehovah. When we think of the way "the god of this system of things," Satan the Devil, "has blinded the minds of the unbelievers," promoting vicious lies about Jehovah, do we not yearn to serve as Witnesses on behalf of our God, setting straight such slander? (2 Corinthians 4:4; Isaiah 43:10-12) And when we contemplate Jehovah's marvelous qualities, do we not feel a desire welling up within us to tell others about him? Really, there can be no greater privilege than helping others come to know and love our heavenly Father as we do.

17 Our worship of Jehovah embraces even more. It touches every aspect of our life. (Colossians 3:23) If we truly accept Jehovah as our Sovereign Lord, then we will seek to do his will in everything—our family life, our secular work, our dealings with others, our private time. We will seek to serve Jehovah "with a complete heart," with integrity. (1 Chronicles 28:9) Such worship leaves no room for a divided heart or a double life—the hypocritical course of appearing to serve Jehovah while carrying on serious sins in secret. Integrity makes such hypocrisy impossible; love makes it repulsive. Godly fear will help too. The Bible links such reverence with our continued intimacy with Jehovah.—Psalm 25:14.

---

16. What is one of the greatest commandments laid upon true Christians, and why do we feel compelled to obey it?
17. What does our worship of Jehovah embrace, and why must we worship with integrity?

Imitating Jehovah

¹⁸ Each section of this book has concluded with a chapter on how to "become imitators of God, as beloved children." (Ephesians 5:1) It is vital to remember that imperfect though we are, we can truly imitate Jehovah's perfect way of using power, of exercising justice, of acting in wisdom, and of showing love. How do we know that it really is possible to imitate the Almighty? Remember, the meaning of Jehovah's name teaches us that he causes himself to become whatever he chooses in order to fulfill his purposes. We are rightly awed by that ability, but is it completely beyond us? No.

¹⁹ We are made in God's image. (Genesis 1:26) Thus, humans are unlike any other creatures on earth. We are not driven merely by instinct, genetics, or factors in our environment. Jehovah has given us a precious gift—free will. Despite our limitations and imperfections, we are free to *choose* what we will become. Do you want to be a loving, wise, just person who uses power aright? Thanks to the help of Jehovah's spirit, you can become exactly that! Think of the good you will thereby accomplish.

²⁰ You will please your heavenly Father, making his heart rejoice. (Proverbs 27:11) You can even be "fully pleasing" to Jehovah, for he understands your limitations. (Colossians 1:9, 10) And as you continue to build good qualities in imitation of your beloved Father, you will be blessed with a great privilege. In a bedarkened world alienated from God, you will be a light bearer. (Matthew 5:1, 2, 14) You will help to spread abroad in the earth some reflections of Jehovah's glorious personality. What an honor!

18, 19. Why is it realistic to think that mere imperfect humans can imitate Jehovah God?

20. What good do we accomplish when we imitate Jehovah?

"Draw Close to God, and He Will Draw Close to You"

21 The simple exhortation recorded at James 4:8 is more than a goal. It is a journey. As long as we remain faithful, that journey will never end. We will never stop drawing closer and closer to Jehovah. After all, there will always be more to learn about him. We should not imagine that this book has taught us all there is to know about Jehovah. Why, we have barely begun to discuss all that the Bible says about our God! And even the Bible itself does not tell us *all* there is to know about Jehovah. The apostle John supposed that if everything that Jesus did during his earthly ministry were put in writing, "the world itself could not contain the scrolls written." (John 21:25) If such a thing could be said of the Son, how much more so of the Father!

22 Even eternal life will not bring us to the end of learn-

21, 22. What endless journey lies before all who love Jehovah?

May you always draw closer to Jehovah

```
┌─────────────────────────────────────────────┐
│             Questions for Meditation           │
│                                                │
│  Psalm 25:1-22 How may we draw closer to      │
│  Jehovah, and what confidence may we have as  │
│  a result?                                     │
│                                                │
│  Hosea 6:3 How does this verse show that      │
│  getting to know Jehovah requires effort and  │
│  brings blessings?                             │
│                                                │
│  Matthew 16:21-27 If we are to imitate         │
│  Jehovah, whose example must we follow, and   │
│  what spirit must we show?                     │
│                                                │
│  Revelation 21:3, 4 As you contemplate the    │
│  future blessings that Jehovah will provide,  │
│  what are you moved to do in response?         │
└─────────────────────────────────────────────┘
```

ing about Jehovah. (Ecclesiastes 3:11) Think, then, of the prospect before us. After having lived for hundreds, thousands, millions, even billions of years, we will know far more about Jehovah God than we do now. But we will still feel that there are countless wonderful things to be learned. We will be eager to learn more, for we will always have reason to feel as did the psalmist, who sang: "The drawing near to God is good for me." (Psalm 73:28) Eternal life will be unimaginably rich and varied—and drawing closer to Jehovah will always be the most rewarding part of it.

²³ May you respond to Jehovah's love now, by loving him with your whole heart, soul, mind, and strength. (Mark 12:29, 30) May your love be loyal and steadfast. May the decisions that you make every day, from the smallest to the greatest, all reflect the same guiding principle—that you will always choose the path that leads you to a stronger relationship with your heavenly Father. Above all, may you draw ever closer to Jehovah, and may he draw ever closer to you—throughout all eternity!

---

23. What are you encouraged to do?

Would you welcome more information?

Write Jehovah's Witnesses at the appropriate address below.

ALASKA 99507: 2552 East 48th Ave., Anchorage. **ALBANIA:** Kutia postare 118, Tiranë. **ANGOLA:** Caixa Postal 6877, Luanda. **ARGENTINA:** Casilla de Correo 83 (Suc. 27B), 1427 Buenos Aires. **AUSTRALIA:** Box 280, Ingleburn, NSW 1890. **AUSTRIA (also Bulgaria, Macedonia, Yugoslavia):** Postfach 67, A-1134 Vienna. **BAHAMAS:** Box N-1247, Nassau, N.P. **BARBADOS, W.I.:** Crusher Site Road, Prospect, St. James. **BELGIUM:** rue d'Argile-Potaardestraat 60, B-1950 Kraainem. **BENIN, REP. OF:** 06 B.P. 1131, Akpakpa pk3, Cotonou. **BOLIVIA:** Casilla 6397, Santa Cruz. **BRAZIL:** Caixa Postal 92, 18270-970 Tatuí, SP. **BRITAIN:** The Ridgeway, London NW7 1RN. **CAMEROON:** B.P. 889, Douala. **CANADA:** Box 4100, Halton Hills (Georgetown), Ontario L7G 4Y4. **CENTRAL AFRICAN REPUBLIC:** B.P. 662, Bangui. **CHILE:** Casilla 267, Puente Alto. **COLOMBIA:** Apartado Postal 85058, Bogotá 8, D.C. **CONGO, DEMOCRATIC REPUBLIC OF:** B.P. 634, Limete, Kinshasa. **COSTA RICA:** Apartado 187-3006, Barreal, Heredia. **CÔTE D'IVOIRE (IVORY COAST), WEST AFRICA:** 06 B P 393, Abidjan 06. **CROATIA:** p.p. 58, HR-10090 Zagreb-Susedgrad. **CURAÇAO, NETHERLANDS ANTILLES:** P.O. Box 4708, Willemstad. **CYPRUS:** P.O. Box 11033, CY-2550 Dali. **CZECH REPUBLIC:** P.O. Box 90, 198 21 Prague 9. **DENMARK:** Stenhusvej 28, DK-4300 Holbæk. **DOMINICAN REPUBLIC:** Apartado 1742, Santo Domingo. **ECUADOR:** Casilla 09-01-1334, Guayaquil. **EL SALVADOR:** Apartado Postal 401, San Salvador. **ESTONIA:** Postbox 1075, 10302 Tallinn. **ETHIOPIA:** P.O. Box 5522, Addis Ababa. **FIJI:** Box 23, Suva. **FINLAND (also Latvia, Lithuania):** Postbox 68, FIN-01301 Vantaa. **FRANCE:** B.P. 625, F-27406 Louviers cedex. **GERMANY:** Niederselters, Am Steinfels, D-65618 Selters. **GHANA:** P. O. Box GP 760, Accra. **GREECE:** 77 Kifisias Ave., GR-151 24, Marousi, Athens. **GUADELOUPE:** Monmain, 97180 Sainte Anne. **GUATEMALA:** Apartado postal 711, 01901 Guatemala. **GUYANA:** 50 Brickdam, Georgetown 16. **GUYANE FRANÇAISE (FRENCH GUIANA):** 328 CD2, Route du Tigre, 97300 Cayenne. **HAITI:** Post Box 185, Port-au-Prince. **HAWAII 96819:** 2055 Kam IV Rd., Honolulu. **HONDURAS:** Apartado 147, Tegucigalpa. **HONG KONG:** 4 Kent Road, Kowloon Tong. **HUNGARY:** Cserkút u. 13, H-1162 Budapest. **INDIA:** Post Bag 10, Lonavla, Pune Dis., Mah. 410 401. **INDONESIA:** P.O. Box 2105, Jakarta 10001. **IRELAND:** Newcastle, Greystones, Co. Wicklow. **ITALY (also Israel):** Via della Bufalotta 1281, I-00138 Rome RM. **JAMAICA:** P. O. Box 103, Old Harbour, St. Catherine. **JAPAN:** 1271 Nakashinden, Ebina City, Kanagawa Pref., 243-0496. **KENYA:** P. O. Box 47788, 00100 Nairobi GPO. **KOREA, REPUBLIC OF:** Box 33 Pyungtaek P. O., Kyunggido, 450-600. **LIBERIA:** P. O. Box 10-0380, 1000 Monrovia 10. **LUXEMBOURG:** B. P. 2186, L-1021 Luxembourg, G. D. **MADAGASCAR:** B.P. 116, 105 Ivato. **MALAWI:** Box 30749, Lilongwe 3. **MALAYSIA:** Peti Surat No. 580, 75760 Melaka. **MARTINIQUE:** 20, rue de la Cour Campêche, 97200 Fort de France. **MAURITIUS:** Rue Baissac, Petit Verger, Pointe aux Sables. **MEXICO (also Belize):** Apartado Postal 896, 06002 Mexico, D. F. **MOZAMBIQUE:** Caixa Postal 2600, Maputo. **MYANMAR:** P.O. Box 62, Yangon. **NETHERLANDS:** Noordbargerstraat 77, NL-7812 AA Emmen. **NEW CALEDONIA:** BP 1741, 98874 Mont Dore. **NEW ZEALAND:** P O Box 75-142, Manurewa. **NICARAGUA:** Apartado 3587, Managua. **NIGERIA:** P.M.B. 1090, Benin City 300001, Edo State. **NORWAY:** Gaupeveien 24, N-1914 Ytre Enebakk. **PANAMA:** Apartado 6-2671, Zona 6A, El Dorado. **PAPUA NEW GUINEA:** P. O. Box 636, Boroko, NCD 111. **PARAGUAY:** Casilla de Correo 482, 1209 Asunción. **PERU:** Apartado 18-1055, Lima 18. **PHILIPPINES, REPUBLIC OF:** P. O. Box 2044, 1060 Manila. **POLAND:** Skr. Poczt. 13, PL-05-830 Nadarzyn. **PORTUGAL:** Apartado 91, P-2766-955 Estoril. **PUERTO RICO 00970:** P.O. Box 3980, Guaynabo. **ROMANIA (also Moldova):** Căsuţa Poştală nr. 132, O.P. 39 Bucureşti. **RUSSIA (also Belarus, Georgia, Kazakhstan):** ul. Srednyaya 6, p. Solnechnoye, 197739 St. Petersburg. **RWANDA:** B.P. 529, Kigali. **SLOVAKIA:** P.O. Box 17, 810 00 Bratislava 1. **SLOVENIA:** Poljanska cesta 77 A, p.p. 2019, SI-1001 Ljubljana. **SOLOMON ISLANDS:** P.O. Box 166, Honiara. **SOUTH AFRICA:** Private Bag X2067, Krugersdorp, 1740. **SPAIN:** Apartado 132, 28850 Torrejón de Ardoz (Madrid). **SRI LANKA, REP. OF:** 711 Station Road, Wattala 11300. **SURINAME:** P.O. Box 2914, Paramaribo. **SWEDEN:** Box 5, SE-732 21 Arboga. **SWITZERLAND:** P.O. Box 225, CH-3602 Thun. **TAHITI:** B.P. 7715, 98719 Taravao. **TAIWAN 327:** 3-12, Lin 7, Shetze Village, Hsinwu. **TANZANIA:** Box 7992, Dar es Salaam. **THAILAND:** 69/1 Soi Phasuk, Sukhumvit Rd., Soi 2, Bangkok 10110. **TOGO, WEST AFRICA:** B.P. 2983, Lomé. **TRINIDAD AND TOBAGO, REP. OF:** Lower Rapsey Street & Laxmi Lane, Curepe. **UKRAINE:** P.O. Box 246, 79000 Lviv. **UNITED STATES OF AMERICA:** 25 Columbia Heights, Brooklyn, NY 11201-2483. **URUGUAY:** Casilla 17030, 12500 Montevideo. **VENEZUELA:** Apartado 20.364, Caracas, DF 1020A. **ZAMBIA:** Box 33459, Lusaka 10101. **ZIMBABWE:** Private Bag WG-5001, Westgate.

Contact your local office for addresses in the following countries: Antigua, Guam, Iceland, Senegal, Sierra Leone.